AF478433

Europeanising party politics?

Manchester University Press

Europeanising party politics?

Comparative perspectives on central and Eastern Europe

Edited by Paul G. Lewis and Radoslaw Markowski

Manchester University Press

Manchester and New York

distributed in the United States exclusively by Palgrave Macmillan

Published by Manchester University Press
Oxford Road, Manchester M13 9NR, UK
and Room 400, 175 Fifth Avenue, New York, NY 10010, USA
www.manchesteruniversitypress.co.uk

Distributed in the United States exclusively by
Palgrave Macmillan, 175 Fifth Avenue, New York,
NY 10010, USA

Distributed in Canada exclusively by
UBC Press, University of British Columbia, 2029 West Mall,
Vancouver, BC, Canada V6T 1Z2

British Library Cataloguing-in-Publication Data
A catalogue record for this book is available from the British Library

Library of Congress Cataloging-in-Publication Data applied for

ISBN   978 07190 8297 9   hardback

First published 2011

Typeset 10.5/12.5pt Times
 by Graphicraft Limited, Hong Kong
Printed in Great Britain
 by CPI Antony Rowe Ltd. Chippenham, Wiltshire

Contents

List of figures

List of tables

Contributors

Lenka Bustikova is a Ph.D. candidate at Duke University. She is currently working on a dissertation on radical parties in post-communist democracies. Her work has been published in *The Journal of Contemporary European Studies*, *Communist and Post-Communist Studies* and the *Czech Journal of Sociology*.

Fernando Casal Bértoa is a Ph.D. candidate at the European University Institute in Florence. His current research focuses on party system institutionalisation, democratic consolidation and the functioning of democracy in East-Central Europe.

Mikołaj Cześnik works as an Assistant Professor at the Institute of Political Studies of the Polish Academy of Sciences and is also a post-doctoral researcher at the Institute of Political Science of the Warsaw School of Social Sciences and Humanities. He is a member of the Polish National Election Study.

Zsolt Enyedi is an Associate Professor at the Central European University, where he also serves as the head of the Political Science Department. His research interests focus on party politics, comparative government, church–state relations, and political psychology. He has published more than fifty articles and book chapters.

Danica Fink-Hafner is Professor of Political Parties, Interest Groups and Policy Analysis at the University of Ljubljana and head of the Centre for Political Science Research at the Faculty of Social Sciences.

Mitja Hafner-Fink is Assistant Professor of Social Science Methodology at the Faculty of Social Sciences, University of Ljubljana, and researcher in its Public Opinion and Mass Communication Research Centre. His specialities include (political) participation, citizenship, (national) identity and social science methodology.

Herbert Kitschelt is George V. Allen Professor of International Relations at Duke University. He has published widely on patterns of party competition in post-communist and established Western democracies, including the challenge of the radical right. His work also deals with the interface between party competition and political economy.

Petr Kopecký is an Associate Professor of Comparative Politics in the Department of Political Science at Leiden University. He has published widely in the fields of comparative democratisation, legislative studies, political parties and East European politics, and recently edited *Political Parties and the State in Post-communist Europe* (Routledge 2007).

Alenka Krašovec is Associate Professor in the Faculty of Social Sciences, University of Ljubljana, Slovenia. She specialises in political institutions and processes.

Robert Ladrech is Senior Lecturer in Politics at Keele University, UK. His research interests cover comparative party politics, European Union politics and Europeanisation studies. His work on Europeanisation and political parties has appeared in *Party Politics* and the *European Journal of Political Research*. He is the author of *Europeanization and National Politics* (Palgrave, 2010).

Paul G. Lewis is Professor of European Politics in the Department of Politics and International Relations at the Open University (UK). He has published extensively in the fields of East European history, post-communist politics and party development. He co-edited *The European Union and Party Politics in Central and Eastern Europe* (Palgrave 2006).

Radoslaw Markowski is head of the Electoral Studies Section at the Institute of Political Studies of the Polish Academy of Sciences and Director of the Centre for the Study of Democracy at the Warsaw School of Social Psychology. His main interests are in electoral behaviour, party systems and democratisation.

Geoffrey Pridham is Emeritus Professor and Senior Research Fellow in European Politics at Bristol University. He has for long worked on problems of democratic transition and consolidation, first in Southern Europe and for the last two decades in Central and Eastern Europe. In 2005 he published *Designing Democracy: EU Enlargement and Regime Change in Post-Communist Europe* (Palgrave).

Maria Spirova is an Assistant Professor of Comparative Relations and International Relations in the Department of Political Science at Leiden University. She works on issues of party development, Europeanisation, and minority politics and policy. In 2007 she published *Political Parties in Post-communist Societies: Formation, Persistence and Change* (Palgrave).

Abbreviations for party names

Abbreviation	Party name	Country
BNRP	Bălgarska Nacionalna Radikalna Partija – [Bulgarian National Radical Party]	Bulgaria
BSP	Bălgarska Sotsialisticheska Partiya [Bulgarian Socialist Party]	Bulgaria
CSSD	Ceská Strana Sociálne Demokratická [Czech Social Democratic Party]	Czech Republic
DPA	Partia Demokratike Shqiptare; Demokratska Partija na Albancite [Democratic Party of Albanians]	Macedonia
DPMNE	Demokratska Partija za Makedonsko Nacionalnoedinstvo [Democratic Party for Macedonian National Unity]	Macedonia
DS	Dělnická Strana; DSSS – Dělnická strana sociální spravedlnosti [Worker's Party]	Czech
EIP	Eesti Iseseisvuspartei [Estonian Independence Party]	Estonia
EK	Eesti Kodanik [Estonian Citizens]	Estonia
ERKL	Eesti Rahvuslaste Keskliit [Estonian Nationalists Central League]	Estonia
ERSP	Eesti Rahvusliku Sõltumatuse Partei [Estonian National Independence Party]	Estonia
Fidesz	Fidesz – Magyar Polgári Szövetség [Fidesz – Hungarian Civic Union]	Hungarian
FPÖ	Freiheitliche Partei Österreichs [Freedom Party of Austria]	Austria
GERB	Grazhdani za Evropeysko Razvitie na Balgariya [Citizens for European Development of Bulgaria]	Bulgaria
Harmony Centre	Saskaņas Centrs	Latvia
HDZ	Hrvatska Demokratska Zajednica [Croatian Democratic Union]	Croatia
HSP	Hrvatska Stranka Prava [Croatian Party of Rights]	Croatia

HZDS	Hnutie za Demokratické Slovensko [Movement for a Democratic Slovakia]	Slovakia
Isamaa	Pro Patria	Estonia
KDH	Krestanskodemokratické Hnutie [Christian Democratic Movement]	Slovakia
Kesk	Eesti Keskerakond [Estonian Centre Party]	Estonia
Koond	Eesti Koonderakond [Estonian Coalition Party]	Estonia
KPRF	Kommunisticheskaya Partiya Rossiskoy Federatsii [Communist Party of the Russian Federation]	Russia
KSCM	Komunistická Strana Cech a Moravy [Communist Party of Bohemia and Moravia]	Czech Republic
KUN	Kongres Ukraiins'kikh Natsionalistiv [Congress of Ukrainian Nationalists]	Ukraine
LC	Latvijas Cels [Latvia's Way]	Latvia
LDDP	Lietuvos Demokratine Darbo Partija [Lithuanian Democratic Labour Party]	Lithuania
LDPR	Liberal'no-Demokraticheskaya Partiya Rossii [Liberal-Democratic Party of Russia]	Russia
LDS	Liberalna Demokracija Slovenije [Liberal Democracy of Slovenia]	Slovenia
LK	Lietuvos Konservatoriai [Lithuanian Conservatives]	Lithuania
LKD	Lietuvos Krikščionys Demokratai [Lithuanian Christian Democrats]	Lithuania
LKDS/LTJS	Jaunoji Lietuva Susivienijimas uz Vieninga Lietuva [Young Lithuania – For United Lithuania]	Lithuania
LLS	Lietuvos Liberalu Sajunga [Lithuanian Liberal Union]	Lithuania
LNDP	Lietuvos Nacionaldemokratu Partija [Lithuanian National Democratic Party]	Lithuania
LNNK	Latfija Nacionalas Nearkarîbas Kustîba [Latvian National Independence Moverment]	Latvia
LNP-JL	Lietuvos Nacionaldemokratu Partija – Jaunosios Lietuvos [Lithuanian National Party – Young Lithuania]	Lithuania
LPR	Liga Polskich Rodzin [League of Polish Families]	Poland
LPR	Liga Prawicy Rzeczypospolitej [The League of the Right of the Republic (League of Polish Families (LPR) + Real Politics Union + Right of the Republic)]	Poland
LSDP	Lietuvos Socialdemokratu Partija [Lithuanian Social-Democratic Party]	Lithuania
MDF	Magyar Demokrata Fórum [Hungarian Democratic Forum]	Hungary
MIÉP	Magyar Igazság és Élet Pártja [Hungarian Justice and Life Party]	Hungary

MIÉP-Jobbik	[MIÉP-Jobbik Magyarországért Mozgalom – Movement for a Better Hungary] Jobbik – Movement for a Better Hungary	Hungary
MSZP	Magyar Szocialista Párt [Hungarian Socialist Party]	Hungary
NDS	Národně Demokratická Strana – [National Democratic Party]	Czech
NDSV	Nacionalno Dviženie za Stabilnost i Văzhod [National Movement for Stability and Progress]	Bulgaria
NS	Národní Strana [National Party]	Czech
NSA	Nacionalen Sayuz Ataka – [National Union Attack, which includes BNRP {Attack Coalition}]	Bulgaria
NSi	Nova Slovenija – Krščanska ljudska stranka [New Slovenia-Christian People's Party]	Slovenia
NU	Nasha Ukrayina [Our Ukraine]	
ODS	Obcanská Demokratická Strana [Civic Democratic Party]	Czech Republic
ÖVP	Österreichische Volkspartei [Austrian People's Party]	Austria
Partia X	Party X	Poland
PBK	BK – Balli Kombëtar [National Front Party]	Albania
PD	Partidul Democrat [Democratic Party]	Romania
PDL	Partidul Democrat-Liberal [Democratic Liberal Party]	Romania
PDS	Partei des Demokratischen Sozialismus [Party of Democratic Socialism]	Germany
PDSR	Polul Democrat-Social din Romania [Democratic Social Pole of Romania]	Romania
PE	Parem Eesti [Right Estonia]	Estonia
PiS	Prawo i Sprawiedliwość [Law and Justice]	Poland
PNG	Partidul Noua Generație – Creştin Democrat [New Generation Party]	Romania
PNL	Partidul National Liberal [National Liberal Party]	Romania
PNTCD	Partidul National Taranesc Crestin si Democrat [Christian Democratic National Peasants Party]	Romania
PO	Platforma Obywatelska [Civic Platform]	Poland
PPCD	Partidul Popular Creştin-Democrat [Christian Democratic People's Party]	Romania
PRM	Partidul (Popular) România Mare [Party for Greater Romania]	Romania
PSD	Partidul Social Democrat [Social Democratic Party]	Romania
PSNS	Pravá Slovenská Národná Strana [Real Slovak National Party]	Slovakia
PUNR	Partidul Unității Naționale a Românilor [Party of Romanian Unity]	Romania
PWN-PSN	Polska Wspólnota Narodowa – Polskie Stronnictwo Narodowe [Pol. Nat. Commonwealth – Polish Nat. Party]	Poland

RL	Eestimaa Rahvalitt [People's Union of Estonia]	Estonia
RMS	Republikáni Miroslava Sládka – [Republicans of Miroslav Sládek]	Czech
ROP	Ruch Odbudowy Polski [Movement for the Reconstruction of Poland]	Poland
Rukh	Narodnyi Rukh Ukrajiny [The People's Movement of Ukraine]	Ukraine
S	Samoobrona [Self-Defence]	Poland
SD	Socialni Demokrati [Social Democrats]	Slovenia
SDKÚ	Slovenská Demokratická a Krestanská Únia [Slovak Democratic and Christian Union]	Slovakia
SDS	Slovenska Demokratska Stranka [Social Democratic Party of Slovenia]	Slovenia
SLD	Sojusz Lewicy Demokratycznej [Alliance of the Democratic Left]	Poland
SLS	Slovenska Ljudska Stranka [Slovenian People's Party]	Slovenia
SN	Stronnictwo Narodowe [National Party]	Poland
SNS	Slovenska Nacionalna Stranka [Slovenian National Party]	Slovenia
SNS	Slovenská Národná Strana [Slovak National Party]	Slovakia
SPO	Srpski Pokret Obnove [Serbian Renewal Movement]	Serbia
SPR-RSČ	Sdružení pro Republiku – Republikánská strana Československa (Sládek)	Czech Republic
SRS	Srpska Radikalna Stranka [Serbian Radical Party]	Serbia
Svoboda	[Freedom]	Ukraine
SZDSZ	Szabad Demkraták Szöversége [Alliance of Free Democrats]	Hungary
TB	Tēvzeme un Brīvībai [For Fatherland and Freedom]	Latvia
TB/LNNK	Apvienība Tēvzeme un Brīvībai/LNNK – Alliance For Homeland and Freedom/LNNK – Latvijas Nacionālās Neatkarības Kustība [Latvian National Independence Movement]	Latvia
TP	Tautas Partija [People's Party]	Latvia
TS	Tevynes Sajunga [Homeland Union]	Lithuania
UD	Unia Demokratyczna [Democratic Union]	Poland
UMP	Union pour un Mouvement Populaire [Union for a Popular Movement]	France
UW	Unia Wolnosci [Freedom Union]	Poland
VMRO	Vnatrešna Makedonska Revolucionerna Organizacija [Internal Macedonian Revolutionary Organization]	Macedonia
VMRO-DP	Vnatreška Makedonska Revolucionerna Organizacija – Demokratska Partija [Internal Macedonian Revolutionary Organization-Democratic Party]	Macedonia

VMRO-DPMNE	Vnatreška Makedonska Revolucionerna Organizacija – Demokratska Partija za Makedonsko Nacionalno Edinstvo [Internal Macedonian Revolutionary Organization-Democratic Party for Macedonian National Unity]	Macedonia
ZChN	Zjednoczenie Chrześcijańsko-Narodowe [Christian National Union]	Poland
ZSLD	Združena Lista Socialnih Demokratov [United List of Social Democrats]	Slovenia

1

Introduction: Europeanising party politics? Central and Eastern Europe after EU enlargement

Paul G. Lewis[1]

Party development and the Europeanisation of party politics in Central and Eastern Europe

Extensive discussion of political Europeanisation has been conducted since the early years of the European Union (EU) and the institutions that preceded it, although investigation of how the process has affected party politics in the member states is a more recent development. With the accession of ten post-communist states in Central and Eastern Europe (CEE) between May 2004 and January 2007 the topic has taken on greater interest in a context where EU membership is also thought to be a reflection of the consolidation of the new democratic regimes and understood to assist their future progress along the path of political virtue. Such a development is, however, by no means assured and not all the changes seen in the context of EU membership have been positive. Major differences in party politics continue to exist, too, between established European democracies and those of more recent provenance.

In this book we aim to explore some of these significant differences on a systematic comparative basis, examine the role of 'European' factors in them and use new empirical material to investigate a range of key comparative topics. In the introductory chapter we survey existing literature and identify areas where relevant comparative work has already been conducted in order to identify the main differences that have already become apparent in the sphere of party politics between older, mostly Western democracies and the newer EU members in the East. Recent studies of party system institutional-isation are examined in the attempt to establish basic parameters of party politics in the new member states. It is clear, however, that many questions remain unanswered. In this context the continuing role of Europeanisation is discussed, and the nature of the comparative contributions made in the following chapters is outlined.

The emergence, development and stabilisation of democratic party politics in CEE on what is broadly understood to be a (West) European model is a topic analysed in several major surveys of the region (Pridham and Lewis, 1996; Kitschelt *et al.*, 1999; Lewis, 2000; Kostelecký, 2002; van Biezen, 2003; Millard, 2004; Jungerstam-Mulders, 2006; Lewis and Mansfeldová, 2006; Webb and White, 2007). On the basis of roughly a decade's experience of post-communist pluralism and competitive party politics, proposals began to be made about levels of party development and party system consolidation throughout the region, with initial suggestions made that the process was more advanced in Hungary, Slovenia and the Czech Republic (Lewis, 2000: 133). A few years later it was similarly proposed that the same countries could loosely be described as having 'stable party systems offering a measure of predictability to their voters', with Estonia also appearing to have reasonably durable parties (Millard, 2004: 143, 153). Amongst five post-Soviet cases Meleshevich (2007: 109, 210) similarly found Estonia to be the only country that displayed a 'steady and consistent trend toward a more autonomous and stable party system'. However, even these few cases of relative stability were put in question by the sudden rise of Res Publica in 2003 in Estonia and the ending of the centrality of Slovenia's Liberal Democracy to the country's party system with the 2004 election. Hungary, Slovenia and the Czech Republic also had the most enduring parties throughout this period, with Poland and Latvia showing the greatest fluidity (Lewis, 2006a).

Other comparative data generally substantiate these conclusions. Electoral volatility measures were uniformly low for Hungary, Slovenia and the Czech Republic, and the structure of party competition in Hungary and the Czech Republic was closed at a relatively early stage (Toole, 2000). The Comparative Study of Electoral Systems (CSES, 2008) data showed Czechs and Hungarians to have rising levels of party attachment from the mid-1990s, although this was not the case with Slovenia. In the area of party competition, the Czech Republic was characterised by a high level of ideological structuring, while representation also seemed to be working effectively in both Hungary and the Czech Republic (Mainwaring and Torcal, 2006: 211; McAllister and White, 2007). Both World Values Study (WVS, 2008) and CSES data showed a high value being attached to democracy in Hungary, Slovenia and the Czech Republic, as well as Slovakia. Early CSES data suggested that Czechs and Hungarians strongly endorsed the role of political parties in the democratic regime. Levels of confidence in parties have been relatively high in Hungary and Estonia (particularly in more recent years), reasonably so in Slovenia but lower in the Czech Republic. Party encroachment on the state is limited in Hungary, Estonia and Slovenia, while politicisation of the state apparatus is more pronounced in Slovakia and Latvia (S. Hanley, 2008: 1165–6). On the whole, though, party-relevant differences between Eastern and Western

Europe in general are still striking in many respects, with Eastern volatility emerging as a major factor. The post-communist CEE democracies have developed competitive European-style parties and equivalent party systems but they have yet, more generally, to display the levels of stability seen in most areas of post-war Western Europe (Lewis, 2007: 190).

Such fluidity makes it difficult to produce any general observation about the form that post-communist party politics has taken. The arena of CEE party politics may have been 'Europeanised' to some extent, then, but it is debatable if it has consolidated sufficiently to resemble any general European party model (to the extent that one can be identified). The precise meaning of Europeanisation in this context raises many questions, too, and existing data often convey mixed messages (Lewis, 2006b). In this earlier discussion I noted a parsimonious definition of Europeanisation that associated it with the 'aim of retracing the effects of the European integration process at national level' (Major, 2005: 177). In Chapter 2 of this volume Europeanisation is defined as 'the effects that EU-level institutions, policies and policy making have on institutions, policies, policy making and politics at the domestic (national or sub-national) level of governance'. In their study of European impacts on British politics Bache and Jordan (2008: 30) similarly define Europeanisation as 'the reorientation or reshaping of politics in the domestic arena in ways that reflect policies, practices and preferences advanced through the EU system of governance'. Many other similar variants have been offered, but as we are here concerned with the impacts of EU accession on national CEE party politics Ladrech's (2009: 6) recent, and brief, understanding of Europeanisation 'in its most generally understood sense' as 'analysis of the domestic impact of the EU' is quite sufficient. As the EU is generally understood to be a democratic entity, too, this also implies continuing progress towards democratic consolidation and a moderating effect on the process of party competition.

Surveys of Europeanisation along various dimensions suggest that the 'return to Europe' and accession to the European Union (EU) have, not surprisingly, had some impact on party politics although any clear pattern of influence or discrete set of consequences remain quite elusive. Signs of some influence or interaction between the European and national levels have been detected in different arenas of party activity by different observers. Enyedi (2007) has identified as many as eleven distinct areas of influence. Ladrech (2008) has surveyed five dimensions of party change based on the classification he proposed some years ago and identifies these in terms of policy and programmatic change, internal organisation, changing patterns of competition, relations between government and party, and relations beyond the national political system. While stressing that the EU has had a considerably greater impact on the party politics of the recent accession states, his account also conveys the impression that the grip of Europeanisation on CEE structures and processes is often curiously weak and its precise influence difficult to define. Lewis (2008) also points to five areas of change in this area and directs attention to the composition of the party system, forms of organisation, standardisation of party ideologies, treatment of European issues, and patterns of representation, but finds it difficult to reach any unambiguous conclusion. Whether the EU exercises a significant impact on CEE party politics, and any concrete implications this might have for the region's democratic politics, remains a topic that is hotly debated.

Most evidence on European party politics, East, Central and West, has tended to suggest that EU influences have in fact had little direct impact. Empirical studies have, too, been quite rare and it is only recently that political scientists have begun to focus on the influence of EU involvement on national parties. Mair's (2000) study of the impact of Europe on the parties of Western Europe is now a standard point of reference, and relatively little divergence can be seen from his view that the direct impact of EU involvement has been strictly limited. Raunio's (2007: 257) assertion that 'European integration has transformed party politics in Europe' is not quite what it seems, as his major observation really concerns the party politicisation of the EU itself. An extensive research project on the Europeanisation of national party organisations was recently completed and it, too, seems to have found little evidence that European-level decision making has greatly changed the balance of power within national political parties (Poguntke *et al.*, 2007a and b; Ladrech, 2007). More publications on Central and East European developments in this area have now begun to appear (Johansson, 2008; Ladrech, 2008; Lefkofridi, 2008; Lewis, 2008; Neumayer, 2008; Spirova, 2008; Vachudova, 2008; Haughton, 2009; Vachudova and Hooghe, 2009). Empirical studies of the Europeanisation of CEE parties have, however, still generally been less common than work on EU effects in related fields (Sedelmeier, 2006). Rather more has been published, for example, on aspects of leverage and conditionality in the accession process as well as on the Europeanisation of specific policy areas (Schimmelfennig and Sedelmeier, 2005; Vachudova, 2005; Grabbe, 2006). There have been more institutional studies in areas like the judiciary and the reform – or effectively Europeanisation – of the core executive than in the sphere of party politics (Dimitrov *et al.*, 2006; Sadurski *et al.*, 2006). It is, further, accepted that EU impact on domestic *policy* has been far greater than its influence on domestic *politics* and institutions (Börzel and Risse, 2007: 495).

Studies of CEE party change also raise rather different questions from those relating to established party systems even in the common environment of European integration. The environmental context has had a major constitutive effect on the development of competitive party politics in the former communist region, to the extent that the Europeanisation of CEE party politics is virtually indistinguishable from the general process of democratisation, although any uniform EU impact or harmonious process of Europeanisation in this area is inherently unlikely. Conditionality also played a part not seen in early accessions, and was yet stronger (if not always successfully applied) in the later accessions of Romania and Bulgaria (Pridham, 2007a and b). The EU itself had become a far more developed and self-aware actor with a broadly coherent and articulated set of objectives and expectations in CEE. European models of party development have certainly been influential in the region since the early days of post-communist change. Close attention was paid by politicians in the region to pan-European models and Estonian Prime Minister Juhan Parts (2004), for one, argued that the country's party system should develop on general European lines and take specific account of European networks.

But European issues have been generally ill defined and not greatly prominent in CEE party competition – although (and also because) the issue of EU membership itself was highly salient for the electorate as a whole (Benoit and Laver, 2006: 110). There were few signs of firm positions being taken on EU issues (apart from a firm commitment to joining it) in early CEE elections. At the time of the 2003 referendums EU enlargement did not emerge as a viable issue for inter-party competition but was often regarded as a matter of national interest and a factor potentially disruptive of internal party unity if discussed in any detail. Elections to the European Parliament (EP) in both 2004 and 2009 seemed to reflect established European experience. Turnout was low, European issues were prominent by their absence, and voters used the opportunity to register their dissatisfaction with the government (although Koepke and Ringe (2006: 341) have argued that CEE practice has in fact not followed that of older EU members in treating EP elections as second-order events).

Subsequent observations and more general surveys confirm that there has been little *direct* impact from the EU on the party politics of the new CEE member states. Continuing interest in the topic is, however, based on evidence of changes in national parties that are 'somehow related to the EU' (Ladrech, 2009: 13). More graphically, Haughton (2009: 424) suggests that the EU is not a driver or navigator of party politics but may appropriately be characterised either as the vehicle's conductor (by ensuring that 'the passengers have paid the fare and abide by the rules') or a fellow passenger who seeks to influence others' behaviour through engagement and force of argument (this being the role that seems to be most appropriate in the sphere of party politics). As with established members, the format of CEE party systems has not been greatly affected, although integration has probably had somewhat greater consequences for their mechanics and general mode of behaviour.

But there are contrasting and more nuanced views. Vachudova and Hooghe (2009: 179) argue that 'the long and demanding process of qualifying for EU membership has had a profound impact on nascent party systems in Central and East European states'. The conditions of more extreme party system instability seen in some CEE countries have produced situations, it has been argued, where the EU and integration issues have become more prominent. In this context, Poland has generally been seen to have provided the prime example of early EU accession fears impacting on the format of a national party system (Lewis, 2005: 185; Markowski and Tucker, 2008; Zuba, 2009). Slovakia, on the other hand, seemed to be the major case where EU influence succeeded in changing the mechanics of a national party system, with EU leverage being used 'very directly and deliberately to change . . . policies and to dislodge [the HZDS (Movement for a Democratic Slovakia) coalition] from power' (Vachudova, 2005: 170). It has been suggested that this pattern was replicated prior to the accession of two further CEE countries in 2007, with Bulgaria seeing a change in party system format and Romania one in party mechanics (Chiva, 2007). Cholova (2008) has also identified a significant Europeanisation of the Bulgarian party system and traced four distinct patterns of European influence through different stages of party development.

In both early cases, however, this degree of EU influence has been contested. Some suggest that the removal of the Mečiar government from power was driven rather by domestic factors, and the fact that issues concerning the EU had a high profile in Slovak politics did not mean that the EU itself exerted any direct influence (Henderson, 2006: 155, 166; Haughton, 2007: 233). Others equally argue that the EU impact on Poland was minimal (Szczerbiak and Bil, 2009). Overall it seems that, as suggested earlier by Marks and Wilson (2000), 'Europe' might have exerted an influence that is both pervasive and quite profound – but also one that is by no means direct. Mair (2007a: 159) has also come to endorse this view more strongly. In related fashion, he also points out that it has become increasingly difficult to separate out what is European and what is national. In this context he draws felicitously on the insights of the great Irish writer and humorist Flann O'Brien to advance a 'molecular theory of Europe', analogous to the process by which 'cyclists who ride their bikes often enough, especially on bumpy Irish roads, will transfer some of their molecules into the bike, while the bike will transfer some of its molecules into the cyclist', each thereby gradually adopting the characteristics of the other (Mair, 2007b).

Differential processes of change have also been considered. One perspective on the specific nature of CEE party politics has been suggested by Ágh (2006: 91–2) in a proposal that the Europeanisation of CEE parties should be distinguished in its external and internal dimensions (although they might also be conceived of as processes of change operating primarily at international and national levels). External Europeanisation is understood to be an elite-based process in which contacts with, as well as membership of, international party organisations have developed and CEE party programmes, values and public discourses have changed accordingly. Internal Europeanisation is a process reaching down to membership and constituency level in which internal party organisation and popular perceptions are also affected. In more extreme cases this distinction suggests that CEE party change may be two-faced and contain significant internal contradictions, with Europeanisation being something of a cosmetic process that leaves the internal roots of the party organisation unchanged. Explanations for the rapid decline of the Polish Union of the Democratic Left (SLD) have, for example, drawn attention to the discrepancy between the party's European image and a domestic political practice that perpetuated organisational practices more associated with the communist period (Lewis, 2008: 154). The same author (Ágh 2003; Ágh, 2008a: 308) has also distinguished between modes of Europeanisation that vary over time, notably one prevailing until 1998 which was anticipatory and a subsequent one that was primarily adaptive.

Variants of Europeanisation may also be distinguished by their intensity and depth of penetration into any political system or institution. In new EU member states the process may, for a variety of reasons, be less deep or far reaching than in older member states and its effects rather shallow, with greater chances of their being reversible (Goetz, 2005: 262). Perspectives on this kind of party change are here explored in the chapter on (Shallow) Europeanisation and Party System Instability. Any Europeanisation effect on the party politics of Central and Eastern Europe is, therefore, clearly not amenable to easy identification. It is an area where much remains uncertain and considerable empirical work is still to be done.

Aspects of party system institutionalisation

In contrast to the new CEE regimes, one characteristic of established European democracies has been the emergence of relatively stable party systems and their institutionalisation in a number of dimensions. Parties and party systems in longer-lasting liberal democracies have, further, been characterised not just by stability but also by a remarkably high degree of durability. Of the twenty-three democracies in existence during the late 1950s only four had a radically different party system thirty years later. By the 1970s major changes were perceived in Denmark, Norway and Ireland in ways that seemed to contradict prevalent ideas of 'frozen' party systems, but over the longer term the changes made did not seem quite so significant (Ware, 1996: 13, 213). In CEE only Hungary and the Czech Republic show signs of developing such stable patterns, and in other countries there was far less evidence of growing party system stability. By one calculation only five major new parties have emerged in Western Europe since 1973 while – leaving aside the first two free elections (which could not fail to see parties emerge to compete for power) – eleven emerged in CEE between 1995 and 2008 (Bågenholm and Heinö, 2009; also Tavits, 2007). There is little evidence to suggest that institutionalisation has made much headway in the region overall in the past two decades.

Major claims have been made for the importance of party system institutionalisation, and it has been argued to have a profound impact on the quality of democracy in any political system (Mainwaring, 1999: 37–8). Four conditions for the process have been specified: the first ('and most important') is stability in the rules and nature of inter-party competition; second, parties also need 'somewhat stable roots in society' that help provide a basic measure of regularity in how people vote; third, major political actors have to accord legitimacy to parties and the electoral process; fourth, party organisations must acquire an independent status and value of their own (Mainwaring and Scully, 1995: 4–5). The conditions remained largely unchanged in subsequent formulations. Much of the party system institutionalisation literature relates to a framework applied to developing systems in Latin America, but the notion of an institutionalised party system fits rather well with the idea of the stable or consolidated party system often thought to be characteristic of established European democracies. Recent work in this area has, moreover, shed significant light on relevant CEE developments, although some conditions of institutionalisation are more intensively researched than others.

Electoral volatility is generally the best-covered area (Tavits, 2005; Lane and Ersson, 2007; Mainwaring and Zoco, 2007) although there are also other foci of analysis: partisanship (Dalton and Weldon, 2007), party stability and durability (Lewis, 2006a), ideology (Horowitz and Browne, 2005), patterns of representation and its effectiveness (Bielasiak, 2005), cleavage patterns (Zielinski, 2002; McAllister and White, 2007), and electoral systems (Bielasiak, 2002). Mainwaring and Torcal (2006) have presented a broader overview of the process, but still focus on just two of the four dimensions. Apart from electoral volatility they also discuss the social rootedness of parties – although mostly in terms of patterns of presidential voting, which is of less relevance to the CEE context. Webb and White (2007) also used elements of the institutionalisation framework to structure their collection of country studies. Apart from this, attempts to present a more comprehensive analysis have been notable by their absence. Existing evidence is patchy, and there are major differences concerning the quantity and quality of evidence relating to the four conditions of the process. We now look at some of the evidence that has recently been presented.

With respect to electoral volatility and patterns of competition Mainwaring and Zoco (2007) have found that CEE party systems are highly fluid, like most of those inaugurated after 1978. This date generally marked the emergence of television as a major factor in election campaigning that enabled politicians to avoid the arduous chore of intensive party building but also had the effect of leaving a gap that parties had previously filled by helping to form strong civic identities and political loyalties. Compared with other cohorts of new democracies, party systems in those inaugurated post-1978 therefore show fewer signs of stabilising over time, a feature associated with several perverse outcomes for party politics. Large numbers of citizens in such polities tend to believe, for example, that parties persistently fail them and they become increasingly disillusioned, disaffected and often hostile towards party organisations. By way of response, their elected representatives tend to engage in collusion and develop predatory attitudes in their professional activity, further feeding civic disillusion and popular anti-political attitudes. From this respective, institutionalisation receives a permanent setback.

Lane and Ersson (2007) have also identified higher levels of electoral volatility in CEE than in Western Europe from 1990 onwards. However, as they also detect a significant impact of socio-economic modernisation on net volatility they expect it to decrease as post-communist economic development continues to make progress. While, too, Western Europe has seen rising volatility since the early 1990s they foresee increasing convergence between such aspects of party system instability in the different regions of Europe. Tavits (2005) also identifies high electoral volatility in Eastern Europe and a tendency for it to increase in the early years of democratic transition. But she also finds it decreasing once the democracies have had time to mature, and argues that the electoral arena moves towards stabilisation after about eleven years of democratic experience, a process facilitated by the growth of supportive institutional structures and good economic performance. She has also argued that volatility results from an increased supply of parties rather than from erratic voting patterns, which casts a different light on processes of stabilisation (Tavits, 2008).

Bielasiak's data, on the other hand, show a further increase in average volatility even in the fifth round of democratic elections in Eastern Europe (Bielasiak, 2005: 338). In common with Tavits, Mainwaring and Torcal (2006: 209) also find that GDP per capita is a powerful predictor of electoral volatility but argue (in line with Mainwaring's later analysis) that the main explanation does not derive from modernisation but is rooted in the different social conditions under which early democratisations occurred and the party systems of new democratic regimes were inaugurated. Weak institutionalisation and high volatility, they argue, 'could go on for an extended period'. While there is substantial consensus on the high levels of electoral volatility in CEE, then, there is disagreement about its extent and the direction of change. One obvious reason for this is the slightly different data sets and groups of countries chosen for analysis. Different forms of statistical manipulation will also introduce an effect, and the coverage of different time periods will further change the picture. There are, too, questions of judgement and expectation that enter into any predictive activity. Lane and Ersson, as well as Tavits, expect steady economic growth to impact on electoral activity in a relatively unproblematic way while Mainwaring and his collaborators see a clear qualitative change having occurred in the conditions under which party systems develop (or fail to do so) in new democracies. Their analysis of volatility is set in a richer account of the changing nature of party politics overall.

The simple factor of time also means that these items of analysis are now quite dated. Four elections took place during 2006 in the new EU member states, two more were held in 2007 (Estonia and Poland), a further three in 2008 (Slovenia, Lithuania and Romania) and one in 2009 (Bulgaria). On the face of it recent elections have shown signs of an unusual stability. In contrast to the established CEE practice of governments losing elections, half of those held in 2006–7 were won by incumbent parties (Hungary, Latvia, Estonia). Even in Poland the 2005 election saw the same six parties being returned to parliament, with no new entrants in 2007 either. Recent calculations show a significant decline in electoral volatility for the Visegrad countries (van Biezen and Caramani, 2007; Ágh, 2008b). The benefits of economic growth and relative stability may have been feeding through to the political system and contributing to voter satisfaction, a dimension where EU impacts may also have played some part.

Investigation of the contemporary conditions for institutionalisation in new CEE democracies will obviously benefit from study of the most recent data but even then, in an area where extensive analysis of electoral volatility has already been conducted, it may still be queried whether the first condition has been fully investigated in anything like a comprehensive fashion. Studies of electoral volatility produce only limited data on how far stability in the rules and nature of inter-party competition has been established. They primarily shed light on the nature of elector–party relations and the degree of regularity in voter choice, but do not generally provide a basis for pronouncements about party system stability in terms of the pattern of relations between electoral contenders, or what Mainwaring (1999) calls 'continuity in the components that form the system'. The capacity of individual parties to survive from one election to another is another critical aspect of party system stabilisation, and this is a dimension that volatility measures shed little light on (Lewis, 2006a). It is a factor prominent in an approach that focuses more directly on relations between parties than on party–voter links.

It is in this context that James Toole (2000) has applied Mair's model of the structure of inter-party competition to estimate the level of party system stabilisation in East-Central Europe. On two out of three measures the structure of competition for government in Hungary and the Czech Republic was already found to be closed by the late 1990s, a situation that reflected a relatively advanced stage of party system stabilisation – particularly over the short time span considered. Stabilisation was less advanced in Poland, where the structure of competition was only closed on one count. Relevant factors here were found to be party systems in Hungary and the Czech Republic with more stable membership (i.e. fewer parties entered or left the system at each election), lower levels of fractionalisation and an electoral system that secured an appropriate balance between disproportionality and fractionalisation (the original Polish system having been highly dysfunctional in this respect). Despite its having been conducted at a relatively early stage, the continuing stability of the Hungarian and Czech party systems suggests that major factors in the institutionalisation process were identified in this analysis.

The second condition for institutionalisation concerns the success that parties have in putting down relatively stable roots in society. In this respect citizens need to develop some attachment to a party, and party labels should have some meaning for the voters they are intended to attract, which in party system terms means that consistency in the relative ideological position of the different parties needs to develop (Mainwaring and Scully, 1995: 5). This is also linked with parties' ability to survive, as the fact that individual parties endure suggests that they have captured the long-term loyalties of some social groups (Mainwaring, 1998: 73). Analysis that contributes to an understanding of these developments has been conducted by Dalton and Weldon (2007: 185–6) on the basis of CSES data. Not surprisingly, they suggest that partisan attachment is generally stronger in older democracies, is less intense for younger generations in new democracies and develops less successfully through the years. Comparison of data from CSES modules 1 and 2 shows Poland starting with a relatively high level of party attachment, which then declines, with the Hungarian and Czech levels of attachment starting low but then increasing, which corroborates other findings in this area.

A second analysis in this area confronts the issue of the programmatic or ideological structuring of party competition, which involves consideration of spatial models of voting, social cleavage theory and location on a left-right continuum. In this context Mainwaring and Torcal (2006: 211) find a strong correlation between ideological voting and the stability of inter-party competition overall. Such voting patterns are, however, much weaker in most post-1978 competitive regimes, personalistic attachments possibly being the most convincing explanation for this tendency. Nevertheless, Bulgaria and the Czech Republic show high levels of ideological structuring but still have moderate to high electoral volatility. On the basis of a study of twenty-three post-communist democracies, Horowitz and Browne (2005: 702) also highlight the strength of ideological voting in the process of party system consolidation and argue, in effect, that stabilisation depends on ideological consolidation as much as on institutional rules like electoral systems or strong presidencies.

A further contribution focuses on parties and the process of democratic consolidation, although in practice its attention is more directed towards the representation of social cleavages and party system consolidation from this perspective. The general conclusion is that parties operate to represent social cleavages less effectively in post-communist countries, although representation is already thought to be working quite well, in view of the short period for which competitive parties have been working – particularly, once again, in Hungary and the Czech Republic (McAllister and White, 2007). There are, however, certain doubts about the relevance of this analysis to the focus of the study – left–right self-placement is used as a surrogate measure of party support, for example – and generally speaking the evidence for this aspect of institutionalisation is quite patchy. If the key point is how far voters develop an attachment to a party, there is little direct evidence over a sustained period, while analysis in terms of ideological structuring represents a somewhat tangential approach to the topic.

The third condition for institutionalisation concerns the legitimation of political parties and the electoral process. At present there do not seem to be any recent publications that address this issue on a comparative empirical basis, neither does there seem to be much material that can be brought directly to bear on it. WVS and CSES data nevertheless provide some related information on the value attached to a democratic system and whether parties are thought to be necessary to make such a system work properly. Support for democratic principles seems to vary roughly in line with other aspects of party system institutionalisation, with the Czech Republic, Slovenia and Hungary all ranking quite high, while variation in the endorsement of parties is somewhat wider. The high ranking of Romania is quite surprising here, although the value attached to parties in the Czech Republic, Hungary (high) and Poland (low) is in line with previous findings (Lewis, 2008). Responses (2008) to questions about feelings of confidence and trust in parties also provide relevant information, and Eurobarometer findings are useful here. In terms of general perceptions of parties the high ranking of Estonia, Hungary and Slovenia is not surprising here. More surprisingly, Romania continues to gain a high score and the Czech Republic rather a low one. Less surprising are the low scores of Poland and Latvia (Eurobarometer, 2009).

In relation to the fourth condition – the development of party organisations that are valued and have an independent status – comparative CEE data are also almost totally lacking. In an article introducing a symposium on party system development issues Joseph LaPalombara (2007: 150) noted with reference to CSES data that, 'Rich though these materials and the research based on them may be, they leave us with scant information regarding the internal organizational nature and dynamics of political parties.' Individual studies of different aspects of party organisation appear on occasion (Spirova, 2005; Linek and Pecháček, 2007; Enyedi and Linek, 2008), but it is hardly possible to produce any comprehensive overview. As editors of a comparative work on party development in new democracies which spans Eastern Europe and Latin America, Webb and White (2007: 356) also find it hardest to summarise the information on party organisation development, given the 'patchy or imprecise nature of much of the data'. They point to the relative organisational strength of (former) communist parties, but this is now a declining asset. In view, too, of the swift demise and marginalisation of the Polish SLD – once thought to be a prime example of a successfully reformed communist party – this may be less of a significant factor in the institutionalisation process in East-Central Europe than the authors suggest.

In terms of the conclusions that can be drawn from the current literature and existing data on party system institutionalisation, the comparative picture is therefore quite limited. Information on electoral volatility presents the fewest problems, although further work needs to be conducted to produce a clearer understanding of the pattern of inter-party competition. Some analysis has been published with respect to levels of partisanship. Eurobarometer surveys are run more frequently than others, and yearly snapshots of popular trust in parties and related topics like satisfaction with democracy are produced. But they suggest either that there is still major fluidity in such sentiments in some countries – including those where other studies point to higher levels of institutionalisation – or that such snapshots are not always reliable and that there may be a significant degree of arbitrariness in the survey results. These might, of course, be accurate reports of popular sentiments – but in that case much will depend on which year the survey is conducted in. If the scores provide an accurate reflection, too, they are hardly likely to provide much evidence of institutionalisation, where a significant degree of stability is a defining characteristic.

Party politics after enlargement

Despite the limited level of party system institutionalisation, post-communist democratic development in Central and Eastern Europe seemed to have progressed comparatively well and was (arguably) further consolidated by the EU accessions of 2004 and 2007. But the process has not been untroubled or completely smooth. After a sequence of national legislative elections – five in a thirteen-month period from September 2005 to October 2006 – the picture began to look rather different: Central Europe seemed to look rather 'unhinged' and its party politics more turbulent. The core Visegrad states 'displayed a worrying tendency to plunge back into populism, nationalism, Europhobia, and reform-aversion, which, according to the EU "script" was supposed to be firmly a thing of the past' (Sobell, 2006: 2). From one perspective, the influence of the EU had vanished like a short-term anaesthetic and it was argued that not too much should be expected of it as a beneficial influence on further progress in the democratisation process (Mungiu-Pippidi, 2007). In the most recent accession countries, Bulgaria and Romania, it has particularly been argued that the 'elitist and highly fragmented policy environment, created by the process of Europeanization, has opened additional space for the rise of populist alternatives' (Andreev, 2009: 389).

But the predictions of a general return to populism and other negative political responses soon turned out to be an exaggeration. Broadly speaking, populist parties and apparently extremist forces have often turned out to be quite restrained in their response to EU accession and receptive to the political opportunities offered by EU membership, although developments in some countries have been quite ambiguous. In Slovakia Fico's rather populist Smer party formed a government in 2006 and incurred the wrath of the Party of European Socialists (of which it was a member) by coalescing with the nationalist SNS. The government as a whole, though, showed no reluctance to follow the path of European integration and was only the second CEE state to adopt the euro in 2009. Equally, the Eurosceptic Law and Justice won the 2005 election in Poland and formed a coalition with the downright Europhobic League of Polish Families and the opportunistic Self-Defence party of the erratic Andrzej Lepper. The public soon tired of the posturings of the hybrid coalition, though, and the two smaller parties were punished by the electorate in premature elections held in 2007. There is little evidence so far, either, that extremist or nationalist responses to the global economic crisis that emerged in 2008 have been stronger in CEE than in Western Europe (Lewis, 2009). It may well be that it is the immediate pre-accession period which provides the greatest opportunities for anti-EU forces – it was the 2001 elections that saw the rise of Eurosceptic parties in Poland and those in Bulgaria during 2005 that saw the rise of the Ataka coalition.

While formal commitment to European integration has become the norm any broadly based political force, nevertheless, finds it difficult to avoid the emergence of Eurosceptic tendencies within its own ranks, and conflict about the integration process has been found to be sharper in Europe as a whole within mainstream parties than between them (Hooghe and Marks, 2004: 3;

Gabel and Scheve, 2007: 41). One account found little variation among mainstream parties in established EU states on integration issues, with parties of the extreme left and radical right both much more likely to take up Eurosceptic positions (Beers and Clark, 2005), although the applicability of this finding to CEE has been challenged in recent analysis of the region (Marks *et al.*, 2006; Vachudova, 2008; Vachudova and Hooghe, 2009). But if there may well be considerable scope for anti-accession activity in party systems overall, it has not taken root in parties close to the political centre (Bartolini, 2005: 312; Bielasiak, 2006: 59–60). Anti-EU parties have tended to cluster on the margins of the party system or, if they persist and continue to show serious political ambitions, moderate their outlook and move towards the political centre.

But there is also little solid evidence that Europarties have had much success in influencing the course of party development. The major EU groups of both right and left have certainly made efforts to change the course of party system development. The emergence of the Bulgarian Euroleft and New Left was strongly promoted by the Party of European Socialists, but domestic considerations and the resilience of the Bulgarian Socialists determined the general failure of the initiative (Spirova, 2007: 138). Equally, the attempt of the European People's Party after 1989 to create a group of Christian Democratic parties in Central Europe met with only limited success (Öhlén, 2008). There are major doubts as to whether transnational groups put real effort into attempts to influence national parties, depending as they did on politicians whose base was essentially national. One major study notes that much depended on how domestic actors behaved while their 'parties were mainly reacting to events and taking up opportunities created for them, in an essentially passive process' (D. Hanley, 2008: 203).

Some observers continue to see European influences having a generally negative effect on domestic politics and a potentially disruptive impact on party systems. When Europeanisation penetrates the domestic arena, Peter Mair (2007b: 157) thus foresees the predominant indirect outcome of a hollowing-out of national party competition, growing constraints on domestic decision making and the devaluation of national electoral competition. Less likely are direct effects in the form of the emergence of anti-European parties or the rise of anti-European sentiments within existing parties. Ágh (2007: 8) also argues that EU accession has had a traumatic impact on the new member states, with the emergence of a general crisis in CEE party systems. Individual parties have often been institutionalised as a form of Europeanisation, although this has not happened with party systems which he sees as having become more nationalised. This also suggests a growing separation between the nature of party politics at national and international levels (Bardi and Mair, 2008).

EU impacts and the nature of any Europeanisation of CEE party politics have thus proved to be elusive and difficult to grasp in any precise way, although there remains a general feeling that they are neither non-existent nor insignificant. Some analysts, particularly those writing more recently, have argued that EU influence has actually been significant and quite strong (Cholova, 2008; Markowski and Tucker, 2008; Vachudova, 2008; Vachudova and Hooghe, 2009; Zuba, 2009). But there is a difference of opinion between those who see 'Europe' impinging on CEE party politics primarily in the pre-accession period (whether positively in terms of the influence of conditionality or negatively by producing resistance to European integration) and others who see more of a continuity of Euro-influences through a range of direct or – more frequently – indirect mechanisms. Studies of older EU member countries also show that Europeanisation is a lengthy process. Bache and Jordan (2008: 271), for example, conclude that the UK showed no 'sharp or immediate change' following accession in 1973, and that change occurred with distinct periods of acceleration and braking. Moreover, comparative empirical analysis of the different areas of Europe – East and West, old and new EU members, as well as EU members in distinction to those who still remain outside the Union – has still not greatly progressed, although some advances have been made in the field of party system institutionalisation. In view of the conceptual and methodological problems involved both in defining and in analysing the process of Europeanisation and its effects, it is likely that further work on comparative lines will be most productive, particularly as there is an increasing range of empirical material now available for analysis. More thoroughgoing comparative analysis will provide a solid basis for identifying the 'European' influences that have been exerted on CEE party politics.

The following chapters will therefore discuss change in a number of key areas and seek to identify EU impacts from several different angles. We start by examining the institutional context of changing party politics in terms of party–state relations and the framework of transnational party cooperation (Chapters 2 and 3). We then move to studies of political participation and seek to establish the patterns that emerge across Europe and within the CEE area (Chapters 4 and 5). Chapters 6 and 7 focus on patterns of party competition, both in general terms and with specific reference to the emergence of far-right parties as examples of non-mainstream parties (in view of the communist background of these countries it is understandable that far-left parties are virtually non-existent in the region and are therefore not considered here). Further chapters (8 and 9) direct attention to key issues of political representation and emerging patterns of partisanship.

We begin this book with the argument, therefore, that there is now a clear need for more focused comparative study of specific aspects of contemporary CEE party politics and aim to meet this need in several key areas by adopting a variety of approaches – theoretical, empirical and descriptive/ speculative. Individual chapters will examine:

- party–state relations and the development, on the one hand, of mechanisms of party management expressed in the formulations embodied in new constitutions and applied through the decisions taken by constitutional courts and, on the other, of the colonisation of the post-communist state through party patronage and perceptions of corruption;
- the role of transnational party cooperation as an agency of party Europeanisation in candidate countries, where this has had considerably more salience for party elite than has been the case in existing member states. Indirect effects are distinguished from those which are more direct, and particular attention is paid to the accession process when political conditionalities have particular prominence;
- patterns of participation analysed in terms both of long-term deep changes and of short-term variation within the longer-term patterns, thus taking account of behaviour before and after EU accession. Comparisons are made between post-communist countries that joined the EU in 2004 and those which joined later or not at all, as well as established democracies that were mostly (but not exclusively) within the EU;
- voter turnout and the implications of declining participation in successive elections – with the exception of Poland, where it was low from the outset, and the partial exception of the Czech Republic, where a recent rise has been noted. While low turnout is generally understood to have negative consequences for democracy, the idea that it facilitated EU accession and contributed to stronger democratic outcomes is also examined;
- patterns of inter-party competition, which cluster in three key areas: volatility and aspects of electoral behaviour; the behaviour of parties in the government arena and particularly the degree to which patterns of party competition in this area are open or closed; and relations between parties beyond the government arena in respect of party number, polarisation, ideological orientation and the nature of party blocs;
- the mobilisation of support for the radical right as a primary example of populist tendencies: the particular appeals of nationalism and normative tendencies that reject social liberalism are identified by linking them with both demand- and supply-side factors, the key group in terms of the former being the losers in successive phases of economic reform. In the current context of welfare retrenchment it is from the right that the extremist challenge to democracy is most likely to come, and this is the area to which we therefore direct our attention. From the supply point of view, however, a distinction is drawn between the legacy of national accommodative and patrimonial regimes;

- the quality of representation, which encompasses a range of different dimensions: general levels of participation, differential voting patterns affecting degrees of inclusion and exclusion, subjective judgements about institutions and practices, correspondence between public preferences and leadership policy, and influences deriving from the institutional context;
- EU effects on post-communist states in terms of producing conditions that maintain party system institutionalisation at a low level, particularly in terms of maintaining significant incongruence between the policy preferences of voters and party elites. This is examined in terms of the limited policy options available to parties committed to EU entry and the opportunities this has offered for more extreme parties and shifts in the overall pattern of party competition.

Note

1 I wish to acknowledge the generous support of the British Academy in funding the Research Network on The Impact of EU Enlargement on Central European Party Systems and Electoral Alignments (2004–9) and the valuable contribution it has made to the activities of the group that has produced this book.

References

Ágh, A. (2003), *Anticipatory and Adaptive Europeanization in Hungary* (Budapest: Hungarian Centre for Democracy Studies).

Ágh, A. (2006), 'East-Central Europe: parties in crisis and the external and internal Europeanisation of the party system', in P. Burnell (ed.), *Globalising Democracy: Party Politics in Emerging Democracies* (London: Routledge), pp. 88–103.

Ágh, A. (2007), 'Bumpy road ahead in East Central Europe: post-accession crisis and social challenge in ECE', in A. Ágh and A. Ferencz (eds), *Overcoming the EU crisis: EU Perspectives after the Eastern Enlargement* (Budapest: 'Together for Europe' Research Centre and Foundation), pp. 7–38.

Ágh, A. (2008a), 'Democratization and Europeanization of the ECE countries: post-accession crisis and catching-up process in the new member states', in Ágh and Kis-Varga (eds), *New Perspectives for the EU Team Presidencies*, pp. 303–65.

Ágh, A. (2008b), 'Deep party polarization as "nationalization" of the polity: structuring the party system in Hungary in an ECE context', paper prepared for ECPR Joint Sessions in Rennes, Workshop on The Nationalization of Party Systems in Central and Eastern Europe.

Ágh, A. and J. Kis-Varga (eds) (2008), *New Perspectives for the EU Team Presidencies: new members, New Candidates and New Neighbours* (Budapest: 'Together for Europe' Research Centre).

Andreev, S. A. (2009), 'The unbearable lightness of membership: Bulgaria and Romania after the 2007 EU accession', *Communist and Post-Communist Studies* 42, pp. 375–93.

Bache, I. and A. Jordan (eds) (2008), *The Europeanization of British Politics* (Houndmills: Palgrave Macmillan).

Bågenholm, A. and A. J. Heinö (2009), 'A new road to electoral success: incentive structures, elite strategies and the emergence of new political parties in the Baltic states', paper prepared for workshop on The Success of New Political Parties in Central and Eastern Europe, Department of Political Science, University of Gothenburg.

Bardi, L. and P. Mair (2008), 'The parameters of party systems', *Party Politics* 14, pp. 147–66.

Bartolini, S. (2005), *Restructuring Europe: Centre Formation, System Building and Political Structuring between the Nation-State and the European Union* (Oxford: Oxford University Press).

Beers, D. J. and N. Clark (2005), 'Euroskepticism in transition: public support for Euroskeptic parties in Eastern Europe and the national and transnational levels', paper prepared for conference of the EU Studies Association, Austin, TX.

Benoit, K. and M. Laver (2006), *Party Policy in Modern Democracies* (London: Routledge).

Bielasiak, J. (2002), 'The institutionalization of electoral and party systems in post-communist states', *Comparative Politics* 34, pp. 189–210.

Bielasiak, J. (2005), 'Party competition in emerging democracies: representation and effectiveness in post-communism and beyond', *Democratization* 12, pp. 331–56.

Bielasiak, J. (2006), 'Party systems and EU accession: Euroskepticism in East Europe', in R. Rohrschneider and S. Whitefield (eds), *Public Opinion, Party Competition, and the European Union in Post-Communist Europe* (Houndmills: Palgrave Macmillan).

Börzel, T. A. and T. Risse (2007), 'Europeanization: the domestic impact of European Union politics', in Jørgensen, *et al.* (eds) (2007), *Handbook of European Union Politics*, pp. 484–504.

Chiva, C. (2007), 'EU enlargement and the Bulgarian and Romanian party systems', paper delivered to a conference on The EU's South-Eastern Enlargement: Romania and Bulgaria in Comparative Perspective, European Studies Research Institute of the University of Salford.

Cholova, B. (2008), 'The Europeanization of the Bulgarian party system', in Ágh and Kis-Varga, *New Perspectives for the EU Team Presidencies*, pp. 185–206.

CSES (Comparative Study of Electoral Systems), at www.cses.org, accessed 30 September 2008.

Dalton, R. J. and S. Weldon (2007), 'Partisanship and party system institutionalization', *Party Politics* 13, pp. 179–96.

Dimitrov, V., K. H. Goetz and H. Wollmann (2006), *Governing After Communism: Institutions and Policymaking* (Lanham, MA: Rowman and Littlefield).

Enyedi, Z. (2007), 'The "Europeanisation" of Eastern Central European party systems', *THE NET Journal of Political Science* 5:1, pp. 65–74.

Enyedi, Z. and L. Linek (2008), 'Searching for the right organisation: ideology and party structure in East-Central Europe', *Party Politics* 14, pp. 455–77.

Eurobarometer 70, at http://ec.europa.eu/public_opinion/index, accessed 10 February 2009.

Gabel, M. and K. Scheve (2007), 'Mixed messages: party dissent and mass opinion on European integration', *European Union Politics* 8, pp. 37–59.

Goetz, K. H. (2005), 'The new member states and the EU: responding to Europe', in S. Bulmer and C. Lequesne (eds), *The Member States of the European Union* (Oxford: Oxford University Press), pp. 254–84.

Grabbe, H. (2006), *The EU's Transformative Power: Europeanization through Conditionality in Central and Eastern Europe* (Basingstoke: Palgrave Macmillan).

Hanley, D. (2008), *Beyond the Nation State: Parties in the Era of European Integration* (Houndmills: Palgrave Macmillan).

Hanley, S. (2008), 'Restating party development in Central and Eastern Europe', *Czech Sociological Review* 44, pp. 1155–76.

Haughton, T. (2007), 'When does the EU make a difference? Conditionality and the accession process in Central and Eastern Europe', *Political Studies Review* 5, pp. 233–46.

Haughton, T. (2009), 'Driver, conductor or fellow passenger? EU membership and party politics in Central and Eastern Europe', *Journal of Communist Studies and Transition Politics* 25, pp. 413–26.

Henderson, K. (2006), 'Slovak political parties and the EU: from symbolic politics to policies', in Lewis and Mansfeldová (eds), *The European Union and Party Politics*, pp. 149–68.

Hooghe, L. and G. Marks (2004), 'European integration and democratic competition' (Bonn: Friedrich Ebert Stiftung International Policy Analysis Unit).

Horowitz, S. and E. C. Browne (2005), 'Sources of post-communist party system consolidation: ideology versus institutions', *Party Politics* 11, pp. 689–706.

Johansson, K. M. (2008), 'External legitimization and standardization of national political parties: the case of Estonian Social Democracy', *Journal of Baltic Studies* 39, pp. 157–83.

Jørgensen, K. E., M. A. Pollack and B. Rosamund (eds) (2007), *Handbook of European Union Politics* (London: Sage Publications).

Jungerstam-Mulders, S. (ed.) (2006), *Post-Communist EU Member States: Parties and Party Systems* (Aldershot: Ashgate).

Kitschelt, H., Z. Mansfeldová, R. Markowski and G. Tóka (1999), *Post-Communist Party Systems: Competition, Representation and Inter-Party Cooperation* (Cambridge: Cambridge University Press).

Koepke, J. R. and N. Ringe (2006), 'The second-order model in an enlarged Europe', *European Union Politics* 7, pp. 321–46.

Kostelecký, T. (2002), *Political Parties after Communism* (Washington: Woodrow Wilson Center and Johns Hopkins University Press).

Ladrech, R. (2007), 'National political parties and European governance: the consequences of "missing in action"' *West European Politics* 30, pp. 945–60.

Ladrech, R. (2008), 'Europeanization and the variable influence of the EU: national parties and party systems in Western and Eastern Europe', *Journal of Southern Europe and the Balkans* 10, pp. 139–50.

Ladrech, R. (2009), 'Europeanization and political parties', *Living Reviews in European Governance* 4, 1: www.livingreviews.org/lreg-2009–1, accessed 10 February 2009.

Lane, J.-E. and S. Ersson (2007), 'Party system instability in Europe: persistent differences in volatility between the west and east', *Democratization* 14, pp. 92–110.

LaPalombara, J. (2007), 'Reflections on political parties and political development, four decades later', *Party Politics* 13, pp. 141–54.

Lefkofridi, Z. (2008), 'An integrated model of national party response to European integration' (Vienna Institute for Advanced Studies, Political Science Series 115).

Lewis, P. G. (2000), *Political Parties in Post-Communist Eastern Europe* (London: Routledge).

Lewis, P. G. (2005), 'EU enlargement and party systems in Central Europe', *Journal of Communist Studies and Transition Politics* 21, pp. 171–99.

Lewis, P. G. (2006a), 'Party systems in post-communist Central Europe: patterns of stability and consolidation', *Democratization* 4, pp. 562–83.

Lewis, P. G. (2006b), 'The EU and party politics in Central and Eastern Europe: questions and issues', in Lewis and Mansfeldová (eds), *The European Union and Party Politics*, pp. 1–19.

Lewis, P. G. (2007), 'Political parties', in S. White, J. Batt and P. G. Lewis (eds), *Developments in Central and East European Politics 4* (Houndmills: Palgrave Macmillan), pp. 174–92.

Lewis, P. G. (2008), 'Changes in the party politics of the new EU member states in Central Europe: patterns of Europeanization and democratization', *Journal of Southern Europe and the Balkans* 10, pp. 151–66.

Lewis, P. G. (2009), 'Party system stabilisation in Central Europe: record and prospects in a changing socio-economic context', paper prepared for ECPR General Conference in Potsdam, section on Reconceptualising the Transition in New EU Member States.

Lewis, P. G. and Z. Mansfeldová (eds) (2006), *The European Union and Party Politics in Central and Eastern Europe* (Houndmills: Palgrave Macmillan).

Linek, L. and Š. Pecháček (2007), 'Low membership in Czech political parties: party strategy or structural determinants?', *Journal of Communist Studies and Transition Politics* 23, pp. 259–75.

McAllister, I. and S. White (2007), 'Political parties and democratic consolidation in post-communist societies', *Party Politics* 13, pp. 197–216.

Mainwaring, S. P. (1998), 'Party systems in the third wave', *Journal of Democracy* 9, pp. 67–81.

Mainwaring, S. P. (1999), *Rethinking Party Systems in the Third Wave of Democratization* (Stanford, CA: Stanford University Press).

Mainwaring, S. P. and T. R. Scully (1995), *Building Democratic Institutions: Party Systems in Latin America* (Stanford, CA: Stanford University Press).

Mainwaring, S. P. and M. Torcal (2006), 'Party system institutionalization and party system theory after the third wave of democratization', in R. S. Katz and W. Crotty (eds), *Handbook of Party Politics* (London: Sage Publications), pp. 204–27.

Mainwaring, S. P. and E. Zoco (2007), 'Political sequences and the stabilization of interparty competition: electoral volatility in old and new democracies', *Party Politics* 13, pp. 155–78.

Mair, P. (2000), 'The limited impact of Europe on national party systems', *West European Politics* 23, pp. 7–15.

Mair, P. (2007a), 'Political parties and party systems', in P. Graziano and M. P. Vink (eds), *Europeanization: New Research Agendas* (Basingstoke: Palgrave Macmillan), pp. 154–66.

Mair, P. (2007b), 'Political opposition and the European Union', *Government and Opposition* 42, pp. 1–17.

Major, C. (2005), 'Europeanisation and foreign and security policy: undermining or rescuing the national state?' *Politics* 25, pp. 175–90.

Markowski, R. and J. A. Tucker (2008), 'Euroskepticism and the emergence of political parties in Poland', downloaded from http://homepages.nyu.edu/~jat7/, accessed 4 November 2009.

Marks, G. and C. Wilson (2000), 'The past in the present: a cleavage theory of party response to European integration', *British Journal of Political Science* 20, pp. 433–59.

Marks, G., L. Hooghe, M. Nelson, and E. Edwards (2006), 'Party competition and European integration in east and west: different structure, same causality', *Comparative Political Studies* 39, pp. 155–75.

Meleshevich, A. A. (2007), *Party Systems in Post-Soviet Countries: A Comparative Study of Political Institutionalization in the Baltic States, Russia, and Ukraine* (Houndmills: Palgrave Macmillan).

Millard, F. (2004), *Elections, Parties, and Representation in Post-Communist Europe* (Houndmills: Palgrave Macmillan).

Mungiu-Pippidi, A. (2007), 'EU accession is no "end of history"', *Journal of Democracy* 18, pp. 12–16.

Neumayer, L. (2008), 'Euroscepticism as a political label: the use of European issues in political competition in the new member states', *European Journal of Political Research* 47, pp. 135–60.

Öhlén, M. (2008), 'Nationalization through Europeanization: the European People's Party and its (potential) sister parties in Poland, Hungary and the Czech Republic', paper prepared for ECPR Joint Sessions in Rennes, Workshop on the Nationalization of Party Systems in Central and Eastern Europe.

Parts, J. (2004), 'We must learn to trust people more', in *Baltic Times* (29 September), available at www.baltictimes.com/art.php, accessed 1 October 2004.

Poguntke, T., N. Aylott, R. Ladrech and K. R. Luther (2007a), 'The Europeanization of National Party Organizations: a conceptual analysis', *European Journal of Political Research* 45, pp. 747–71.

Poguntke, T., N. Aylott, R. Ladrech and K. R. Luther (2007b), *The Europeanization of National Political Parties* (London: Routledge).

Pridham, G. (2007a), 'Change and continuity in the European Union's political conditionality: aims, approach, and priorities', *Democratization* 14, pp. 446–71.

Pridham, G. (2007b), 'The scope and limitations of political conditionality: Romania's accession to the European Union', *Comparative European Politics* 5, pp. 347–76.

Pridham, G. and P. G. Lewis (eds) (1996), *Stabilising Fragile Democracies: Comparing New Party Systems in Southern and Eastern Europe* (London: Routledge).

Raunio, T. (2007), 'Political parties in the European Union', in Jørgensen *et al.* (eds), *Handbook of European Union Politics*, pp. 247–62.

Sadurski, W. *et al.* (eds) (2006), *Après Enlargement: Legal and Political Responses in Central and Eastern European States to the EU* (Florence: Robert Schumann Centre).

Schimmelfennig, F. and U. Sedelmeier (eds) (2005), *The Europeanization of Central and Eastern Europe* (Ithaca, NY: Cornell University Press).

Sedelmeier, U. (2006), 'Europeanisation in new member and candidate states', *Living Review of European Governance* 1:3, www.livingreviews.org/lreg-2006-3, accessed 8 October 2008.

Sobell, V. (2006), 'Central Europe unhinged', Tokyo: Daiwa Institute of Research Ltd. (October).

Spirova, M. (2005), 'Political parties in Bulgaria: organizational trends in comparative perspective', *Party Politics* 11, pp. 601–22.

Spirova, M. (2007), *Political Parties in Post-Communist Societies: Formation, Persistence, and Change* (Houndmills: Palgrave Macmillan).

Spirova, M. (2008), 'Europarties and party development in EU-candidate states: the case of Bulgaria', *Europe-Asia Studies* 60, pp. 791–808.

Szczerbiak, A. and M. Bil (2009), 'When in doubt (re-)turn to domestic politics: the (non-)impact of the EU on Polish party politics', in *Journal of Communist Studies and Transition Politics* 25, pp. 447–67.

Tavits, M. (2005), 'The development of stable party support: electoral dynamics in post-communist Europe', *American Journal of Political Science* 49, pp. 283–98.

Tavits, M. (2007), 'Party systems in the making: the emergence and success of new parties in new democracies', *British Journal of Political Science* 38, pp. 113–33.

Tavits, M. (2008), 'On the linkage between electoral volatility and party system instability in Central and Eastern Europe', *European Journal of Political Research* 47, pp. 537–55.

Toole, J. (2000), 'Government formation and party system stabilization in East Central Europe', *Party Politics* 6, pp. 441–61.

Vachudova, M. (2005), *Europe Undivided: Democracy, Leverage, and Integration after Communism* (Oxford: Oxford University Press).

Vachudova, M. (2008), 'Tempered by the EU? Political parties and party systems before and after accession', *Journal of European Public Policy* 15, pp. 861–79.

Vachudova, M. and L. Hooghe (2009), 'Postcommunist politics in a magnetic field: how transition and EU accession structure party competition on European integration', *Comparative European Politics* 7, pp. 179–212.

van Biezen, I. (2003), *Political Parties in New Democracies* (Houndmills: Palgrave Macmillan).

van Biezen, I. and D. Caramani (2007), 'Cleavage structuring in Western vs Central and Eastern Europe: state formation, nation-building and economic modernisation', paper prepared for ECPR Joint Sessions in Helsinki, Workshop on Politicising Socio-Cultural Structures: Elite and Mass Perspectives on Cleavages.

Ware, A. (1996), *Political Parties and Party Systems* (Oxford: Oxford University Press).

Webb, P. and S. White (eds) (2007), *Party Politics in New Democracies* (Oxford: Oxford University Press).

WVS (World Values Study), at www.worldvaluessurvey.org/ accessed 30 September 2008.

Zielinski, J. (2002), 'Translating social cleavages into party systems', *World Politics* 54, pp. 184–211.

Zuba, K. (2009), 'Through the looking glass: the attitudes of Polish political parties towards the EU before and after accession', *Perspectives on European Politics and Society* 10, pp. 326–49.

2

Party management and state colonisation in post-communist Europe: the European dimension

Petr Kopecký and Maria Spirova

Introduction

The way parties and the state relate to each other in contemporary democracies is an important aspect of the political system. This has become even more so in the current age of the cartel party when, as Katz and Mair (1995) have argued, parties have moved away from society and entrenched themselves in the state. The nature of this relationship influences the immediate development of both parties and the state and, especially in new democracies, can have long-term consequences for their development, performance and popular legitimacy. The relationship between parties and the state can be conceptualised in a variety of ways, but following van Biezen and Kopecký (2007), we think of it as having three dimensions: the dependence of parties on the state, the management of parties by the state and the colonisation of the state by political parties. The dependence of parties on the state, most often conceptualised as state financing and other material support for political parties, is well documented and analysed in the general literature as well as elsewhere in this volume. Here we focus on the other two aspects of the party–state relationship: party management by the state and party colonisation of the state.

The chapter starts by defining these two dimensions of the party–state relationship and then describes the existing patterns of party–state relations in post-communist Europe and compares them across countries. The second part of the chapter investigates the 'Europeanisation' of party–state relationships, a process broadly conceived in this chapter in terms of the impact of EU integration on the evolution of observed patterns of party management and state colonisation. Empirically, the chapter focuses on the ten Central and Eastern European (CEE) countries that have become EU members: Bulgaria, the Czech Republic, Estonia, Hungary, Latvia, Lithuania, Poland, Romania,

Slovakia and Slovenia. We show that parties in post-communist Europe are quite extensively regulated by the state and that the state, via the rulings of constitutional courts, is also willing to apply those regulations in practice. We also document a relatively high level of state colonisation by the parties in the region but, in contrast to uniformly extensive levels of state regulation, we highlight important differences that are emerging in those patterns of state colonisation among the post-communist countries. Finally, we contend that, in the short term, the impact of the EU on rent seeking within the state has been relatively limited. Seen in the light of party patronage, the EU might actually be seen as an incentive rather than a constraint on those practices.

Parties and the state in post-communist Europe

If we think of the position of political parties as being either closely linked to society or closely linked to the state, parties in post-communist Europe have been particularly likely to build close links with the state. With the exception of the successor parties, parties there developed in relative isolation from the wider society; they emerged as elite groups with very loose organisations and meagre membership (van Biezen, 2003: 31; Lewis, 2001; Toole, 2003). As a result, parties have had to look elsewhere for resources and legitimacy, and the newly established democratic states provided the logical alternative. It appears that now, after almost twenty years of democratic development, parties in post-communist Europe are closely managed by the state, while at the same time they also use the state extensively in order to cement themselves in the political system.

Party management by the state in post-communist Europe[1]
Following van Biezen and Kopecký (2007) and Kopecký (2008) we define party management by the state as the 'extent of state involvement in internal party affairs' and operationalise it as the constitutional recognition of political parties and the regulation of party activities, financing, ideology and organisation through public law, including the constitution. To estimate the extent of state regulation we thus look at the basic laws of the country and analyse the extent to which parties are subject to state regulation through them. However, we improve on this operationalisation by adding another, more practical dimension of the state involvement of party life, that of the *application* of the regulation through the rulings of the constitutional courts.

Constitutional courts or their equivalents exist in most modern democracies and are usually granted powers to interpret the constitutionality of laws and policies and are thus a very important arm of the state. Their rulings can deal with political parties in a direct and an indirect way – they can concern the very survival of individual political parties by banning (or refusing to ban) their existence or declaring some of their actions and features (un)constitutional. Constitutional court rulings on related issues – such as the constitutionality of the electoral system, electoral campaigns, or the system of party financing – can also impact the development of political parties. The concept of state management of political parties is thus incomplete without a consideration of the extent to which the parties are managed not only formally – by the word of the law – but also in practice – through the rulings of the highest judicial organ.

Table 2.1 summarises the four indicators of state management of political parties in Central and Eastern Europe. It reports data on: whether a system of finance regulation exists in the country as of 2006, where there is constitutional recognition of political parties in the system and whether, during the post-communist period as a whole, the constitutional court has been involved in party activities. For the latter, we report data on two distinct indicators: whether the constitutional court in each system has been involved in decisions related to parties in general and whether any of them have been of direct consequence to the survival of political parties by either banning or refusing to ban one or several political parties or some of their fundamental activities, such as running in an election.

Table 2.1 Party management by the state in Central and Eastern Europe

Country	System of regulation of party finances (as of 2006)	Constitutional recognition of parties (as of 2006)	Constitutional court rulings related to parties (1990–2007)	
			Total	Decisions on the survival of parties
Bulgaria	Yes	Yes	10	Yes
Czech Republic	Yes	Yes	10	No
Estonia	Yes	Yes	3	Yes
Hungary	Yes	Yes	6	Yes
Latvia	No	No	2	Yes
Lithuania	Yes	Yes	2	No
Poland	Yes	Yes	6	Yes
Romania	Yes	Yes	4	Yes
Slovakia	No	Yes	12	Yes
Slovenia	Yes	Yes	22	Yes

Source: Kopecký (2008) and authors' own calculations based on data from the constitutional courts.

As discussed in more detail in Kopecký (2008), the data on the system of finance regulation and constitutional recognition of parties portray a picture of a close link between parties and the state. Eight of the ten states included in the analysis have a system of regulation of party finances; all but one provide constitutional recognition of the parties in their basic laws. The regulation of party finances is not that surprising, given that all but one country in our sample (Latvia) subsidise parties from the state budget. It appears that as soon as a country provides state support to political parties, it also tends to establish a system of enforcement and regulation of party finances. Only Slovakia appears as an exception to this pattern, as it introduced state subsidies without regulation. However, even Slovakia now provides a certain minimal regulatory framework, for example by setting limits on campaign expenditures. In Latvia, too, parties are at least obliged to submit detailed annual financial declarations, and face potential penalties if they fail to do so.

Constitutional recognition of political parties is also not that atypical in the context of contemporary democracies. Most post-World War II democracies with new constitutions tend to recognise political parties and regulate them in some way; in new democracies that have appeared as part of the Third Wave of democratisation, constitutional recognition of parties is a near-universal pattern (see van Biezen and Kopecký, 2007). However, it is also interesting to note different patterns in the way political parties are constitutionally recognised in the post-communist world. There are, for example, very few post-communist countries which do not issue some orders or instructions as to how parties should behave and/or organise. Most post-communist constitutions unquestionably fall under what Janda calls the 'prescription model' of party regulation (Janda, 2005). A frequent form of this prescriptive model is represented by constitutional formulae, including a ban on advocating totalitarian methods of political activity (e.g. Poland) or dictating that parties must be separated from the state (e.g. Bulgaria, Hungary, Slovakia). There are also a significant number of post-communist constitutions that appear to have elevated parties into a privileged position within the democratic system. Pluralism, political participation and competition have come to be defined in many of these documents almost exclusively in terms of party, as for example in the Czech Republic, Romania, Bulgaria or Hungary.

Constitutional courts have also been used extensively to manage the life and activities of political parties. The judicial bodies have been active in most of the post-communist countries from the early years of democracy and intervened to solve issues of policy and politics on numerous occasions. The only exception is Estonia, where the power of constitutional review is in the hands of the national Supreme Court (article 152 of the constitution). The courts vary in their activism and involvement in political life, so the indicators on their decisions on political parties need to be seen through the prism of their overall position, but it is telling that even the most inactive of the courts, that in Latvia, has been involved in decisions related to the activities of political parties.

Some examples of this more general involvement include decisions on the electoral system and its regulation, such as the Czech Constitutional Court decision of 24 January 2001. The Court overruled parts of electoral law that introduced a larger number of electoral districts and shifted from the Hagenbach-Bischoff to the d'Hondt method of seat distribution on the grounds that it favoured large parties too much (EECR 11: 1/2). Another example is the decision of the Estonian judicial body of 15 July 2002. The Constitutional Review Chamber declared unconstitutional parts of the Local Government Election Act, which prohibits electoral coalitions in local elections (EECR 11: 3, EECRCL 10: 1, pp. 1–19). Both of these decisions had clear consequences for smaller political parties, as the respective provisions would have made it more difficult for them to get seats in parliament or local councils and might have influenced their survival in the long run.

Party laws and the system of financing of political parties have also been subject to court decisions. For example, the Slovenian Constitutional Court decided on 11 March 1999 that article 23.1 of the Political Parties Act, which states that parties that did not obtain mandates at the last parliamentary elections do not receive financing, was unconstitutional and should be changed in such a way that 'the legislation prevents running in elections for the purpose of obtaining funds from the state budget' (Slovenian Constitutional Court website, U-I-367/96). Another instance is the decision of the Romanian Constitutional Court of 2 April 1996, in which it dismissed a number of challenges to the Law on Political Parties by nationalist parties. However, the Court did rule that article 3.2 of the same law, which stated that parties could initiate constitutional amendment procedures, was unconstitutional, while this paragraph was challenged by no one (Romanian Constitutional Court website, decision no. 35 of 1996, EECR 5: 2/3, pp. 19–20). While these decisions do not directly influence the existence of a political party, similar to those on elections, they do have an impact on the functioning and activities of the political entities and thus have longer-term consequences for the parties. The most direct outcomes, however, come from the decisions that relate to the very existence of parties. The number of these cases is more limited and they include both decisions to ban or refusals to ban the existence of a party and decisions that impact on the conditions under which a party can be formed, such as the number of members a proto-party must have in order to be registered as a political party.

The decision of the Bulgarian Constitutional Court regarding the constitutionality of the Movement for Rights and Freedoms, for example, ensured its persistence in the system and thus greatly influenced the political life in the country. In 1992, the Court rejected a petition by 93 MPs (virtually all affiliated with the former Communist Party) to declare the political party Movement for Rights and Freedoms unconstitutional because of its ethnic base (Ganev, 2004: 66; EECR 4: 2, p. 7). Similarly, in 1996 the Slovenian Constitutional Court rejected a request of the National-Social League of Slovenia to ban all the following parties: the Liberal Democracy of Slovenia, Associated List of Social-Democrats, Social-Democratic Party of Slovenia, Slovenian People's Party, Slovenian Christian-Democrats, Christian-Social Union and Slovenian National Right Wing (Slovenian Constitutional Court website, U-I-115).

Of less symbolic significance, but of substantial practical consequence, have been decisions regarding the requirements for a political party to form or persist in the system. For example, in 2005 the Estonian Constitutional Review Chamber denied a request by the Chancellor of Justice to declare article 6.2 of the Political Parties Act unconstitutional. The article states that a political party needs at least 1,000 members in order to be registered as a political party (Estonian Constitutional Review Chamber Website, 3-4-1-1-05, EECRCL 12: 1, pp. 1–27). On similar lines, in 1997 the Hungarian Court rejected a motion to declare unconstitutional the law 'Governing the Operation and Administration of Political Parties', which required parties to present at least one parliamentary candidate in two elections in order to retain their status as political parties (EECR 6: 1, pp. 16–17).

These examples represent only a small selection of the varied cases that the constitutional courts have dealt with in relation to political parties. Their overall involvement in cases related to or directly dealing with political parties is another indication of the substantial level of state management to which parties are subject in CEE. On many occasions, the highest judicial bodies have been involved in deciding whether parties persist or disappear, whether their candidates can run in elections and how they should behave in the system overall. This trend provides further evidence not only about the close links between parties and the state in post-communist Europe, but also about the willingness of the state to intervene in the functioning, organisation and ideology of political parties.

Party colonisation of the state in post-communist Europe

The second dimension of party–state relations that we discuss in this chapter is party colonisation or exploitation of the state. This concept usually encapsulates one or several of the main forms of rent-seeking by political parties – corruption, clientelism and patronage. All these forms of state colonisation allow the political parties to use state resources to their advantage for the purposes of party building, electoral gain, party enrichment or even personal enrichment. Here we focus specifically on two of these phenomena – party corruption and party patronage.

Political corruption is usually defined as the abuse of public office for private gain, and parties are often seen as one of the main culprits that sanction individual corruption or engage in corrupt practices as a collective actor. Whether by vote buying, accepting illegal donations or taking bribes in exchange for favourable decisions or state jobs, parties often 'abuse their powerful position in the political system' (Blechinger, 2002). Political parties in post-communist systems have not been an exception to this trend – if anything, they have benefited from the uncertain and fluctuating rules and the absence of enforcement mechanisms and supervisory bodies to engage in various forms of corrupt behaviour, or other forms of state colonisation (van Ham and Spirova, 2007; see also O'Dwyer, 2006 and Grzymala-Busse, 2007).

The first column of Table 2.2 reports the value of our indicator of party corruption. We use a measure derived from a cross-nationally comparable survey carried out by Transparency International (TI) which reflects the extent to which political parties are perceived to be affected by corruption. With all the values of this indicator around 4 (out of a maximum of 5), parties in post-communist Europe seem to be highly corrupt.[2] Moreover, parties in the new EU member states seem to be *uniformly* corrupt: there is little variation in the value of the indicator across countries. This contrasts with the trend in 'old' EU member states, where the average is not much lower (3.7) but the variation among states is much higher. However, we do

Table 2.2 Party colonisation of the state in Central and Eastern Europe

Country	Corruption of political parties (most corrupt = 5)	Impact of patronage on business (%)
Bulgaria	4.3	42.5
Czech Republic	3.8	16.0
Estonia	3.5	34.8
Hungary	n.a	5.5
Latvia	4.2	31.5
Lithuania	4.3	24.4
Poland	4.2	27.5
Romania	4.0	41.8
Slovakia	n.a	32.6
Slovenia	n.a	11.3
Average	4.04	26.79

Sources: Transparency International (2005) and Kopecký (2008).

need to keep in mind that the TI Corruption Barometer captures the public perception of, rather than the actual level of, political corruption. How engaged parties are in corrupt practices thus might be over- or under-represented, based on the public awareness of corruption in each given country. In addition, the higher rankings for the corruption of parties in the post-communist countries might be a reflection of the overall trend there to view parties as, at best, necessary evils. Twenty years after the fall of the Berlin Wall, political parties still remain the most distrusted political institutions in the region. The perception of their corruptness may well therefore be a reflection of general anti-party sentiment rather than of the actual level of corruption.

We thus need to go further to explore the extent of party colonisation of the state. The second aspect of rent-seeking behaviour that we discuss here is party patronage. In contrast to most studies of particularistic exchanges and state colonisation, we use a relatively narrow but also more precise concept of party patronage, limiting the phenomenon to perhaps its most widespread form: appointments (Müller, 1989, 2006; Kopecký and Mair, 2007; see also Sorauf, 1959; Wilson, 1973 for similar definitions). Unlike many other studies in the field of patronage politics, which include various personal rewards and gifts, allocation of public service projects, contracts or licences, pork-barrel legislation etc. as the forms of patronage, we are concerned only with the ability of political parties to appoint members and other individuals to positions in the public and semi-public sector and the practical exercise of this ability. Consequently, our major empirical concern is to establish the 'reach of the party' (Daalder, 1966); that is, to ascertain to what extent parties in the post-communist context are in control of the state job allocation process.

We therefore see patronage as related to, but conceptually and empirically distinct from, both clientism (i.e. the exchange of benefits to secure votes) and corruption (i.e. illegal exchange of money for favourable public decisions). Patronage appointments are not inherently clientistic, since jobs can be handed out in order to control policy formulation and implementation, and not just to buy votes or reward organisational loyalty. Nor are they inherently corrupt, since many jobs within the gift of party politicians are legally sanctioned. However, this does not mean that jobs cannot be used in a clientistic way. Similarly, obtaining a high-profile job in state administration can merely be the first step in the illegal personal enrichment of party politicians or their supporters; controlling key state positions, for example in the police apparatus, can also be used by parties to prevent criminal investigations into their questionable funding. In those cases, patronage comes perilously close to corruption. In that sense, though distinct, patronage is a necessary condition for both clientism and corruption. For without the ability to control the state via appointments, parties would not be in the position to provide targeted selective benefits to their constituencies, or have something to offer in order to secure illicit party funding.

Patronage is notoriously difficult to study – because of both the semi-legal nature of the practice and its wide scope. However, various studies of patronage practices in the CEE countries reveal evidence about the high level of state colonisation by political parties. Patronage practices are apparently rampant in the post-communist world. If we use the classification made by Kopecký and Scherlis (2008), which divides the empirical cases into four categories, one dimension reflecting the scope of patronage (broad or narrow), and the other reflecting the motivation (reward or control) behind patronage, all of the post-communist states for which data is available fall into the category of 'broad' patronage practices. What this means is that in the post-communist countries, similar to Greece, Italy, Spain, France and Germany, parties can and do reach beyond their legally sanctioned positions to appoint people to state and semi-state institutions. In practice, this suggests that positions which are not officially supposed to be political, either *de jure* or in terms of general expectations and sentiments, such as deputy heads of sections in ministries, heads and deputy heads of various regulatory agencies, chief executive officers and other leadership positions in state-owned companies, hospitals and schools will be subject to political control in these countries, and their incumbents will most likely change after each election. This trend is in contrast to the practice in countries such as Britain, Norway, Sweden and Denmark, where patronage appointments reach only the top levels of state institutions (Kopecký and Scherlis, 2008: 362).

In Poland, for example, as many as 90,000 jobs are estimated to be objects of party patronage, a large share of which are used by parties as a reward for party loyalty (Gwiazda, 2006; Szczerbiak, 2008). In Bulgaria, every change of government has provided new incumbents with the chance to distribute jobs, reaching even the lowest levels of government institutions to replace people in technical and support positions (Spirova, 2006). In Hungary, governing parties 'can potentially control the staffing of the entire ministerial bureaucracy' (Meyer-Sahling, 2008: 25). The practice has probably been even more extensive in Slovakia, where the Mečiar government (1994–98) is considered an 'exemplary case of party patronage linking state building and party building' (Rybář, 2008: 84). Comparable accounts reveal very similar trends of party patronage in Romania and Latvia (Roper, 2008; Ikstens, 2006). It is only in Estonia that the tendency of parties to fill state positions with people connected to them seems to be more restrained; there, Sikk (2008: 109) has argued, a professional civil service has developed that is often in fact recruited into the political party, leading to patronage of a different kind.

The general post-communist pattern seems to be one of extensive patronage practices. It seems that the simultaneous processes of party building and state building created ideal conditions for patronage politics (O'Dwyer, 2004 and 2006). Not only did the parties there have the opportunity to take advantage of a relatively weak and non-professionalised civil service, but a sweeping replacement of state employees was also legitimised by the nature of the regime change. As O'Dwyer notes, the anti-communist coalitions of the early 1990s considered their first task to be replacing 'red' officials wherever possible. In addition, most parties in post-communist countries either originated within the state or gained rapid access to it, which gave them the opportunity to compensate for their feeble position in society by gaining a strong grip over the public sector, similar to Portugal and Spain during the 1970s.

However, this is not to say the scope and nature of patronage is uniform throughout the whole region. The data in the second column of Table 2.2 report our proxy measure of party patronage. It is based on the data from the Business Environment and Enterprise Performance Survey (BEEPS) of the World Bank conducted in 1999–2000. The data reflect answers from a sample of company leaders to the question of what impact patronage (defined as public officials hiring friends and relatives for official positions) has on their business. The figure reported is a sum of percentages of those who answered that the impact was either significant or very significant (as opposed to minor or no impact). The data show that, overall, patronage does not appear to have a very major impact in the post-communist countries: fewer than 27 per cent of the respondents in our countries considered the employment of friends and relatives for official positions as having a (very) significant impact. This finding stands in a stark contrast with the generally high perceptions of corruption of political parties presented in the first column. Of course, what is measured here is the impact of patronage on economic firms. This is potentially very different than the impact of patronage on both political institutions and state administration. However, what the data reveal are differences between post-communist countries. Indeed, these cross-national differences are rather significant, certainly more so than the differences between countries on corruption of political parties. Hungary, Czech Republic and Slovenia, for example, score very low on impact of patronage, while more than 40 per cent of respondents consider patronage to have a (very) significant impact in Bulgaria and Romania.

Indeed, we believe that patronage practices in the post-communist world differ not just in terms of their scope, as the data in Table 2.2 suggest, but also in terms of the other dimension used in Kopecký and Scherlis' categorisation, their motivation. The general literature on party patronage often distinguishes between two major reasons why parties might appoint people in state institutions: one is to reward them for their support at election time and during election campaigns, or for other services rendered to parties (reward function); the other is to ensure that the party is in control of the decision-making and implementation process or, much more simply, that the party is present within important state institutions (control function). While the former motivation is generally seen as 'corrupt' or illegitimate, the latter motivation is of course perfectly compatible with the party government model, especially if the reach of patronage appointments does not strongly undermine bureaucratic autonomy. In this regard, the examples of Bulgaria and the Czech Republic, the two post-communist countries for which we have the most detailed data, are indicative of the trends and variation in the region.[3]

In the Czech Republic, we observe patronage more limited in scope and dominated by the control motivation. Although political parties in general face relatively few legal constraints on staffing state institutions with their appointees, in no small part due to the continuing absence of new civil service legislation, their actual exercise of this opportunity appears to be relatively modest in comparison to other CEE countries. To be sure, top civil service positions, including the state secretaries, usually change with each government, or even with each minister. Similarly, key positions within the regulatory and oversight bodies, such as the media watchdogs or key financial and economic quangos, are also politically appointed, as are governing boards of state companies. However, parties rarely reach into the middle management of state institutions, let alone the technical and service personnel. It should be noted, though, that this is in no small part simply because Czech parties do not have enough people to fill those positions, rather than because of the legal constraints on patronage, or the parties' intrinsic belief in bureaucratic and state autonomy.

Moreover, with the exception of some foreign embassies and governing boards of state companies, the key motivation for party appointments tends to be control of institutions for policy making and other purposes linked to the exercise of political power within the state. As Figure 2.1 illustrates, in an expert survey of about 45 respondents, a clear majority (66 per cent) listed control of institutions as the dominant motivation for making patronage appointments. Only about 10 per cent thought patronage was motivated exclusively by the desire to reward members and activists with state jobs. In the regional comparative sense, the Czech Republic therefore represents a country with a relatively modest scope of patronage, the exercise of which can largely be seen as one of the sinews of party government, rather than as questionable state exploitation.

In contrast to the Czech situation, in Bulgaria we observe larger-scale patronage, dominated by a reward motivation. While variation among different policy areas and specific institutions exists, overall, parties in Bulgaria

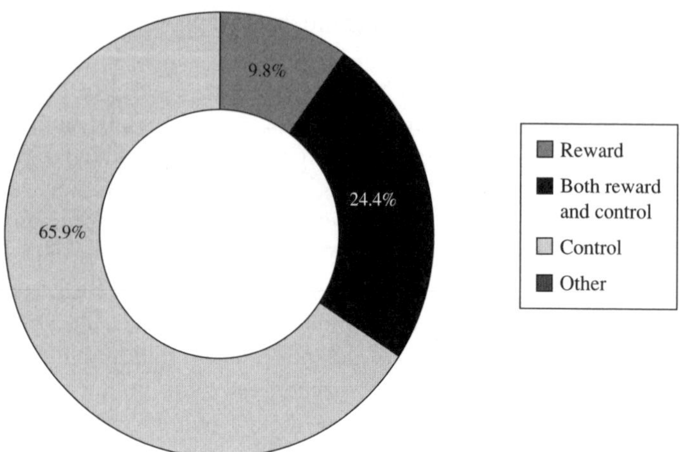

Figure 2.1 Motivation for patronage in the Czech Republic
Source: Authors' database.

tend to appoint people in a wide variety of state institutions and at various levels, including top and middle management as well as technical and service personnel. The difference from the Czech Republic is especially pronounced as we move further away from the core ministerial bureaucracy. While the ministries are arenas for patronage in both countries, the Bulgarian parties are in a more favourable position to make appointments when it comes to regulatory agencies and, particularly, institutions such as state-owned companies, hospitals and schools. In addition, unlike the Czech Republic, where there is a clear dominance of the control function of patronage, in Bulgaria rewarding activists still remains a popular goal in making appointments. In fact, our data indicates that control of the policy-making process is a much rarer motivation for the practice of patronage. Figure 2.2 illustrates this point.

Even when parties appoint with the aim at controlling certain institutions, this is often linked to their ability to distribute resources or further control the appointment process. This was certainly made clear by the problems that arose in the Bulgarian Socialist Party after 2005. The party had spent eight years in opposition and its activists and members had been 'deprived' of access to state institutions during that time. As a result, upon their ascent as a governing party, there was a strong push from regional and local leaders to reward the 'party cadre' with positions in state institutions. Although the leadership of the party realised that it should 'rely on professionals rather than appoint loyal comrades to the state institutions' a high number of state positions were still distributed as rewards (Stanishev, 2005).

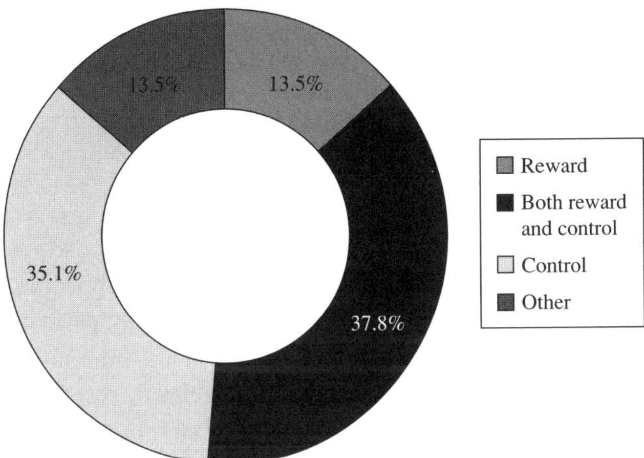

Figure 2.2 Motivation for patronage in Bulgaria
Source: Authors' database.

The impact of Europeanisation on party–state relations

Our data on both state management of political parties and party colonisation of the state suggests a very intricate connection between parties and the state in post-communist Europe. It seems that states both manage parties closely but are also used and abused by the parties for their own particularistic needs. The establishment of such links has clearly been influenced by a host of domestic factors, such as the legacy of the communist regimes, the dynamics of party and party system development, and social and cultural trends. However, just like the overall political and policy-making process in the region, this relationship has emerged and solidified in the context of European integration. While an examination of all the factors that have contributed to closeness of parties and the state in post-communist Europe is beyond the scope of this chapter, the impact of the EU is of specific interest to this volume and so we extend our analysis by briefly exploring the Europeanisation dimension.

We see 'Europeanisation' in broad terms. Cini has defined it as the 'the effects that EU-level institutions, policies, and policy making have on institutions, policies, policy making and politics at the domestic (national or sub-national) level of governance' (Quaglia *et al.*, 2007: 406). This is a very general definition, much in contrast to definitions that focus on the Europeanisation of party politics in particular, but, given the nature of party–state relations, it is well suited for our purposes. We look for the effects of 'European' institutions and policies on the one area of party–state relations for which we have most data: party patronage. While anybody's gut reaction will make us think that personnel decisions are certainly a prerogative of domestic political actors, there are several ways in which the EU has come to leave an imprint on the extent of this practice.

First, the EU strongly encouraged the introduction of an independent civil service, thus limiting, albeit slightly, the number of positions available for patronage distribution. The EU made 'administrative capacity' a condition of entry for all candidate states and encouraged reform of the civil service in both formal and informal ways (Dimitrova, 2002: 178–9; Meyer-Sahling, 2006). Candidate states obliged for the most part and introduced legislation that provided for a 'Weberian-style' bureaucracy by the turn of the century, thus making discretionary appointments more difficult, at least formally (Dimitrova, 2002: 183). Informally, as well, the new, EU-related, responsibilities and experiences of the bureaucracy allowed them to assume a stronger position within the political system, at the expense of parties (Meyer-Sahling, 2006).

However, while the extent of parties' free rein to make patronage appointments has decreased since the adoption of civil service legislation in the region, its impact has been limited. Other research and our own both speak to the ability of parties to bypass the formal rules and continue to make appointments to state institutions. In Bulgaria, for example, five particular ways have been used to replace people with civil-servant status following the 2005 elections: restructuring of the ministry/agency in which the position of the person in question is eliminated; a bad evaluation of the employee's performance; resignation of the employee at the urging of somebody at ministerial level; a claim that the person had violated the civil service code and tarnished the image of the state institution; and finally, and most rarely, transfer of the employee to an out-of-country position (Kapital, 2006). Similar mechanisms have been used in Hungary and Romania to maintain a relatively high level of politicisation of the civil service (Meyer-Sahling, 2008; Roper, 2008). In Slovakia, Rybář argues, patronage has decreased since 2001, but the parties in government have managed to ensure that even when the rules for appointing civil servants are respected, it is the party appointees that receive the jobs (Rybář, 2008: 86).

Second, the EU (among other international actors such as NATO) has been deeply involved in the reform of other sectors in the candidate countries and, in fact, of their very governance. The presence of this additional political authority has made political parties more leery of making sweeping political appointments in some sectors, while its absence in others has allowed parties more of a free rein. Such 'islands of excellence' are, for example, the finance sector in Bulgaria, or the EU units in the Hungarian bureaucracy (Meyer-Sahling, 2006; Spirova, 2006). In contrast, the healthcare sector in Bulgaria, for example, has been left outside the realm of EU involvement, leading to extreme levels of politicisation of its state institutions (Spirova, 2006).

Finally, the EU integration process has also increased the number of state jobs through the creation of new ministries or new administrative units (regions) and thus increased the potential number of patronage appointments. A good example was the newly created Ministry of State Administration in Bulgaria. Officially justified by the need to build a strong bureaucracy because of the EU accession process, according to media reports, the ministry allowed the governing parties to distribute even more patronage positions by creating 140 new staff positions (Stanev, 2005). The introduction and strengthening of the regions at a intermediate level of authority, also required by the EU, also added to the pool of administrative jobs available for patronage distribution (on the Czech Republic, see Novotný, 2003).

Conclusion

The nature of the party–state relations is likely to have both a short-term and a long-term impact on the development of political parties, and thus, also on the institutionalisation of the party system. To begin with, the state has intervened to influence the survival of some political parties directly, and their development indirectly, by providing a strong system of party regulation and ensuring that it is applied through the activities of the constitutional courts. The party systems in post-communist Europe have thus evolved in the context of close scrutiny by the state, and the format they have taken is certainly influenced by this scrutiny. Further, parties have been able to use the state as a resource to provide their members and supporters with selective benefits. Patronage appointments are only one example, but they are indicative of the overall process of party development. Parties' access to the state is one of their most important features in attracting and holding electoral support or in performing as governors of state institutions. Thus, one could argue that the high level of state colonisation by political parties has, in fact, promoted the institutionalisation of the newly formed political parties in post-communist Europe, leading to more stable patterns of electoral and political competition.

However, if we look beyond the short term, the consequences of this process are not so clearly positive. Engagement in patronage, corruption and other rent-seeking behaviour, especially if geared towards rewarding party members or for the personal enrichment of politicians, detracts from the programmatic appeal of the parties and, even more importantly, can only work to attract support in the short run. Parties inevitably fall out of power, and membership organisation, support base and organisational loyalty built exclusively on access to selective benefits are bound to crumble during periods when state access is denied. The legitimacy of the parties as central actors in the political system is also clearly challenged by their engagement in corrupt practices, especially in the context of already pre-existing popular anti-party sentiments and distrust of the state.

As for the impact of the EU integration process on the party–state relationship, the evidence provides a mixed picture. The very presence of the EU as a political and policy-making authority that is not part of the domestic political game raises justifiable hopes that the Europeanisation of the new member states will provide them additional incentives to increase their state capacity and improve processes of governance, including creating hindrances to the continued colonisation of the state by political parties. The insistence of the EU on the adoption of new civil service legislation in the candidate states to create an effective and politically neutral bureaucracy is one example of such potentially constraining formal rules. The irony, from the evidence that we have presented in this chapter, is that the country which has been perhaps most reluctant among the new EU member states to adopt such legislation, the Czech Republic, also shows signs of the least pervasive practices of party patronage. In that sense, understanding the domestic political context, including institutional legacies and patterns of party organisation and party competition, appears indispensable for appreciating the relative importance of international factors in the processes of state and party building.

Notes

1 We are grateful to Edward Koning for his research assistance in this part of the chapter.
2 Data are, unfortunately, only available for seven of our ten countries. The mean value of the indicator is 4 and the standard deviation .27.
3 The basis for this comparison is the extensive data on patronage practices in Bulgaria and the Czech Republic collected by the authors as part of a major research project on party patronage in new democracies (see Kopecký *et al.*, 2008).

References

Blechinger, V. (2002), *Corruption and Political Parties*, USAID, available at: www.usaid.gov/our_work/democracy_and_governance/publications/as/sector/ politicalparties, viewed 13 November 2009.
Daalder, H. (1966), 'Parties, elites, and political developments in Western Europe', in J. LaPalombara and M. Weiner (eds), *Political Parties and Political Development* (Princeton: Princeton University Press), pp. 43–77.
Dimitrova, A. (2002), 'Enlargement, institution-building and the EU's administrative capacity requirement', *West European Politics* 25, pp. 171–90.

Dimitrova, A. (2005), 'Europeanization and civil service reform in Central and Eastern Europe', in F. Schimmelfennig and U. Sedelmeier (eds), *The Europeanization of Central and Eastern Europe* (Ithaca, NY: Cornell University Press), pp. 71–90.

EECRCL (*East European Case Reporter of Constitutional Law*), Den Bosch: BookWorld Publications, various issues.

EECR (*Eastern European Constitutional Review*), various issues, New York: New York University School of Law, available at www1.law.nyu.edu/eecr/, accessed 4 October 2009.

Ganev, V. (2004), 'History, politics, and the constitution: ethnic conflict and constitutional adjudication in postcommunist Bulgaria', *Slavic Review* 63, pp. 66–89.

Grzymala-Busse, A. (2007), *Rebuilding Leviathan. Party Competition and State Exploitation in Post-Communist Democracies* (Cambridge: Cambridge University Press).

Gwiazda, A. (2006), 'Party patronage in Poland: the Democratic Left Alliance and Law and Justice compared', paper prepared for the ECPR Joint Sessions of Workshops, Nicosia, Cyprus, 25–30 April.

Ikstens, J. (2006), 'Patronage as party building tool: the case of Latvia', paper prepared for the ECPR Joint Sessions of Workshops, Nicosia, Cyprus, 25–30 April.

Janda, K. (2005), *Political Parties and Democracy in Theoretical and Practical Perspectives* (Washington DC: National Democratic Institute for International Affairs, available at www.ndi.org/files/1948_polpart_janda_110105.pdf, accessed 4 October 2009.

Kapital (2006), 'Politicheskite metli oshtetyavat danukoplateca [The Political Sweeps Hurt the Taxpayers]', available at: www.capital.bg/show.php?storyid=234609, accessed 15 October 2009.

Katz, R. and Mair, P. (1995), 'Changing models of party organization and party democracy: the emergence of the Cartel Party', *Party Politics* 1, pp. 5–28.

Kopecký, P. (ed.) (2008), *Political Parties and the State in Post-Communist Europe* (Routledge: London and New York).

Kopecký, P. (2008), 'Political parties and the state in post-communist Europe: the nature of symbiosis', in Kopecký (ed.), *Political Parties and the State in Post-Communist Europe*, pp. 1–23.

Kopecký, P. and P. Mair (2007), 'Political parties and patronage in contemporary democracies: an introduction', paper prepared for the Workshop on Political Parties and Patronage, ECPR Joint Sessions of Workshops, Florence, 25–30 April.

Kopecký, P. and G. Scherlis (2008), 'Party patronage in contemporary Europe', *European Review* 16, pp. 355–71.

Kopecký, P., G. Scherlis and M. Spirova (2008), 'Conceptualizing and measuring party patronage', Working Paper 25, Series of the Committee on Concepts and Methods, IPSA, September 2008, available at: www.concepts-methods.org/papers_list.php?id_categoria=1&titulo=Political%20Concepts.

Lewis, P. G. (2001), 'The "third wave" of democracy in Eastern Europe; comparative perspectives on party roles and political development', *Party Politics* 7, pp. 101–18.

Meyer-Sahling, J.-H. (2006), 'De-politicization through the backdoor? EU integration, administrative reform and party patronage in East Central Europe', paper prepared for the ECPR Joint Sessions of Workshops, Nicosia, Cyprus, 25–30 April 2006.

Meyer-Sahling, J.-H. (2008), 'The rise of the partisan states? Parties, patronage and ministerial bureaucracy in Hungary', in Kopecký (ed.), *Political Parties and the State in Post-Communist Europe*, pp. 24–48.

Müller, W. C. (1989), 'Party patronage in Austria. Theoretical considerations and empirical findings', in A. Pelinka and F. Plasser (eds), *The Austrian Party System* (Boulder, CO: Westview Press), pp. 327–55.

Novotný, V. (2003), 'The Creation of Regional Government in Czechia in the 1990s', PhD dissertation (Glasgow: University of Strathclyde).

O'Dwyer, C. (2004), 'Runaway state building: how political parties shape states in post-communist Eastern Europe', *World Politics* 56, pp. 520–53.

O'Dwyer, C. (2006), *Runaway State Building: Patronage Politics and Democratic Development* (Baltimore: Johns Hopkins University Press).

Quaglia, L., M. Neuvonen, M. Miyakoshi and M. Cini (2007), 'Europeanization', in M. Cini (ed.), *European Union Politics* (Oxford, Oxford University Press), pp. 405–21.

Roper, S. D. (2008), 'The influence of party patronage and state finance on electoral outcome: evidence from Romania', in Kopecký (ed.), *Political Parties and the State in Post-Communist Europe*, pp. 112–33.

Rybář, M. (2008), 'Powered by the state: the role of public resources in party building in Slovakia', in Kopecký (ed.), *Political Parties and the State in Post-Communist Europe*, pp. 70–91.

Sikk, A. (2008), 'From private organizations to democratic infrastructure: political parties and the state in Estonia', in Kopecký (ed.), *Political Parties and the State in Post-Communist Europe*, pp. 91–112.

Sorauf, F. (1959), 'Patronage and party', *Midwest Journal of Political Science* 3, pp. 115–26.

Spirova, M. (2006), 'Political parties and patronage in Bulgaria: a case study of the 2005 "Red Sweep"', paper prepared for the ECPR Joint Sessions of Workshops, Nicosia, Cyprus, 25–30 April.

Stanev, I. (2005), 'The coalition is sinking in bureaucracy', *Kapital* 1–7 October (Sofia), available at www.capital.bg/show.php?storyid=233075, accessed 13 November 2009.

Stanishev, S. (2005), Political Report at the 46th Congress of the BSP, 12 December 2005, available at: www.bsp.bg/shownews.php?id=648, accessed 2 February 2009.

Szczerbiak, A. (2008), 'State party funding and patronage in post-1989 Poland', *Journal of Communist Studies and Transition Politics* 22, pp. 298–319.

Toole, J. (2003), 'Straddling the East-West divide: party organization and communist legacies in East Central Europe', *Europe-Asia Studies* 55, pp. 101–18.

Transparency International (2005), *Global Corruption Barometer*, available at www.transparency.org/policy_research/surveys_indices/gcb/2005, accessed 2 February 2009.

van Biezen, I. (2003), *Political Parties in New Democracies: Party Organization in Southern and East-Central Europe* (Houndmills: Palgrave Macmillan).

van Biezen, I. and P. Kopecký (2007), 'The state and the parties: public funding, public regulation and rent-seeking in contemporary democracies', *Party Politics* 13, pp. 235–54.
van Ham, C. and M. Spirova (2007), 'Cleaning-up politics: parties and corruption in the "New" Europe', paper prepared for delivery at the 2007 Annual Meeting of the American Political Science Association, 30 August–2 September.
Wilson, J. Q. (1973), *Political Organizations* (New York: Basic Books).

3

Political parties and their consolidation in post-communist new democracies: indirect and direct impacts from EU enlargement

Geoffrey Pridham

Introduction

One significant outcome of European Union (EU) accession for countries from post-communist Europe is an evolving change in the systemic environment which should have short- and long-term consequences for domestic politics and its various actors, like political parties. Countries from Central and Eastern Europe (CEE) joined the EU as member states at what may be called a fairly advanced stage of its integration capacity and its politicisation not only at the level of European institutions but also in the domestic arenas of member states. Such politicisation is not new in the development of European integration, if one recalls the internal controversies over the integration treaties of the 1950s. What is new is the degree and intensity this has acquired over the past decade and more, reflecting the ever-greater political embrace of the EU, with its widening and deepening policy concerns and often stimulated by the now regular question of institutional reform – of which the Lisbon Treaty is the latest example.

This systemic impact of European integration is particularly evident in the considerable administrative, economic and political requirements now facing candidate countries in adapting beforehand to EU membership. That development argues convincingly for including such candidate countries on course for membership in discussion of 'Europeanisation' impacts, which should therefore not be confined to member states. Candidate countries have to undergo their own specially intensive 'Europeanisation' under the relentless time pressure of accession negotiations over the whole range of integration policy concerns, while being required to meet stringent conditionality demands which older member states did not face. At the same time, their

'Europeanisation' is conducted within a power context that is asymmetrically driven by a coercion and leverage on the part of the EU that it does not enjoy over member states (Grabbe, 2006: 39–40). That asymmetry largely disappears once a candidate becomes a member state, qualified only for some years by being excluded from Schengen and the eurozone.

Accordingly, one may suppose that parties and party systems in CEE have encountered mounting Europeanisation challenges over the past nearly two decades. However, that does not, of course, mean they have, as such, become automatically Europeanised, given their rootedness in national systems and familiar national constraints on integration impacts. Central to the advance of Europeanisation is the dynamic created by interactions between European and national levels and their respective actors. Political parties are conventionally seen as central actors in these new democracies, which are variations on the parliamentary model, even though in most CEE countries they display deficiencies of development when compared with their Western European counterparts and – not least – there is a continuing unsettledness of party systems, with new parties arriving and old ones in decline.

It has sometimes been maintained that assessing Europeanisation impacts on political parties is complex, not so much for reasons of absent empirical evidence (on what so far has been an under-researched area) as because there are methodological and conceptual difficulties over distinguishing European causality from other forms of causality, notably that deriving from national politics (Lewis and Mansfeldová, 2006: 6). This is of course a general conundrum in studying integration/national interactions, such as over policy matters, but it is nevertheless an interesting and challenging one. This chapter argues in favour of focusing as well as contextualising the discussion of Europeanisation effects on political parties in candidate countries and new member states. It directs attention to the fact that there is a particularly suitable and manageable comparative arena for observing and assessing such effects, albeit one with its own limitations. That is, the role of transnational party cooperation (TPC) by means of the various EU-wide parties and their groups in the European Parliament (EP), with its own benchmarks for measuring Europeanisation effects. It may be said at once that TPC's effects are directed at individual parties in these organisations which, as in national politics, are ordered ideologically. However, it should be worth exploring whether the collective and cumulative effects of this transnational activity may have some noteworthy impacts on party systems as a whole.

This chapter proceeds as follows. The first section highlights some relevant features of party-political Europeanisation in the light of the change in systemic environment that comes with the EU accession process, looking at the national level in which parties are basically rooted. Any integration impacts here are conceived as indirect and are treated as background to discussion of transnational party cooperation and its direct impacts on national parties in the rest of the chapter. Conclusions are drawn about whether this special activity has promoted the consolidation of party systems in post-communist countries or not, and also whether it has contributed in any way to the deepening of democratisation in post-communist countries. Throughout, the focus is on domestic impacts of TPC in post-communist countries rather than on the European level of this activity.[1]

Political parties and the EU accession environment

The theme of 'Europeanisation' has first and foremost been applied to European impacts on national policy content for the purpose of harmonising policy approaches among member states. There is the liberal market economy conformity implied in much of the *acquis* and required in the economic conditions so far as candidate countries are concerned. Additionally, there is pressure for institutional rationalisation along European lines in order to cope with the demands of EU policy making, although this may run into difficulties deriving from the resistance of national administrative traditions. All these changes, both policy and institutional, may impact persistently on political parties, especially when holding government responsibility in accession countries.

This line of reasoning provides us with one obvious opportunity for a focus in analysing Europeanisation effects on political parties: we can concentrate on the process of EU accession. This has two advantages: it defines a specific period (in fact, one lasting up to a decade) – a slice of time in integration history, as it were; but this is also one in which integration impacts are particularly intensive and wide ranging in terms of policy scope, even though this period's relative brevity might suggest that the scope for deeper effects will be rather limited.

In other words, indirect effects on political parties from accession derive from EU impacts on the domestic political environment as a result of accelerating accession business, and particularly the substance of membership negotiations. Politicisation around European policy took a new turning-point with the shift to membership negotiations. These opened up scope for more party-political differentiation, notably between government and opposition parties over specific policy proposals, despite the continued broad cross-party consensus over the strategic aim of EU membership (Pridham, 2005: chapter 5.2). This tendency, one likely to continue and increase following EU entry, when the constraints of accession have disappeared, questions the argument that integration has generally depoliticised or reduced political competition over policy choice in the CEE countries. There was still scope for interpreting European policies and for determining the pace at which they were applied, not to mention the room for political competition over policy areas that remained essentially a national responsibility or were only partly Europeanised. Accordingly, accession business became sucked into government/opposition dynamics – and markedly so in countries like Hungary and Poland.

Indirect effects on parties may also come from political events linked to EU accession, like the referenda on EU membership and even the first elections to the European Parliament, with inevitable impacts on political parties. Of course, to confuse matters – and suggesting some artificiality in the distinction between the indirect and the direct – events like European elections may also have a rather direct impact on parties and not just on their domestic environments. Such events create a mobilising pressure on parties by introducing a new dimension into the regular schedule of elections – national, local, regional and now European.

The Lewis and Mansfeldová (2006) volume examines Europeanisation effects on political parties in the eight post-communist countries that joined the EU in 2004 and the further two that joined in 2007, with particular attention paid to the EU referenda of 2003 and the European elections of 2004. Despite the policy intrusiveness of the EU during accession, the outcome of this study, with its concentrated time focus, is to emphasise there was little direct impact of the EU on CEE party systems. There is a similarity here to those in Western Europe (i.e. older member states), with their party system formats being hardly affected. Certainly, EU accession produced no crisis of the CEE party systems, with major shocks resulting instead from domestic developments (Lewis and Mansfeldová, 2006: 231–2). At the same time, this study emphasises that parties in CEE were shaped by the existence of the EU, which provided the means of political change (Lewis and Mansfeldová, 2006: 16). That indicates a contextual and therefore indirect influence of some potential and one that came into play gradually over some time, looking beyond accession.

Perhaps a more telling distinction than the indirect/direct one might be that between primary or systemic impacts, on the one hand, and secondary or party-specific (though not party-existential) impacts, on the other. Thus, referring to Lewis's list of changes in party development (Lewis and Mansfeldová, 2006: 16), the acceptance of the rule of law would obviously be a primary impact, while that of adopting professional campaigning and organisation management would probably be secondary. According to this, EU impacts during accession tended to be of a secondary rather than systemic order.

All the same, some party developments during accession had their own individual significance which did not always fit easily with such a dual categorisation. For instance, as noted, there were significant policy constraints deriving from accession business, in effect moving parties to the centre of the political spectrum; just as there were signs of extremist parties being constrained by the accession dynamic and becoming more marginalised because they did not qualify for transnational party membership (Lewis and Mansfeldová, 2006: 233). Political parties in these candidate countries were subject to observation and various monitoring constraints from the EU institutions. Accordingly, various parties of a nationalist tendency moderated their line towards the EU, not least because membership was very popular in their countries (and they were publicly attacked by Enlargement Commissioner Verheugen when they failed to do so). This last outcome may be seen as having some systemic importance in terms of greater, albeit perhaps superficial, EU-supportiveness.

Cross-national variation was apparent, with, for example, Estonia showing an EU impact on centre-right ideology (through membership of the European People's Party [EPP]) as accession strengthened the already existing neo-liberal consensus, but having little impact on party organisation. By comparison, in Slovakia the greatest impact was on political competition through the way parties interacted with EU affairs, producing a more solid consensus behind integration, clearly as a result of the pressures of the accession process. The 2003 referendum on EU membership highlighted this change. Somewhat in contrast, in this period Poland saw the emergence of Euroscepticism as a significant force.[2]

Indeed, Europeanisation impacts through accession business showed considerable cross-national variation. This becomes more apparent when discussion of the accession process is broadened over its whole time span and not just focused on certain specific albeit relevant political events. Party-political Europeanisation as such may affect various forms, like identity and ideology, programme, organisation, electoral politics and personnel (Pridham, 2001: 184); and some of these changes may take time to develop. If this seems like a recipe for considerable change, it should be remembered, however, that integration impacts may be both varied and limited.

At this point, it is necessary to emphasise the longer-term problem that most CEE party systems remained unsettled through the accession period and even beyond. This broader time perspective suggests a potential in them for major influences, or certainly for integration impacts greater than in old member states, which usually had settled party systems before EU membership impacted on their domestic systems. In CEE, such impacts began in the first years after 1989 and began to speed up with the Europe (i.e. association) agreements from the mid-1990s, with a further intensification once membership negotiations started in 1998 or 2000. During this period, one may look back and find cases of serious party decline (like the centre-right Union of

Democratic Forces (UDF) in Bulgaria, Latvia's Way in Latvia and the Movement for a Democratic Slovakia (HZDS) in Slovakia), serious party rise (the right-wing Fidesz in Hungary and the Social Democrats (CSSD) in the Czech Republic) and of new party emergence (the centre-left Smer in Slovakia and New Era in Latvia). How much the EU had a bearing on these changes in the party systems in question is a matter for close and detailed national analysis which is outside the brief of this chapter.

That last methodological point strengthens the case for examining Europeanisation effects on individual parties rather than on party systems as a whole, thus allowing for intra-national differentiation as well as cross-national variation. Thus, in a given polity, there is likely to be some variation in Europeanisation between different parties in light of their ideologies, their receptiveness of integration messages, their own stages of development and their different transnational party memberships. Hence, there may be variations in the nature of European/national interactions producing Europeanisation trends.

For instance, in Slovakia, Mečiar's HZDS owed little in the 1990s to European impacts (in contrast, its then nationalism included a rejection of European standards). But it began to bend to the inevitability of accession from around 2002, although its transnational membership remained unresolved because of Mečiar's controversial past. A different trajectory of party development was followed by Dzurinda's SDKÚ, founded in late 2000 after negotiations started. It became the most pro-European of the Slovak parties (as demonstrated for instance by its slogans and party cosmetics during the 2002 election) and enjoyed a straightforward choice of transnational membership in the European People's Party. In Latvia, as always, party development has been powerfully affected by the ethnic divide between Latvians and Russians in that country. Centre-right and right-wing parties based largely on support from the former have tended to be more pro-EU (i.e. pro-West) than parties – essentially on the left – representing the Russian minority. The latter, obviously influenced by a certain Russophilia, came only late in the accession period to adopt a more favourable position on EU membership and to become more open to European influences (Pridham, 2007a: 569–70).

Thus, in view of the wider time span of the accession period, it is difficult to argue that the changed systemic environment that came with the growing impact of European integration had simply secondary or even minimal Europeanisation effects on political parties, especially if one takes due notice of cross-national variation and also of cross-party variation. Party development, with its multifarious aspects, is a complex as well as rich area of analysis, and not enough attention has been paid to interactive dynamics between European and national levels, where indirect effects can have a powerful and maybe sustaining influence.

One important further test of indirect effects on political parties through the changed systemic environment may be applied. The EU had – and certainly aimed to produce – systemic improvements in candidate countries during accession with its political conditionality policy, with thus intended effects on the environment in which parties and other domestic actors operated. At the same time, the EU's insistence on the economic conditions intensified and speeded up the process of post-communist marketisation, with familiar consequences for economic 'winners' and 'losers', and they in turn impacted on party policy positions and on political competition.

However, it was the EU's political or democratic conditionality which ambitiously aimed to modify CEE systems in reinforcing or modifying the nature of their democratic politics in preparation for membership. Originally, the political conditions as set out at Copenhagen in 1993 required that candidate countries 'achieved stabilisation of institutions guaranteeing democracy, the rule of law, human rights and respect for and protection of minorities'. But in the course of the 2004 enlargement these conditions were extended to include the independence of judiciaries, the fight against corruption and a range of economic, social and cultural rights. With the application of political conditionality to the Western Balkans (with more difficult cases of post-communist democratisation) in the present decade, further conditions have been introduced, such as over state capacity (a greater historical legacy problem than in East-Central Europe), capturing war criminals (an outcome of the recent Balkan wars) and regional cooperation, with its overtones of countering destabilisation and conflict in that region (Pridham, 2007b). Altogether, this wide range of conditions amounted to an ambitious effort to modernise and reform new post-communist democracies. The discussion is now taken forward by looking at how these various conditions may have changed the political environment in which CEE parties have functioned, with a brief note on the outcome of conditionality by the time of EU entry.

The stabilisation of newly created democratic institutions, including the reinforcing of executive accountability, as well as underpinning the rule of law obviously aimed to strengthen and help consolidate the already existing post-communist democratic structures. This, once achieved, automatically conditioned the major parties in these countries, i.e. those working within the governmental and parliamentary institutions. Similarly, respect for human and minority rights sharpened the sensitivity of parties to these problems, along with other actors.[3] Also, once such rights became values, racist or nationalist parties were deterred from their worst rhetoric, as indeed was one purpose of Brussels, judging by Commissioner Verheugen's denunciations of extremist parties at various moments during the 2004 enlargement (Pridham, 2005: 152–3).

Rather pertinent were those political conditions which represented a powerful challenge to party-political interests, especially judicial independence and the fight against corruption. The first required ceding an influential area of political control and patronage, while the second struck at the heart of party links with business and therefore financial leverage in post-communist politics. Particular difficulties have been encountered in post-communist countries for this very reason, namely in convincing political leaderships to pursue anti-corruption drives with some persistence; and this problem has become more apparent in the years since EU entry. Romania's great difficulties in meeting these two conditions, for instance, had much to do with the strong counter-pressure from the vested interests of the ruling Social Democrats (PSD) during the Nastase government which ruled during the negotiations. The Party of European Socialists, with the EU's conditionality as a reference point, sought to put pressure on the PSD to respond more effectively in dealing with its own corruption.[4] Similarly, the European People's Party acted as a pressure over corruption involving its member parties from CEE, although this issue was not included in its own conditionality when these parties first joined (Kremer, 2007).

In this way, the EU parties could informally reinforce EU official demands over the political conditions, while domestic opposition parties sometimes attacked those in government for their corrupt practices. Despite the counter-pressures it encountered, fighting corruption has nonetheless for some years been fixed on the political agenda of these countries and some modest progress has been recorded. Some of the other conditions, like gender equality and children's rights, had less immediate impact on party life, although they possibly offered some scope for influence, in the course of time, on special sectors of voting behaviour.

In general, there were real inherent difficulties of implementation with some of the political conditions. The outcome as a whole, by the May 2004 enlargement, was one of incomplete implementation; and this was also true in the case of the two 2007 entrants, especially over fighting corruption and organised crime. This deficiency was partly due to the top-down fashion in which conditionality had been carried out and also to the relatively short time span in which Brussels had imposed conditionality on the candidate countries. There had, as a whole, been more success in producing formal responses than in changing the reality on the ground. For instance, there was progress in creating new judicial structures and introducing anti-corruption agencies, but less in securing effective judicial independence and pushing back the fairly widespread practice of corruption in post-communist societies. As indicated by the record on these two conditions as well as that on certain minority rights (notably those of the Roma), the greatest obstacle to change came from rooted behavioural patterns which resisted accession-driven change.

Post-accession tendencies in conditionality follow-up have so far produced a varied picture, with some further progress but also some cases of relapse (Pridham, 2008a).

This sustained but time-restricted effort by Brussels to push the candidate countries along the road of European standards, together with the potentially substantial impact from the *acquis communautaire* as well as the experience of managing and debating accession business, must in the round be seen as amounting to a considerable change in the political environment in which parties in CEE operated, despite all the imperfections of accession business. There were, as a result, more firmly and clearly defined democratic procedures, new political issues placed on policy agendas and a vast extension of legislation although, at the same time, an enhancement of executive power coming from the requirements of institutional reform during accession. But more time was needed for this totality of change to work itself through and affect political behaviour in party systems.

Transnational party cooperation: a particular case of Europeanisation

While the EU accession process introduced new influences on domestic environments, with a potential for conditioning party development, TPC in the form of EU-wide party organisations and parliamentary groups provided a more immediate and direct framework in which party-political Europeanisation could occur. To some extent, this transnational activity was complementary to Europeanisation pressures that impacted on domestic environments – such as in operating its own version of political conditionality for aspiring member parties and in its influence on policy positions of national member parties – but it was also unique as the most institutionalised form of party-political Europeanisation. It was an activity that started to embrace parties from CEE from the early 1990s, somewhat in advance of accession business, and therefore had a better chance of instilling change, whether formative or relating to subsequent party development. It remains, therefore, to assess its scope and limitations and identify its Europeanising influence on parties from post-communist Europe.

Party-political integration or Europeanisation has only recently begun to attract serious research (Poguntke *et al.*, 2007). But its transnational version has a long history going back to the early post-war years of European integration, as Ernest Haas demonstrated in his book on the 1950s (Haas, 1958). While arguing that 'the major indices of behaviour make ECSC [European Coal and Steel Community] parties quite similar to the American or Canadian prototypes' – suggesting the early emergence of possibly European federal parties – he also, significantly, warned that the lack of political weight and constitutional powers of the 'supranational' institutions, notably the EP (following the Common Assembly of the ECSC), provided the most important restriction on the operation, scope and potential of European parties (Haas, 1958: 437–8). This last lesson was most important, for it became a defining feature of the slow evolution towards some kind of European party system, i.e. this was essentially dependent on the status and institutional power of the EP.

Party groups along familiar ideological lines were present from the beginning in the Common Assembly of the ECSC (they were in fact introduced in the Consultative Assembly of the Council of Europe) and they were repeated in the EP. They have thus a respectable lineage, while the different groups have varied over time, with greater diversity coming from successive enlargements (that of 2004 introducing a noticeable contingent of Eurosceptic MEPs) and, at the same time, a concentration of strength in the two main groups of the centre-right and the centre-left. This latter change was enhanced by the greater policy controls acquired in stages by the EP.

Transnational party cooperation has traditionally taken various forms in organising national parties of the same ideological tendency. The transnational party groups which play a dominant role in the procedural life of the EP have remained the principal focus of this activity by virtue of their institutional location. It was not until the mid-1970s, in the few years before the first direct elections to the EP in 1979, that serious thought was given to developing complementary extra-parliamentary organisations, initially called European party federations, the most important three being the Party of European Socialists (PES) – successor to the previous Confederation of Socialist and Social Democratic Parties of the EC, the centre-right EPP and the European Liberal, Democrat and Reform Party (ELDR), now called the Alliance of Liberals and Democrats for Europe (ALDE). There are similar federations for some smaller forces like the European Federation of Green Parties (EFGP), but some minor groups in the EP do not possess such extra-parliamentary structures. In addition, the party internationals (Socialist, Liberal and Christian Democratic) have played a parallel and sometimes overlapping role in European transnational activity, although they have memberships from across the world. Furthermore, not to be forgotten (and often omitted from analyses of TPC), there is a certain amount of bilateral TPC, often between neighbouring countries and also involving local or regional party branches from different countries. This has sometimes been modelled on and influenced by the developed practice in Europe (including now also CEE) of town twinning. Bilateral TPC has always occurred within the ideological framework of TPC organisations; and it has extended to involve CEE countries, especially in East-Central Europe. Bilateral TPC may either express a particularly close relationship between two parties – such as between some

Swedish parties and their ideological counterparts in the Baltic states – or it may involve a combination of joint political and social activities, notably at the local level, between party branches on both sides.

There have always been problems in defining TPC in terms of a European party system within the complex institutional structure of the EU system. The EP, albeit now more of a recognisable parliamentary institution, is still one without an organic relationship with executive power in the EU, which is, in any case, fragmented. This transnational activity has, over time, acquired more political influence, essentially as a consequence of the EP's enhanced constitutional status as a result of successive integration treaties. At the same time, the party federations have autonomously asserted themselves, such as in attempting to influence policy decisions at the European Council by holding prior summits of party leaders. The practice of the EU parties relating directly to EU executive institutions has become more developed over time, with, for instance, the EPP now holding meetings of both foreign ministers and also finance ministers from member parties prior to their respective Council of Ministers sessions (Kremer, 2008).

Alternatively, a useful distinction may be drawn between this activity's relatively weak constitutional position (formal integration) and its significant political networking capacity (informal integration). As a form of transnational networking, TPC has intensified and acquired ever more political influence, not least as senior party politicians (some of them in government leadership) have been involved; and there have emerged transnational multi-party elites which are usually well linked with national party structures.

This networking opportunity was particularly attractive for political parties and their elites from the accession countries. Coming from states not yet members of the EU and therefore not yet participating directly in its main institutions, they could gain entry to transnational organisations, usually as associate member parties, well in advance of actual accession. Accordingly, CEE party elites tended therefore to give TPC a somewhat greater importance than party elites from EU member states. From the latter half of the 1990s onwards, TPC increasingly came to be regarded and utilised as a channel for furthering enlargement chances as well as for party-political networking. For CEE party leaders and officials, transnational activity gave them relatively easy access – on the basis of ideological fraternity – to top politicians in EU member states. Networking included lobbying influential people (especially those holding government positions in member states) to promote their countries' accession chances – a phenomenon that, obviously, increased with the advance of negotiations.[5] Even political bonds established with opposition politicians might become useful in the event of their elevation to national office, hence with some possible influence on EU enlargement decisions. This networking capacity of TPC for higher political motives was also recognised by high government officials from accession countries (as witnessed by the author's elite interviews during this period), who were more constrained by official procedures and therefore appreciated the freedom that party contacts allowed their co-nationals.

Moreover, association with the different transnational organisations allowed parties from CEE to receive regular and not merely ad hoc assistance over different aspects of party development, including electoral campaign management. This kind of experience had a certain influence on party-political learning and professionalisation and also party elite socialisation, opening leadership personnel to pressures and influences from their equivalents in established democracies of the older member states. All these impacts from the EU may readily be described as direct ones on the parties themselves.

At the same time, the main three EU parties applied a fairly strict form of political conditionality to aspiring member parties concerning democratic principles or attitudes and procedures. This conditionality strongly disapproved of nationalist tendencies, as evident in the policy on admission adopted by the centre-right European People's Party; and it was most in evidence from the early mid-1990s once there began a rush of applications from parties in CEE countries. At that time, the Socialist International and PES proved a decisive influence on former communist-regime parties moving towards social-democratisation and seeking international legitimacy in doing so. The conditionality adopted by the EU transnational organisations allowed some scope for established member parties to veto applicants on grounds of failure to respect individual political conditions – which at times could be controversial. Altogether, this transnational conditionality became a mechanism for encouraging and persuading new parties from post-communist countries to adopt European political standards.

On the other hand, it has to be said that European party activity had its serious limitations. It was less engaging and less demanding than that at the national level, which retained the main loyalty of party leaders and activists. The EU parties operated to a large extent through their member parties, which accorded them more or less political weight according to their own commitment to integration work. The latter has become, over time, somewhat reinforced by the practice of politicians alternating between European and national parliamentary careers; and this has begun to develop too in the new member states of CEE.

The number of national party personnel involved directly in Euro-party activity is usually small. They include especially party leaders (who tend to place enough importance on this activity to attend meetings),[6] international secretaries and selected MPs as well as selected groups of activists (such as for mutual visits between member parties and training programmes). Member parties from CEE countries were already integrated into this activity from the mid-1990s onwards, although full membership was not formally granted until accession occurred. Entry to the EU saw the election of MEPs from these countries who then provided an important addition to European party elites. Party international secretaries interviewed in some of these countries indicated that they devoted the majority of their time to European transnational activity, although the amount actually spent per week could fluctuate according to immediate demands, such as upcoming meetings and whether they were also busy as MPs or not.[7] The question that remains is how much transnational impacts and experiences have percolated downwards through parties more widely, given that their transnationally engaged personnel usually have a certain influence within party structures.

The main basic restriction on the role of the transnational organisations, apart from the constraints that come from the constitutional position of the EP, comes from their member parties remaining largely embedded in and gaining their principal drive from national politics. Indeed, no study of TPC with any depth can avoid taking account of the often influential part played by individual and, particularly, certain national member parties.[8] Any debate about an EU party system has, therefore, to include both levels to have any meaning, just like any discussion about the EU in general as a type of political system. That does not have to mean that the domestic levels have always prevailed over the European level in transnational activity. Rather, it may be argued that the gradual but limited growth in importance of TPC has involved a shift in the relationship between the logics of domestic and European politics in favour of the latter – as a consequence primarily of the expansion of the EP's powers and more broadly of the greater politicisation of EU affairs in member states.

In conclusion, there is certainly a convincing case for considering transnational party cooperation as a viable area for exploring Europeanisation effects, notwithstanding its limitations. It provides a framework rather more analytically manageable than trying to identify broad effects on national party systems coming from a country's participation in the integration process. Furthermore, it provides a significant arena for assessing direct Europeanisation impacts by virtue of the organisational character of transnational parties which may not fit easily with views in the early literature in this field that there has been little direct impact of the EU in general on party systems from CEE (Lewis and Mansfeldová, 2006: 231).

Political parties and EU accession: direct effects through transnationality

For at least a decade and a half now, parties from CEE have been involved with TPC, initially as applicants and subsequently as participants. Their status changed during this period according to the official position of their countries concerning accession. Thus, in the case of the EPP, parties were accepted as observers in the years before their countries were recognised as candidate countries, they were granted associate member status once this was granted and, of course, acquired full membership when their countries entered the EU (Kremer, 2008). It may be said that during this period the main political parties from CEE underwent a process of transnationalisation in European terms from their growing involvement in the party internationals and the EU parties. The above discussion has clarified the general scope and also limitations of this transnationalisation and further demonstrated the supplementary role of the EU parties in party development and professionalisation and even party self-identification. The discussion is now taken forward more schematically by noting different patterns affecting CEE parties and their transnational activity and examining these in the light of comparative party analysis.

Several features generally distinguish CEE parties from those in older member states, apart from their shorter time as members in their respective EU parties. For a while, they continued to reveal legacies from the communist experience, such as in generational mentalities, although this remained mainly a problem for the PES. Communist successor parties, albeit suitably social-democratised for transnational membership, encountered problems in opening up to pluralist debate, due to residual party culture, although that was more evident among activists than leaders or parliamentarians, who were those most involved in proceedings of the EU parties. Generational turnover among the latter, bringing in new party leaders and officials who were more linguistically versatile and confident than their older party cohorts, made a significant difference, as revealed in the author's elite interviews with transnational party officials.[9] Communist legacies were also evident in other forms, notably the tendency for parties from CEE – especially those on the centre-right – to declare anti-Russia positions; and this was also evident among their MEPs.[10] The relevance of these various historical legacies is that they conditioned and to some extent restricted the degree to which CEE parties became transnationalised although, obviously, there was much cross-party variation here, especially between Left and Right.

In some respects, too, parties from CEE took their time in shuffling off behavioural patterns from the accession years, when, like their own countries, they had been in an asymmetrical relationship with the EU and its representatives. This was shown in some cases by CEE parties playing a somewhat less active or less assertive part in EU party affairs, including meetings of party organs usually held in Brussels.[11] Clearly, the fact that older member parties often had better developed organisations in comparison with those from CEE made a difference, such as in resources which supported effective transnational activity. There was still something of a learning mentality evident on occasions among CEE personnel in transnational party business.[12] It should be added at this point that the cost of sending their representatives to the fairly frequent meetings of the EU parties in Brussels was more burdensome for most parties from CEE, which were usually less prosperous than those in Western Europe, and of course had further to travel.

Other patterns indicated that parties from CEE were moving away from accession mentalities. While post-communist countries had in common their compelling desire, when still in negotiations, to join the EU, their parties had, with respect to their transnational organisations, acted sometimes like a grouping or bloc, at least over enlargement matters. This gradually became less prominent, especially after EU entry, when these parties became full members; and regional or bilateral contacts and alliances came more to the fore, as had been the case for some time among West European member parties. That was noticeable, for example, between parties from Scandinavia and the Baltic states, the former having played often a formative part when parties from the latter – especially on the Left – had first developed after the fall of communism. For the Estonian Social Democrats, links with fraternal parties in Sweden and Finland have been especially important. Contacts with the Swedish have been extensive over time, involving political advice, electoral training and organisational help as well as some financial help and participation by district and local branches. Since EU accession in 2004, relations have become less one-sided and more balanced, with more emphasis on joint activities in addition to mutual conference attendance (Johansson, 2008: 168–9).

Direct effects of the EU parties on member parties from CEE could be categorised as threefold (Pridham, 2005: chapter 5.3). Firstly, there was a democratising influence coming essentially from the political conditionality exercised by the different EU parties with respect to applicant parties. This of course happened earlier on, back in the 1990s, for most principal parties from CEE. However, some parties took longer to acquire membership, like the Bulgarian and Romanian parties wishing to join the Socialist International (SI) and PES, because they took longer to overcome communist legacy problems and develop democratically (in the case of the Romanian PSD there was a complicating factor in that a rival Romanian party already in the PES blocked the PSD's chances for some years). One may suppose that over time CEE parties' experience of participation in EU parties, which operated according to established West European party norms, would reinforce any early effects that might have come from transnational conditionality.

It is nevertheless possible in extreme cases for parties to be suspended from membership, or even expelled should they persist in violating European political conditions. But this may be difficult to maintain for any length of time. In autumn 2006, the membership of the Slovak party Smer was suspended by the PES, as it had just formed a coalition with the Slovak National Party, whose leader was renowned for his ethnic prejudice towards Hungarians, the largest minority in Slovakia. This offended a PES political principle embodied in its 2001 Berlin declaration opposed to the incitement of racial or ethnic prejudice (Pridham 2006: 1, 8). The ban on Smer's involvement in PES business lasted for well over a year, until it was lifted early in 2008. The intervening period proved unfruitful, as no real dialogue developed between the two sides, not least because Prime Minister Fico took a hard-nosed approach in not being bothered by the ban and because he was determined to maintain the coalitional relationship. In the end, the crisis was resolved by a common statement on human and minority rights by the leaders of Smer and the SNS, sent to the PES.[13]

Secondly, the EU parties could exercise an ideological influence, depending on the opportunities created by domestic circumstances. This was particularly obvious during the early years after communism, when political parties were trying to discover their preferred identities. In such cases, they sometimes looked to European party links, whether transnational or bilateral, not only for political advice and material assistance but also as a means for establishing their basic political position on the national stage. The Internationals and the EU parties allowed interested parties to benefit from their established identities as legitimate European forces and to simplify if not shorten their own transformation into recognisable parties of the left or centre-right.

In Hungary, for instance, the Free Democrats underwent a formative influence from transnational choice, because their internal debate in the early 1990s over whether to join the Socialist or the Liberal International affected party identity at this early stage (Pridham, 1996: 207). Fidesz was, on the other hand, not so much influenced by European factors; rather, it used them to promote or confirm domestic ambitions, both initially to gain visibility through European Liberal circles (the young Victor Orban was an energetic member of the Liberal International bureau then) and later to underline and legitimate its shift to the right by switching membership from the European Liberals to the European People's Party (Ledenyi, 1993; Duhac, 2000). Both changes illustrated interactions between transnational links and domestic logics, although of rather different kinds.

This use of transnational allegiance was particularly significant on the political Left, since the dominant formative problem was that of overcoming association with the previous communist regime. Membership of the Socialist International, the first stage of transnational acceptance for parties of the Left, allowed former regime parties to convert themselves more readily into parties of the centre-left in the company of European Social Democracy, a process that was led by the Hungarian party in the early mid-1990s and continued into the following decade. The Bulgarian Socialist Party took some time to undergo this change, because of internal as well as legacy problems, and it became quite dependent on its relationship with the SI and PES to break out of domestic isolation and demonstrate its commitment to change. It finally became a member of both organisations in 2003 and 2005 respectively (Stoyanov, 2006: 199). In Estonia, the Social Democratic Party benefited from both its closeness to Nordic parties of the Left (which provided inspiration for its position over social policy and welfare matters) and to the PES, whose name helped to counter adverse domestic feelings about 'socialism' in a former Soviet republic now an independent country (Johansson, 2008: 162, 165).

One interesting feature worth mentioning is some evidence that ethnic parties have moved in the direction of adopting a more overt ideological positioning in line with their Euro-parties. Thus, the Hungarian party in Slovakia (SMK) has consciously sought to redefine itself as centre-right by virtue of its membership in the EPP; while the (Turkish) Movement for Rights and Freedoms in Bulgaria has underlined its liberal credentials through its allegiance to the European Liberals (Pridham, 2005: 170–1).[14] Clearly, the influence of EU party programmes may play some part in this gradual transformation. But, perhaps more influential, electoral considerations have been at work in trying to appeal to new (i.e. non-ethnic) voters while not alienating traditional support among the national minority.

Altogether, these different examples of ideological positioning or reinforcement cannot easily be categorised as secondary or marginal in terms of European influence. In most cases, they involved major political parties utilising European links as part of – or at key moments in – their own developmental processes. There was a common tendency for domestic actors to look outwards for European opportunities as a variant of the transnational/domestic dynamic. Thirdly, there was a direct effect in the form of an integrative influence. This is best discussed in more general terms with respect to parties becoming gradually integrated into European politics. One may perceive here some overlap with the other two influences: the democratising one reinforced CEE parties' acceptance of European political standards, while the ideological one allowed them to approximate to the established European political families. In both cases, this was by and large achieved during accession; while the integrative influence is one that commenced during accession and has continued and strengthened after EU entry. For example, the main parties now became full members of the EP, having briefly been observers just prior to entry, and before that confined to more informal links with EP party groups by virtue of their relationships with the transnational party organisations. Equally, their MEPs became a new element in party structures and sometimes acquired a certain weight there because of the special expertise in integration matters that came from working in the EP.

This reminds us that there was an integrative influence that focused on the European policy positions of parties. The education of CEE parties in integration policy really began in the 1990s through their involvement in the EU party organisations. Clearly, there was an air of professionalisation attached to party elites acquiring growing expertise in EU affairs, a process that began to accelerate once countries entered the negotiations stage of accession. And, obviously, this expertise broadened out once post-communist countries became member states, when governing parties (and opposition parties too, following any alternations in power) were compelled to deal with the whole range of policy making in the EU.

A final question is whether this deepening of EU experience has tended to strengthen the cross-party pro-EU consensus in most of these countries and make parties more supportive of integration as such, as has often been the case following previous EU enlargements (the British Conservatives being a major exception to this rule). Here, Central and Eastern Europe is unusual because it has been noted for the presence of various Eurosceptic parties, some of which have entered the EP. Certain of these parties have found it difficult to relate to the transnational parties, while others, invariably of the soft Eurosceptic variety, have managed to accommodate transnational links and increase their networking capacity (Pridham, 2008b). Finally, to provide transnational party cooperation with a more systemic perspective, the four conditions of party system institutionalisation presented by Mainwaring and Scully (1995: 4–5, see also discussion in Introduction) allow some scope for estimating the wider meaning of this activity. This is a pertinent test in the case of CEE parties, as party system institutionalisation is central to democratic consolidation, which it has been the intention of the EU's political conditionality to promote in accession states (even though that does not in fact embrace political parties). A brief survey applying the four conditions to TPC produces the following results:

Stability in the rules and nature of inter-party competition: the influence of TPC is likely to be minimal here. This is because it has no obvious direct impact at this level, especially concerning problems of electoral volatility, which have persisted and reflect the difficulties and longevity of post-communist transformation. A high level of party system instability in most countries (excepting Hungary and the Czech Republic) continued through the accession period into early EU membership. The only possible exception could be European elections, when transnational actors played a part in partnership with their domestic allies; but on this occasion – as the first time showed in 2004 – political competition, and certainly turnout, was weaker because of the perception of the EP's institutional limitations compared with national parliaments. In the Latvian European elections (June 2004), for instance, parties were more restrained in producing election material, and sponsorship for them was much less forthcoming from business circles precisely for this reason (Pridham, 2007a).[15] However, TPC could be seen as having at the margins an indirect influence, through election training and advice as well as assistance with party organisation, as a factor strengthening the ability of the main parties to compete or even to consolidate their political base.

The acquisition of stable roots in society: similarly, there has been a minimal influence from transnational activity, since the grass-roots of parties were too distant from the EU. Furthermore, societal factors were as much at work here as the efforts of parties to root themselves. However, European top-down pressures for party-political professionalisation and the provision of material and other resources from fraternal parties within the transnational organisations could be helpful in achieving some degree of societal presence. There is, nevertheless, one area where transnational activity could notionally have a more than marginal effect. That was in influencing the ideological location of individual parties, beginning in the earlier stages after communism and over time encouraging a shift towards centrist positions, such as in the moderation of nationalist rhetoric on the right. Once parties engaged in European elections they were required to adopt programmes from those formulated by their EU parties. In turn, any ideological redirection – where, however, domestic factors probably played the decisive part – could have some impact on electoral support, although this point can be overrated. Any transnational influences, which were likely to be quite cross-nationally variable, eventually confronted the reality that social cleavages were usually weakly represented through parties in CEE.

The legitimation of parties and the electoral process: the impact of TPC is most likely to be evident here, for being granted membership of a prestigious European organisation – in which important parties from older member states are present – is a major boost to party legitimation, especially in countries like the then CEE accession states, where support for EU membership was in most cases rather high. At least, that was the common assumption among CEE party elites from the early 1990s. Most decisively, it was the case with certain former regime parties seeking to establish their credibility in democratic politics and shuffle off their controversial associations. But European legitimation has also been important for new parties which have entered the political stage later on in post-communist democratisation. Of these there are quite a few examples, reflecting on the instability of their party systems, with major parties declining or disappearing. One may, for example, refer to the SDKU (a member of the EPP), founded only in autumn 2000, which became the senior governing party under Dzurinda and also the most pro-European of the Slovak parties. In Latvia, New Era (also a member also of the EPP) was founded in early 2002 and then went on to win the parliamentary election half a year later and to form a coalition government under its leader,

Repše. New Era chose as its primary election issue the problem of corruption and was able to gain credence here, since this was one of the EU's political conditions.

One should not, however, assume too readily that European legitimation of this kind brought with it an extra appeal to national publics. There has persisted in CEE a marked mistrust towards political parties (as demonstrated in successive Eurobarometer surveys) which is a result of both the communist experience and also public awareness of corrupt links between parties and economic interests since then. The prestige of the EU and the recognition factor coming from transnational party membership have not always been successfully harnessed by political elites for domestic reasons, because of their own involvement in a vicious circle of dubious party interests (Pridham, 2007a: 582). Evidence from the EU parties suggested they either denied that this problem affected their activity or, while recognising it, concentrated their attention instead on the EU's more visible legitimacy question (Cordery, 2007; Kremer, 2005). Busy transnational actors did not appear to have the time to engage with this problem, which was essentially rooted in domestic politics. But their sense of distance from it also reflected somewhat on the fact that their activity was rather elitist.

The autonomy of party organisations: many of the conventional activities of the EU parties were in one way or another favourable to party organisational development. This applied to their conditionality (e.g. internal party structures had to respect democratic procedures) as well as professional advice on election campaigning and party membership policy. This service was more common back in the 1990s; but even recently member parties from Poland and Romania have called on their transnational parties for help with rebuilding themselves following electoral defeat (Cordery, 2007). There was also the fairly regular involvement of parties in programme formulation and policy debate at the transnational level. This promoted some expertise transfer coming from both the EU party organisations and also from member parties on a bilateral basis, although it directly affected relatively small numbers of party personnel. One area where the SI and PES were fairly influential was in acting as mediating agents in the unification of the political left in Slovakia, Romania and Bulgaria. Their influence came from filling a gap as an acceptably neutral actor using diplomacy, persuasion and much patience to get the different left parties in each country to converge around and eventually merge with the largest party in question (Roll, 2001; Podgoreanu, 2003; Wiersma, 2005; Weiss, 2006; Petras, 2006). The motivation of the Brussels Social Democrats was to simplify the party system structure with a view to having a more viable partner party (and hopefully a greater numerical presence in the EP group of the PES). But it also had an important consequence for party system institutionalisation; and, of course, it had a direct impact on political competition.

All these influences from TPC on party system institutionalisation have to be viewed within the context of the lack of party system consolidation in most countries that joined the EU in 2004 and 2007. Dealing with this basic problem was beyond the capacity of the EU parties, since the deeper causes lay first and foremost within the domestic environments. Nevertheless, these EU parties found themselves called on sometimes to deal with certain party consolidation problems. The PES Secretary-General noted that member parties from CEE were more unstable than those from Western Europe, and different in that there were 'still discussions how a party can develop'; while the Deputy Secretary-General of the EPP remarked that the lack of party system consolidation, such as currently in Bulgaria, was placing special demands on the EPP which 'consume much energy' (Cordery, 2007; Kremer, 2007). This may be seen, on the one side, as providing the EU parties with (maybe sometimes tedious) opportunities for a formative influence. On the other side, clearly, persistent party system instability called into question whether the efforts of transnational party activity were having a productive and durable impact with respect to CEE.

Conclusion: European integration and the consolidation of post-communist party systems

The two processes of party system consolidation and of EU accession have, in most post-communist countries, occurred at the same time, in parallel. It is therefore reasonable to suppose these two processes have influenced each other and interacted in particular ways. While it is commonly assumed that securing EU membership provides an important guarantee of eventual democratic consolidation, it is necessary, however, to discuss how this comes about and, in particular, whether it applies so readily to party systems. In doing so, it is a reasonable working hypothesis that European integration has significantly more potential for impacting on party development in democracies that are new. Hence, early work on Europeanisation (mainly concentrating on established party systems in older member states) emphasising minimal effects on party systems should be treated with some scepticism.

It is clear that Europeanisation effects do not stop with EU entry, but continue and deepen thereafter, although concentrating (as in this chapter) on the accession process has its advantages, not least as this is an occasion for particularly intensive Europeanisation. As shown, accession had important impacts on the political environment of parties in CEE countries as well as having a variety of direct influences on them through the transnational European parties. But was that the same as democratic consolidation?

Some features of accession had a debatable value for democratic consolidation, such as the strengthening of executive power and time-pressure restrictions on political debate and, perhaps, scrutiny about accession matters (which is a general problem in the EU linked to the recognised problem of its 'democratic deficiency'). However, the onset of negotiations more often than not led to greater party-political differentiation on policy specifics within the context of a wide consensus on the broad aim of EU membership.

Alternatively, one might argue that the EU represented a form of 'political system' (albeit one still evolving) and that the wide cross-party backing for its membership implied a kind of systemic supportiveness. This could only benefit democratic consolidation, because the EU was committed to liberal democratic values and consisted of established democracies in the older member states. Furthermore, in pressuring candidate countries to modernise their new democratic systems and open them up to new policy challenges, the EU conceivably made them more effective and responsive as new democracies. The consequence of this was that the different political environment that resulted could – in terms of indirect effects from the EU – only encourage the consolidation of party development. That is underlined by looking at the relevance of political conditionality for political parties from CEE, for in summary this tended to enhance parties' observation of and commitment to the democratic rules of the game.

The discussion of transnational party cooperation showed that its direct effects on party development proved to be important, as they were complementary to these indirect effects. This is summarised above by applying the four conditions of party system institutionalisation. However, the outcome here is a varied one and it is clear that transnational influences had little impact on deeper (i.e. societal) problems of party system instability, including the public disaffection with political parties. In the last respect, there was no compelling evidence that the prestige of the EU in post-communist countries somehow rubbed off on parties through close association with European party formations. The greatest achievement of transnational influences has been to help professionalise parties and to strongly favour elite adaptation.

The consolidation of post-communist party systems is still not fully achieved in most new member states from CEE. It remains to be seen whether both indirect and direct effects from integration present during the accession process and thereafter continue to work through these party systems and eventually help them to secure their consolidation. Lessons from the analysis in this chapter suggest that the record of Europeanisation effects during accession has set patterns for the future. But they are likely to remain limited in the direct sense, while indirect effects coming from the changed political environment may well strengthen as integration deepens through EU membership. At the same time, it is evident that domestic factors will nonetheless play a vital part, especially where the societal dimensions of party system consolidation are concerned.

Notes

1 This paper draws on research for an ESRC Fellowship during 2004–7 on 'Europeanising democratisation? EU accession and post-communist politics in Slovakia, Latvia and Romania' as well as subsequent work as Senior Research Fellow at Bristol University. The Fellowship project involved elite interviews with European and national party personnel in Brussels as well as Bratislava, Riga and Bucharest.
2 See Lewis and Mansfeldová (2006) for chapters by A. Sikk on Estonia, K. Henderson on Slovakia and R. Markowski on Poland.
3 According to Philip Cordery, PES Secretary-General, there had been a noticeable shift in the attitudes of PES member parties in that they became more positive towards the Roma (Cordery, 2007).
4 The PES made several representations to the PSD leader, Geoana, to 'clean up' his party (Cordery 2007 and Wiersma 2007).
5 Although noticeable among party elites from different CEE accession countries, this practice was particularly evident in the case of Romanians, whose country had at the time the least secure chances of gaining EU entry. According to the Deputy Secretary-General of the EPP, the member parties from Romania 'use the EPP to lobby the Romanian case in the EU', for they 'could meet EU leaders in [EPP] Bureau meetings' (Kremer, 2005). This activity was emphasised by different party leaders interviewed in Bucharest (David 2001; Frunzaverde 2005). According to the former, 'we have done it [such lobbying] from the beginning, used this structure [the ELDR] to come closer to EU demands', for 'EU leaders have no time so when you can capture them for an hour of discussion they might understand what your problems are'. Time was usually given at Euro-party executive meetings for bilateral discussions.
6 It has become the standard practice for 80–90 per cent of prime ministers from member parties to attend the EPP's executive meetings (Kremer, 2008).
7 The international secretaries of two of the three Slovak parties in the EPP interviewed in March 2004 in Bratislava said they spent 60 per cent and 80 per cent of their time on EPP business.
8 Work on transnational party cooperation has tended more often than not to concentrate on the European level, such as on the party groups in the EP, although see Pridham and Pridham (1981: chapter 4) on the national party frameworks and transnational party cooperation.
9 E.g. the Deputy Secretary-General of the EPP remarked that for some years CEE member parties had been sending 'different people, especially young, who were not very different from people from the West European parties' (Kremer, 2008).
10 In the EPP, there were strong differences over Russia between member parties from CEE and those from Western Europe (Kremer, 2008).
11 The EPP Deputy Secretary-General recalled that CEE parties tended to play a somewhat less active part in programme activity ('this was natural to West European parties') although there was a change compared with a decade earlier (Kremer, 2008).

12 In the EPP, these differences in the level of party organisation and professionalism were, for instance, apparent in meetings of campaign managers 'where most of the CEE parties are there to listen' (Kremer, 2007).
13 It was understood that the fact the PES had few government parties among its members – Smer being a notable exception – may have influenced this solution (Polet, 2008).
14 Pridham, 2005: 170–1.
15 See the comment of Ikstens (2006: 103) that Latvia's EU accession hardly affected the general pattern of party competition in that country.

References

Cordery, P. (2007), author interview with, PES Secretary-General, in Brussels (May).

David, C. (2001), author interview with, International Secretary of the liberal National Liberal Party in Bucharest (May).

Duhac, J. (2000), author interview with, Konrad Adenauer Foundation, in Budapest (April).

Frunzaverde, S. (2005), author interview with, Vice-President of the Democratic Party for international relations and member of parliament, in Bucharest (November).

Grabbe, H. (2006), *The EU's Transformative Power: Europeanization through Conditionality in Central and Eastern Europe* (Basingstoke: Palgrave Macmillan).

Haas, E. B. (1958), *The Uniting of Europe: Political, Social and Economic Forces, 1950–1957* (Stanford, CA: Stanford University Press).

Ikstens, J. (2006), 'Does EUrope matter? The EU and Latvia's political parties', in Lewis and Mansfeldová (eds), *The European Union and Party Politics*, pp. 86–106.

Johansson, K. M. (2008), 'External legitimization and standardization of national political parties: the case of Estonian Social Democracy', in *Journal of Baltic Studies* 39, pp. 157–83.

Kremer, C. (2005), author interview with, Deputy Secretary-General of the EPP, in Brussels (October).

Kremer, C. (2007), author interview with, Deputy Secretary-General of the EPP, in Brussels (May).

Kremer, C. (2008), author interview with, Deputy Secretary-General of the EPP, in Brussels (November).

Ledenyi, A. (1993), author interview with, International Secretary of Fidesz, in Budapest (March).

Lewis, P. G. and Mansfeldová, Z. (eds) (2006), *The European Union and Party Politics in Central and Eastern Europe* (Basingstoke: Palgrave Macmillan).

Mainwaring, S. and Scully, T. (1995), *Building Democratic Institutions: Party Systems in Latin America* (Stanford, CA: Stanford University Press).

Petras, M. (2006), author interview with, Friedrich Ebert Foundation, in Bratislava (September).

Podgoreanu, R. (2003), author interview with, Executive Secretary of the PSD, in Bucharest (October).

Poguntke, T., N. Aylott, E. Carter, R. Ladrech and K. R. Luther (eds) (2007), *The Europeanization of National Political Parties* (London: Routledge).

Polet, Y. (2008), author interview with, responsible for PES links with CEE, in Brussels (November).

Pridham, G. (1996), 'Transnational party links and transition to democracy: Eastern Europe in comparative perspective', in P. G. Lewis (ed.), *Party Structure and Organisation in East-Central Europe* (Cheltenham: Edward Elgar), pp. 187–216.

Pridham, G. (2001), 'Patterns of Europeanisation and transnational party cooperation: party development in Central and Eastern Europe', in P. Lewis (ed.), *Party Development and Democratic Change in Post-Communist Europe: the First Decade* (London: Frank Cass, 2001), pp. 179–98.

Pridham, G. (2005), *Designing Democracy: EU Enlargement and Regime Change in Post-Communist Europe* (Basingstoke: Palgrave Macmillan).

Pridham, G. (2006), 'Fico's break with the European Socialists' in *The Slovak Spectator*, 23–29 October.

Pridham, G. (2007a), 'Legitimating European Union accession? Political elites and public opinion in Latvia, 2003–2004', in *Party Politics* 13, pp. 563–86.

Pridham, G. (2007b), 'Change and continuity in the European Union's political conditionality: aims, approach and priorities', in *Democratization* 14, pp. 446–71.

Pridham, G. (2008a), 'The EU's political conditionality and post-accession tendencies: comparisons from Slovakia and Latvia', in *Journal of Common Market Studies* 46, pp. 365–87.

Pridham, G. (2008b), 'European party cooperation and post-Communist politics: Euroscepticism in transnational perspective', in A. Szczerbiak and P. Taggart (eds), *Opposing Europe? The Comparative Party Politics of Euroscepticism, volume 2: Comparative and Theoretical Perspectives* (Oxford: Oxford University Press), pp. 76–102.

Pridham, G. and P. Pridham (1981), *Transnational Party Cooperation and European Integration: the Process towards Direct Elections* (London: George Allen & Unwin).

Roll, F. (2001), author interview with, PES official, in Brussels (February).

Stoyanov, D. (2006), 'The impact of EU integration on the Bulgarian party system', in Lewis and Mansfeldová (eds), *The European Union and Party Politics*, pp. 190–209.

Weiss, P. (2006), author interview with, former SDL chairman, in Bratislava (September).

Wiersma, J. (2005), author interview with, prominent PES member, in Brussels (October).

Wiersma, J. (2007), author interview with, prominent member of the PES and MEP, in Brussels (May).

4

Changing patterns of political participation

Mitja Hafner-Fink, Danica Fink-Hafner and Alenka Krašovec

Purpose of the chapter

In this chapter we focus on patterns of political participation in the post-socialist countries that became full members of the European Union (EU) in May 2004. When looking at possible changes in national political participation patterns before and after full EU membership we distinguish between: (a) long-term, deep change in the pattern of political participation, and (b) short-term variations within a longer-term participation pattern. This distinction is important for understanding the difference between deep-rooted participation patterns characteristic of a cluster of similar countries (including those with long-lasting communist legacies), and short-term variations in the amount and mode of political participation that are linked to party-system dynamics through electoral cycles and can be identified in all countries.

Deep patterns of political participation are understood in the terms used in the participation literature based on international comparative research mainly conducted on the basis of public opinion survey data (Dalton, 1996; Dalton and van Sickle, 2005; Deželan *et al.*, 2007). It has been established that these patterns have been co-determined by several crucial factors that may be treated as 'exogenous' to the political system (such as affluence) as well as by citizen competence – measured by either education or a subjective perception of competence. Research so far (e.g. Dalton, 1996) has indicated that such patterns of political participation seem to change only in the long term, over whole generations. There is no evidence that regional integration processes (like EU membership) have had any direct impact on deep patterns of political participation.

Short-term variations in political participation cannot be grasped without looking at factors endogenous to the political system, such as constitutional characteristics, the degree of provision for the rule of law, the operation of different institutions, and levels of corruption (see, for example, the findings of Lane and Ersson (2003) on the endogenous factors favouring democracy).

When looking at post-socialist countries it should not be forgotten that a significant number of citizens were politically socialised under a one-party system, where all permissible political participation was institutionalised and/or channelled by official institutions, in some aspects even by a repressive state apparatus. Party systems – like the entire political systems of a young post-communist democracy – have been developing in the context of multiple transitions (economic, social and political) and the consolidation of their outcomes. Some post-socialist party systems were consolidating while 'their' countries were striving for full integration with the European Communities and, later, with the EU. During the accession process post-communist candidate states were obliged to fulfil various criteria while adopting the *acquis*. They were closely monitored in many respects, including their fulfilment of the Copenhagen political criteria.

Nevertheless, European incentives and pressures have not intervened directly in the national politics of the 2004 accession countries, except in the case of Slovakia (see Rybář, 2005; Haughton and Malová, 2007). Also in the context of full EU membership, young (like old) EU member states have maintained a high level of autonomy so far as domestic politics is concerned. In that sense, it is unlikely that May 2004 (the start of full EU membership) marks a clear milestone in the domestic politics of the post-communist newcomers. Our main thesis is that *formal EU membership does not represent a deep change in domestic politics but rather the opposite*. As the accession countries had already proved to be sufficiently modernised politically (and otherwise) they were accepted first as accession countries and later (after positive evaluation by the Commission and the political decision of older EU members) as full EU member countries. This also constitutes an argument in favour of our thesis that *there are some domestic factors exogenous to a national political system that are decisive in changing a deep political participation pattern*.

The chapter is organised in several sections. After a short overview of the theory and previous research findings the empirical sections relate to two distinctive notions of change in participation patterns. First, we examine variations in national patterns of political participation among all countries that were EU members in May 2004 and (a) a few post-communist countries which were not – Ukraine, Russia and Bulgaria;[1] and (b) two old democracies which were not EU members – Norway and Switzerland (in order to control our findings). The aim is to identify clusters of countries according to similarities in their participation patterns as shown on the basis of individual data (European Social Survey (ESS[2]) data). A more thorough investigation of changes in patterns of political participation from 2002 to 2006 is presented in three cases (Slovenia, Hungary and Poland) – the only three new EU-member countries where ESS data gathering took place at both points in time.

While the first empirical section of the chapter is based on ESS data gathered in 2002, 2004 and 2006, the second empirical section complements analysis of the 2002, 2004 and 2006 ESS data with ESS contextual data,[3] as well as that drawn from the *European Journal of Political Research Political Data Yearbook*. Our research findings are summarised in the conclusion.

Theory and findings of previous research

Political participation has usually been understood as a general set of political activities of people within a certain society. In this chapter we build on Myron Weiner's definition of political participation (Weiner, 1971: 164), which refers to any voluntary action undertaken with the intention of influencing policy choices, the management of public affairs or the choice of political leaders at any level (here we should add the regional/EU and global level to the local and national levels mentioned by Weiner). For our research it is important to stress the voluntary dimension and democratic context which together draw a major contrast between participation under communism and activity in the democratised post-communist context – in addition to the democratic context of old(er) democracies. It is precisely voluntary political activity that characterises participation, a feature which is distinctive of participation in democratic regimes as compared to participation in non-democratic regimes (see McClosky, 1968).

Only since the transitions to democracy has it been possible to use contemporary concepts and methodologies in a comparable way when looking at old and young democracies (including those within the European Communities/EU). There are also communist legacies that have developed as a form of democratic mimicry of communist political culture which need to be accounted for when analysing changing patterns of participation over time. The democratic mimicry of socialist systems is reflected in institutions and political practices which, on the surface, look like the institutions and practices of liberal democratic politics but exclude indispensable liberal-democratic freedoms and elements of political competition. Transitologists consider the transformation of the cultural dimensions of participation of an authoritarian regime to those appropriate to a liberal-democratic regime as one of the most difficult and long-term forms of change, involving a process that takes several generations. This kind of change not only involves a quantitative dimension (the amount of political participation) but also affects the range of and relations between different modes of participation.

Although participation has gained a positive normative connotation in all political systems, including non-democratic regimes, it is only in participatory liberal democracies that the emphasis lies on various forms of free democratic participation, including the referendum, the activities of various kinds of social groups (for example, protest, pressure and interest groups) and the use of political strikes and demonstrations (Lane and Ersson, 2003: 255). Even in old democracies, however, protest activities have only been considered part of 'normal' political activism for the past few decades (Barnes, Kaase *et al.*, 1979). Research on participation undertaken so far has shown that on the micro level the key distinction between different modes of participation lies in the relationship between an individual and the collective level (see e.g. Dalton, 1996; Fink-Hafner and Kropivnik, 2006). In developed countries a tendency towards the individualisation of politics is visible and reflected in the shift from an electoral decision making based on group or party activities to one based on a more inwardly oriented style of political choice (Dalton, 1996: 7). This style is eclectic and egocentric, characterised by autonomous political decisions by individuals about complex political matters and their activities in various forms of non-institutionalised, non-hierarchical collective behaviour.

Social science research has so far also shown that it is possible to identify not only individual patterns of participation but also national patterns which are not necessarily the same as individual patterns in the same country. One paradox that illustrates this phenomenon is that, while in most countries a correlation has been established between education and the propensity to vote, in two of the most highly educated countries in the world (the United States and Switzerland) there is quite a low level of voter turnout overall (Newton and Montero, 2007). In addition, electoral participation is not a good predictor of various other conventional political activities. Although Newton and Montero (2007: 222) stress that 'participation is participation is participation', they also point out that illegal protest differs from other forms of political activity (Newton and Montero, 2007: 219–20). Taking account of the literature on the problems of party development in young democracies – especially post-communist countries (Lewis, 2000; Lewis, 2001; Kostelecky, 2002; van Biezen, 2003) – we expect that in young democracies *participation in elections will be a better predictor of political participation as a whole than in old democracies.*

Much of the social science literature published since the 1920s confirms that those highly active politically are limited in number, that most people are not very interested in politics, while some people are nevertheless willing to be exposed to political stimuli as observers or spectators (see e.g. Merriam and Gosnell, 1924; McClosky, 1968; Weiner, 1971; Verba *et al.*, 1995). Factors outside the political system (the economy, ethnicity and religion) have proved to have a major impact on democracy (Lane and Ersson, 2003). From established research we can conclude that some domestic factors are crucial to the differences seen between predominant patterns of participation in different countries and even world regions (see e.g. Dalton and van Sickle, 2005; Deželan *et al.*, 2007; Schwartz, 2007).

Although each country has an idiosyncratic pattern of political participation, one can still see some similarities in the patterns that emerge in different countries (Newton and Montero, 2007). In a book by Deželan *et al.* (2007) based on the International Social Survey Programme – Citizenship module data a typology of three worlds of political participation was presented. It involves: (a) the world with high levels of participation (i.e. above average) in which we find most individuals engaged in individually demanding forms of political participation (mainly in the most developed countries); (b) the world with mid-levels of participation (in terms of quantity, and including both collective and individual forms); it is here that we find the post-communist group of countries – with some exceptions, such as Poland, which has a very low level of participation and high levels of alienation; and (c) the world with a relatively small amount of political participation, which mainly involves collective political participation (generally in less developed countries). Within the EU the first two worlds mentioned have recently started to live together, operating within the framework of a supranational political system.

The typology is in line with the findings of other national and international comparative research based on survey data showing a correspondence between some major social characteristics and patterns of political participation. The characteristics of political participation in developed countries differ from those in other countries with regard not only to amount but also to the quality of participation. This has recently become particularly obvious with regard to recent trends toward a new individualisation of politics (Dalton, 1996: 7). The latest comparisons among countries or world cultures have shown an unexpected pattern, with a larger share of unconventional political participation or support for it in the wealthiest countries, which also usually have the highest democracy scores (see Dalton and van Sickle, 2005). Although social and economic development is often linked to democratisation, which fosters political activity, it should not be forgotten that a cultural-value climate supportive of autonomous thought and activity also adds to the variations seen among countries (Schwartz, 2007: 196). Research findings which have identified the particular characteristics of post-communist countries primarily point to a decline in political activity immediately after a transitional period (e.g. Kluegel and Mason, 1999) as well as to lower levels of political participation generally, as compared with older democracies (Kluegel and Mason, 1999; Barnes, 2004; Deželan *et al.*, 2007; Newton and Montero, 2007).

In this chapter we are seeking to identify the predominant national patterns of political participation. We follow a research stream where countries are taken as autonomous political systems and participation is investigated within national frameworks. Following on from the previously mentioned research findings, we have excluded electoral participation from the analysis – except for its appearance in a typology of political participation. In view of the characteristics of post-communist countries we have also directed attention to activities related to political parties.

As a rule, political participation has been researched on the basis of social survey data. Here the unit of analysis is the individual, who can be placed in a social milieu by taking account of social variables in relation to the characteristics of political behaviour under investigation. Our expectation was that differences in participation patterns among the current EU member states would be identified in line with previous research findings relating to differences among older and younger democracies. The more developed EU member states, with their longer democratic traditions, richer resources and the subjective competence of their citizens, were expected to have a predominant pattern of rich and complex participation. The less developed EU member states, with shorter democratic traditions, poorer resources and lower levels of subjective competence, were expected to have an overall pattern of a less extensive and less complex participation. The key cleavage we expected to find was one between young and old democracies (this was anticipated regardless of whether the countries were EU members or not). The main expectation was that institutional participation would prevail in young democracies (unlike the situation in old democracies). Since patterns of political participation only change over the long term and relate to deeper currents of social change as well as to generational transformation, the integration of these countries (together with their citizens) with the European Union was not likely to cause any immediate change in national participation patterns.

The general cross-national view of national patterns of political participation in 2002, 2004 and 2006

In this section research findings based on the 2002 ESS data as presented by Newton and Montero (2007) are compared with: (a) our own general research findings based on the 2002, 2004 and 2006 ESS data; and (b) an in-depth analysis of the 2006 ESS data.

The ESS 2002 research findings of Newton and Montero (2007)
Newton and Montero's (2007) analysis of the 2002 ESS data for twenty countries shows that for any particular country the participation level in any kind of association is generally repeated in most of the others. Spain, Slovenia, Italy, Portugal and Hungary appeared to have generally low levels

of participation across each type of organisation and, in all but a few cases, were around the twenty-nation average. Sweden, Denmark, the Netherlands and Finland generally had higher levels of participation and in most cases were well above the average. Luxemburg, Ireland, Germany, Israel, the United Kingdom and France were close to the average. Conventional political activity (the following activities undertaken during the past twelve months: voting, involvement in political campaigns; contacting political and governmental officials; joining, working for, or giving money to political organisations; being interested in politics; and talking about politics) appeared to be the most widespread form of involvement in democratic politics. But it was also apparent that protest behaviour had become part of the normal repertoire of politics. As with conventional political participation, Austria, Norway, Switzerland, Sweden and Denmark were well above average in three of the four measures of protest politics (lawful demonstrations, signing a petition, boycotting products and deliberately buying certain products for political, ethical or environmental reasons), while Poland, Greece, Hungary and Portugal were well below and had lower figures overall (lawful demonstrations were the exception to this rule).

In the search for an explanation of the national patterns, the authors compiled a set of indicators defining the social, economic and political characteristics of the twenty-two countries included in this part of their analysis: the Gini index, Freedom House ratings, World Bank indicators related to the rule of law, World Bank indicators of government effectiveness, Transparency International indicators of corruption, the degree of religious, linguistic and ethnic fractionalisation, government expenditure and some social and economic indicators (population size and density, degree of urbanisation, size of the agricultural sector, life expectancy, educational level of the population). The general findings are that high rates of all kinds of participation appear in wealthy countries with effective and stable governments that are governed by the rule of law (have low levels of crime, theft, corruption and black market activity, a predictable judiciary and enforceable private and government contracts). Newton and Montero (2007: 228) believe it is possible to talk about three families of countries with a strong resemblance to each other: the northern countries (Finland, Sweden, Norway, Denmark and the Netherlands) at the top of the participation tables; Mediterranean countries (Greece, Portugal, Italy and Spain), which generally have low participation rates on all measures; and Central European countries (Poland, Hungary, Slovenia and the Czech Republic). Common borders and comparable cultures also seem to correlate with similar participation rates – examples are Austria and Switzerland; Norway, Sweden and Finland; the Benelux countries; Ireland and the UK; Portugal and Greece; Hungary and Poland.

General comparisons: ESS 2002, 2004 and 2006
We can observe the following seven forms of citizens' active participation (for each of the forms, respondents were asked whether they had engaged in the activity during the previous twelve months) at three points in time (ESS, 2002, 2004 and 2006; Jowell and Central Co-ordinating Team, 2003, 2005, 2007):

- contacting a politician, government or local government official;
- work in a political party or action group;
- work in another organisation or association;
- wearing or displaying a campaign badge/sticker;
- signing a petition;
- taking part in a lawful public demonstration;
- boycotting certain products.

Based on the data for each form of political participation presented in Table 4.A1 in the Appendix, we can summarise the main comparative characteristics for the three time points (there are no major or systematic changes from 2002 to 2006). More citizens participate in old and established democracies. The most widespread forms (not including voting at elections) are work in various organisations/associations and signing a petition. When compared to other forms of participation, the proportion of citizens working in political parties is the lowest.

The ESS 2006 research findings
In producing a more detailed picture for 2006 – ESS Round 3 (Jowell and Central Co-ordinating Team, 2007) – we focused on the following:

- dimensions of citizen participation – principal component analysis within the 'space' of the seven forms of activities (prepared as binary variables);[4]
- a 'typology of citizen participation' on the basis of the dimensions identified;
- classification of countries;
- predictors of political participation (linear regression analysis).

To discover any general structure underlying the seven observed forms of political activity we used a principal component analysis for the pooled data set (twenty-three European countries; more than 38,000 respondents)[5] and identified two components (which explain 47.7 per cent of the total variance) representing *two general dimensions of political participation*. The first one – *institutionalised activities* – consists of three items (forms of activity): work in a political party, work in other organisations/associations, contacting a politician, government or local government official. The second one – *individualised actions* – also consists of three items: signing a petition, boycotting certain products, taking part in a demonstration. The seventh form of activity (wearing a badge) was not clearly connected to any dimension (it has the lowest loading on both components) and we therefore decided to exclude it from the two composite indexes produced for these two dimensions of participation.

In addition, several principal component analyses conducted for selected individual countries (Bulgaria, Estonia, Hungary, Poland, Russia, Slovenia, Slovakia, Ukraine, Austria, Germany, France, Portugal and Sweden) support the results presented above on the basis of a pooled data set, although they show some variation between countries. Besides 'wearing a badge', some other forms of activity were not clearly attached to a single component. From our data analysis it is not clear whether they were of a conventional or unconventional nature. For example, in some countries 'taking part in a lawful demonstration' appears to be of this kind, while in some other countries this is the case with 'contacting a politician'. Our decision about the two dimensions (and particular actions related to them) was finally made on the basis of three elements: (a) results of our analysis; (b) results of other research (e.g. Dalton, 1996; Newton and Montero, 2007); and (c) some theoretical ideas related to a post-modern concept of citizenship (e.g. Vandenberg, 2000; Beck and Beck-Gernsheim, 2002).

For further analyses two composite indexes for two dimensions of political participation were developed: *institutional activities* and *individualised actions*. Three dimensions of participation were our starting point for creating a *simple typology of citizens' (political) participation*: (a) both of the above-presented dimensions – institutional activities and individualised actions; and (b) voting at elections. We prepared all three dimensions as binary variables (yes/no) and thereby formed the following typology:

1. No actions ('excluded' citizens);
2. Only vote at elections;
3. Only institutional activities (+ elections);
4. Only individualised actions (+ elections);
5. Combined institutional and individualised (+ elections).

When we compare the group of countries included in the 2006 survey[6] we see some differences between them (Table 4.1). In general, in all countries the proportion of citizens who *only* participate at elections is the biggest. In older democracies, however, these proportions are smaller than in younger democracies. This is because in older democracies more citizens practise a greater variety of forms of political participation. It is also in older democracies that the proportion of citizens participating in the individualised participation mode is the largest. It is the difference between old and young democracies that appears to be crucial – and *not* membership in the EU. Switzerland and

Table 4.1 Typology of political participation (%)

	No activities (excluded)	Only vote at elections	Institutional activities	Individualised actions	Combined – institutional and individualised
2004 EU members – former communist countries[a]	25.8	50.5	8.9	9.3	5.5
Other former communist countries[b]	21.3	61.6	7.1	6.1	4.0
2004 EU members without former communist countries[c]	7.1	36.0	16.8	19.7	20.3
EU members before 1990 – young democracies[d]	18.4	55.1	7.6	10.6	8.3
Old EU member – old democracies[e]	11.8	35.1	12.5	23.0	17.7
Non EU members – old democracies[f]	12.3	24.9	11.0	28.7	23.0
Total	15.7	43.0	11.2	16.7	13.4

Notes: Weighted N = 38692; χ^2 = 5208.1; df = 20; Cramer's V = 0.184; sig. < 0.0005.
[a] Estonia, Hungary, Poland, Slovenia, Slovakia.
[b] Bulgaria, Russia, Ukraine.
[c] 1996 EU members and Cyprus.
[d] Portugal and Spain.
[e] all countries integrated with the European Communities by 1990, except for Portugal and Spain.
[f] Switzerland and Norway.
Source: ESS 2006.

Norway are examples of the typical pattern seen in other old democracies in the ESS country sample, although they are not EU members. Further, the proportion of citizens taking part in individualised actions is the largest in these two countries. Similarly, we see that Ukraine, Russia and Bulgaria (not EU members in 2006) share the young democracies' predominant participation pattern, although with some variation (their national patterns are extreme examples of having a high proportion of citizens who only vote at elections and at the same time very small numbers of those who participate in other political activities as well).

As shown in Table 4.1 and illustrated in Figure 4.1, the key difference lies between two groups of countries – old and young democracies regardless of EU membership. The group of young democracies includes Portugal and Spain, which are usually treated as countries that form part of the third wave of democratisation. This main picture persists even after clustering countries based on the proportion of citizens participating in each of the seven forms of activities (contacting a politician, government or local government official; work in a political party or action group; work in another organisation or association; wearing or displaying a campaign badge/sticker; signing a petition; taking part in a lawful public demonstration; boycotting certain products; see the dendrogram in Figure 4.A1 in the Appendix). In addition, the clustering reveals some sub-groups within each of the two groups. Within the old democracies there are three sub-groups: (a) Belgium, the Netherlands, Austria and Ireland (Spain is on the border between young and old democracies); (b) three Scandinavian countries (Finland, Norway and Sweden); and (c) Germany, Denmark, Switzerland, Great Britain and France. Within the young democracies cluster there appear to be two sub-groups: (a) Estonia, Russia, Poland, Hungary, Ukraine, Bulgaria and Portugal; and (b) Slovenia, Slovakia and, a special case, Cyprus.

Looking at the relationship between the two main dimensions of political participation (individualised and institutionalised) as shown in Figure 4.1 and from additional analysis we can clearly distinguish between two groups of countries: (a) there is clear positive correlation ($r = 0.618$, $n = 9$) between the two dimensions in the group of young democracies – the larger proportion of individually active citizens goes together with the larger proportion of institutionally active citizens; and (b) there is no clear pattern within the group of old democracies ($r = -0.106$, $n = 10$). Such a result reflects a new emerging trend: a greater diversity of political participation patterns based on individual choice.

As we expected, the young democracies' patterns of political participation seem to be affected by idiosyncratic legacies of the non-democratic old regime and transitional party politics. In young democracies trust in political parties is lower than in longer-established regimes. In both clusters (old and

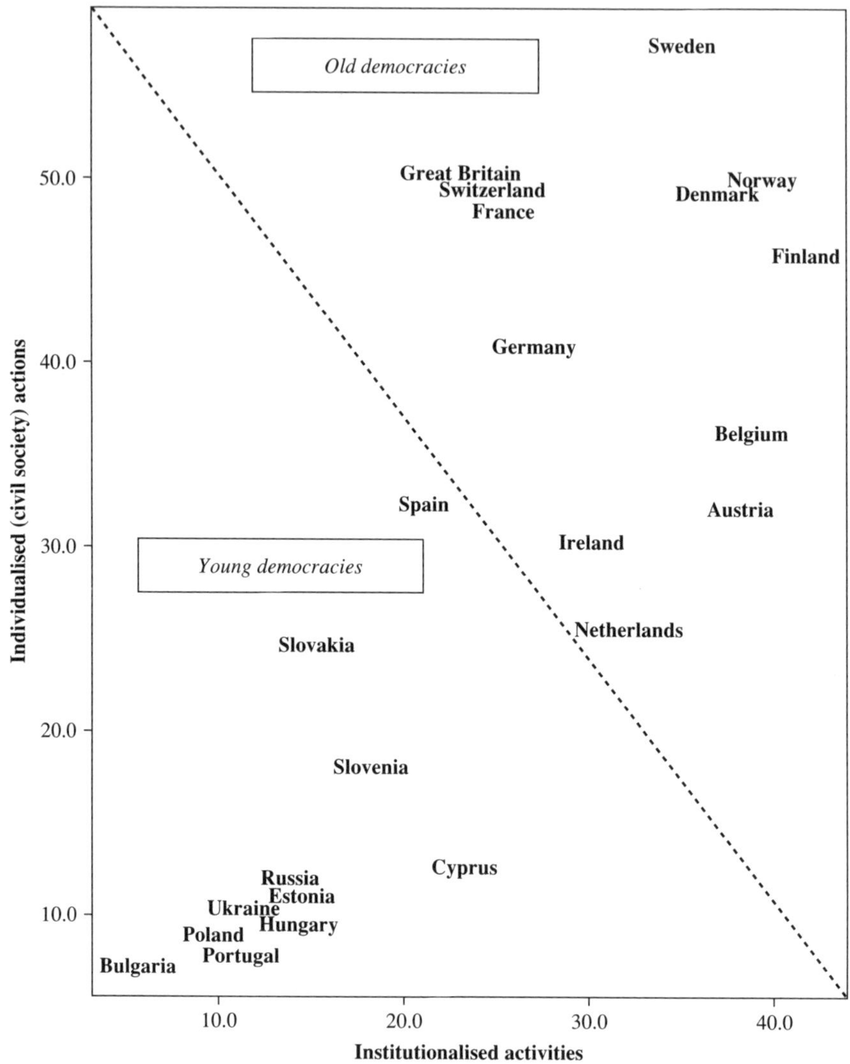

Figure 4.1 Classification of European countries by level of citizen participation (in %) in two broad groups of political activities

Note: Each scale presents the proportion of citizens who have practised at least one of the three activities included in each index. The index *institutionalised activities* consists of three items: work in a political party, work in other organisations/associations and contacting a politician, government or local government official. The index *individualised actions* also consists of three items: signing a petition, boycotting certain products, taking part in a demonstration.

Source: ESS 2006.

young democracies) trust in parties is highest among individuals active in most other ways. But there are some variations between the young and old democracies. In old EU member countries (most of the old democracy group), among the politically active the most party-sceptical seem to be involved in individualised actions only, while in young democracies, as a rule, they comprise those who only vote at elections. And there is one more finding showing differences between old and young democracies: it seems there is a stronger association between the political participation typology and level of trust in a political party in young democracies than in old democracies (Table 4.2). As a hypothesis for further research we may conclude with the general statement that in developed democracies citizens' trust in (political) institutions is becoming less related to citizens' political involvement (type and amount).

In the search for possible *predictors (factors in) of political participation* we applied a linear regression analysis. The analysis was conducted on the 2006 data set separately for a group of post-communist countries and for a group of other countries. Although several (individual) variables appeared to be significant predictors of political participation (due to a high N in both groups, even coefficients with absolute values below 0.03 are formally significant), only for two of them did we discover considerable effects in both groups: *subjective competence* and *education* (Table 4.3). Apart from this common conclusion, there are some hints of differences between both groups concerning the following predictors: (a) trust in the European parliament (a weak negative effect in non-former communist countries); (b) generalised trust (a weak positive effect in non-former communist countries); and (c) religiosity (a weak effect in post-communist countries) (Table 4.3). Since the coefficients suggest very weak effects, it is hard to make any clear conclusion at the level of pooled data – country-specific contexts should be taken into account.

Comparisons (2002–6)

Comparisons of Newton and Montero's (2007) cross-national analysis of the 2002 ESS data and our cross-national analysis of the 2006 ESS data (ESS Round 3) do *not* show a shift to deep political participation patterns in any individual country. From Newton and Montero's as well as our analysis, it is clear that there are two large clusters of countries – the developed countries/old democracies with higher levels and richer political participation activities (a wider variety of political participation activities) and the third wave of democratic transition countries/young democracies. In spite of that, Montero and Newton treat the Mediterranean and CEE countries separately, although they in fact show very similar national patterns of low political participation. Patterns of participation correlate with factors largely determined

Table 4.2 Trust in a political party – relation to modes of political participation in different groups of countries (mean values on a 0–10 scale, where 10 means the highest level of trust; ESS 2006)

Groups of countries	Types of political participation					
	No activities (excluded)	Only vote at elections	Institutional activities	Individualised actions	Combined – institutional and individualised	
2004 EU members – former communist countries[a]	2.51	3.07	3.34	3.14	3.71	N = 7014 F = 37.90* Eta = 0.145
Other former communist countries[b]	1.68	2.44	2.74	2.49	3.22	N = 5022 F = 33.95* Eta = 0.162
2004 EU members without former communist countries[c]	3.34	4.17	4.39	4.22	4.46	N = 6370 F = 22.39* Eta = 0.118
EU members before 1990 – young democracies[d]	2.45	2.79	2.99	3.41	3.60	N = 3655 F = 21.50* Eta = 0.152
Old EU members – old democracies[e]	3.32	4.08	4.48	3.83	4.15	N = 12562 F = 60.31* Eta = 0.137
Non EU members – old democracies[f]	4.19	4.64	4.56	4.45	4.80	N = 2911 F = 6.99* Eta = 0.098

Notes: * sig. < 0.0005.
[a] Estonia, Hungary, Poland, Slovenia, Slovakia.
[b] Bulgaria, Russia, Ukraine.
[c] 1996 EU members and Cyprus.
[d] Portugal and Spain.
[e] all countries integrated with the European Communities by 1990, except for Portugal and Spain.
[f] Switzerland and Norway.

Table 4.3 Predictors of political participation (number of different forms of activities taking place over the last 12 months – maximum 7): results of linear regression analysis (standardised regression coefficients, R^2, F) (ESS 2006)

Predictors	Post-communist countries	Other countries
Trust in the country's parliament	**0.036	**0.041
Trust in the European parliament	*0.027	**−0.047
Generalised trust (social trust) (composite index)	0.005	**0.059
Subjective competence (composite index)	**0.129*	**0.144*
Religiosity (self-estimate)	**0.048	0.006
Gender (male)	0.015	**−0.019
Age	0.018	−0.001
Years of full-time education completed	**0.157*	**0.216*
Place of living (rural)	0.006	0.006
Weighted N	9332	24018
R^2	0.057	0.095
F	**62.9	**279.0

Note: ** sig. < 0.01; * sig. < 0.05.

by factors from outside the political system – especially welfare, education and subjective competence. According to Newton and Montero (2007), important within-system factors are effective and stable government as well as government under the rule of law. Although with the 2006 ESS data we did not repeat Newton and Montero's analysis involving non-survey data (we only made an analysis of survey data), the patterns of political participation and especially the clustering of countries according to shared characteristics confirm previous findings (e.g. by Newton and Montero, 2007; Deželan *et al.*, 2007). In the empirical section that follows we look more thoroughly at the three countries included in all three ESS rounds (2002, 2004 and 2006).

Comparing political participation patterns in three post-communist countries before and after the official start of their EU membership

Poland, Hungary and Slovenia are all considered to be successfully consolidating young democracies. They all experienced a period of liberalisation before the actual transition to democracy. Civil society in the form of many oppositional social movements and newly emerging associations created pressure 'from below' in all three countries, although with some variation in the type of civil society organisations. Further analysis of the changing patterns of participation over time in the three countries[7] reveals some variations over the 2002–6 period, whilst they all remain within the basic participation framework characteristic of post-communist countries. In line with the analysis shown in Table 4.3 we cannot see any clear pattern regarding changes in major predictors of political participation at the individual level. *Education* and *subjective competence* remained the most important predictors of political participation at all three points in time – 2002, 2004 and 2006 (see Table 4.A2 in the Appendix). However, there are other findings that indicate possible new tendencies. First, it seems that in the 2002–6 period trust (generalised or institutional) was becoming a more important predictor. Second, only in Hungary does religiosity appear to be a significant predictor of participation (Table 4.A2).

In general, we can establish an association between party identification and political participation: *those who feel closer to a particular political party*[8] *are also more active* (taking part in several different political activities). But for the three post-communist countries subject to analysis (Hungary, Poland and Slovenia) we can also see some changes between 2002 and 2006. Comparing institutional and individualised participation, we see that in 2002 both are related to party identification at the same level, while in 2006 the comparison shows that the relation of individualised participation to party identification is weaker than for institutional participation (Table 4.4). It seems in this context that we can identify a tendency towards a clearer distinction emerging between (institutional) party politics and civil society activities.

The changes described are based on survey data and seem to have a logical relationship with political developments in the three countries investigated over the 2002–6 period (see the condensed overview in Table 4.5).

While political participation in Slovenia is a little higher in 2006 than in 2002, in Poland and Hungary some decline in political participation can be observed when both institutionalised and non-institutionalised activities are taken into account (Figures 4.A2 and 4.A3 in the Appendix).

The changes in political participation in Poland seem to be related to some negative trends in domestic politics. For example, in 2002 Poland faced the 'Rywin' scandal, in which some high-ranking politicians were involved. Further, the following year saw the 'Starachowice scandal' followed by the 'Orlen corruption affair' in 2004, which involved the prime minister. What is more, such scandals rarely reached any kind of legal finality. These developments were accompanied by several conflicts between opposition and government parties as well as tensions within parties, all of which contributed to government instability. Although Poland also faced quite an unfavourable economic situation during the 2002–6 period, it seems that some social

Table 4.4 Relationship between party identification and general modes of political participation (institutional and individualised) in Hungary, Poland and Slovenia (% of those who took part in at least one of the three activities included in each of the two indices – within the group of those who identify with a particular party and within the group of those who do not identify)

		Institutional activities	*Individualised activities*
2002			
Hungary	Identify with a party (%)	21.7	12.5
(N = 1587)	Don't identify (%)	9.3	3.7
	χ^2; df; phi*	41.7; 1; 0.162	35.6; 1; 0.150
Poland	Identify with a party (%)	21.2	16.1
(N = 1916)	Don't identify (%)	11.7	8.0
	χ^2; df; phi*	28.7; 1; 0.122	29.9; 1; 0.121
Slovenia	Identify with a party (%)	21.5	23.0
(N = 1385)	Don't identify (%)	10.3	11.9
	χ^2; df; phi*	32.6; 1; 0.153	29.7; 1; 0.146
2006			
Hungary	Identify with a party (%)	18.3	13.0
(N = 1439)	Don't identify (%)	8.9	6.8
	χ^2; df; phi*	26.3; 1; 0.135	15.2; 1; 0.103
Poland	Identify with a party (%)	19.8	15.9
(N = 1610)	Don't identify (%)	6.1	6.3
	χ^2; df; phi*	67.9; 1; 0.205	36.1; 1; 0.150
Slovenia	Identify with a party (%)	26.3	22.5
(N = 1342)	Don't identify (%)	18.8	15.9
	χ^2; df; phi*	32.4; 1; 0.155	9.4; 1; 0.084

Note: * sig. < 0.01.
Source: ESS.

reforms (like those in the fields of education and healthcare policy) mobilised citizens to some extent. In any case, however, such developments did not seem to reflect any EU membership impact on the pattern and degree of political participation in Poland.

Hungarian developments were similar to those in Poland in terms of certain negative trends in domestic politics – like domestic corruption scandals, intensive political conflicts between party elites and between the political elite as a whole and other social groups; ineffective government contributing to a poor economic situation, attempts at political mobilisation from above fed by an individual party's short-term political interests. Negative trends in the Hungarian economy also seemed to be crucial. In 2002 such conflicts led

Table 4.5 Main contextual data in three countries

Country	2002	2003	2004	2005	2006
Slovenia	• Presidential and local elections • Conflict between the Triglav insurance company and control agency • Debate on national interests (border with Croatia, brewery war)	• 5 referendums and more mistrust of politicians • Social pact for 2003–5 period concluded • Conflicts over social minority policy issues	• 1 referendum, EP and national elections • Ministerial interpellations • Accusations of corruption and clientism • Strike of 120,000 workers.	• 1 referendum • Conflicts caused by the new government's policy and political actions • Demonstrations against reforms proposed by the new government.	• Local elections • Conflicts between the PM and the President of the Republic • Several scandals in public sectors
Hungary	• Parliamentary elections • Former PM organised civil circles as a tool for mobilisation of citizens – frequent demonstrations • New PM accused of being member of intelligence service in the communist regime • Public divisions on lustration	• EU referendum • Number of changes to ministerial posts • Poor economic situation	• Two referendums, EP elections • PM resigned, new PM elected • Unpopular radical social cuts and education reform • Corruption scandals • Start of long-term negotiations of two of the biggest parties in elections for president of the republic • Poor economic situation	• Presidential elections ended only in the third round • Demonstrations by farmers • Conflicts between the government and national bank • Poor economic situation	• Parliamentary and local elections • Secret speech of PM and accusations of party lies about economic situation • Demonstrations against the government, indirectly supported by president of the republic (bipolarisation) • PM demands a vote of confidence and wins • Closing down of parts of public infrastructure • Demonstrations against these measures • Lowest level of trust in politicians

Poland				
• Several laws adopted after heated debates and conflict (labour law and tax abolition – later declared unconstitutional by the Constitutional Court) • Open conflict between two ministers • Conflict in parliament due to disrespect of statutory rules • Beginning of the Rywin scandal involving high-ranking politicians of the ruling socialist party • Poor economic situation	• EU referendum, local elections • Corruption in the ruling party (Starachowice scandal) • Two radical and populist parties against EU membership • Exclusion of a coalition partner – minority government	• EP elections • Corruption, scandals involving high-ranking politicians from the ruling party (new Orlen scandal involving the PM) alongside the old scandals • Splits in the ruling party • PM resigns right after Poland's accession to EU • Poor economic situation	• Parliamentary and presidential elections • Unexpected victory of Law and Justice • Disrespect of previously agreed coalition agreement after presidential elections • Minority government • Conflict over elections of House Speakers • Lustration • Better economic situation	• Stabilisation Pact among several parties, formation of a new coalition with radical and populist parties (PM: J. Kaczynski) • President pardons politician most involved in the Starachowice scandal; corruption in main parliamentary party and accusations of sexual harassment in coalition party • New lustration law targets broader circle of people • Disagreements within the coalition and search for a new coalition • Conflicts in the biggest opposition party • Conflict between government and national bank • Radical foreign policy actions involving EU and Russia • Demonstrations: (a) reforms in education and healthcare policy; and (b) against and for the government (low turnout)

Source: EJPR Political Data Yearbooks 2002–7, ESS event data.

to the organisation of the 'citizens' circles' co-organised by a former prime minister. They represented an attempt to mobilise citizens to take part in frequent demonstrations. But they did not bring about the level of mobilisation that was anticipated, and the circles were abandoned in 2003.

Some radical reforms and consequences of the poor economic situation nevertheless provoked demonstrations and protests by various social groups, like farmers and employees in the fields of education and healthcare systems. In 2006 there were even violent demonstrations against the government or, more precisely, the prime minister. A direct source of the dissatisfaction with the prime minister was the public revelation of a 'secret speech' at the party caucus where he explained that the economic situation was actually much worse than had been publicly admitted. It can be concluded that in Hungary there were attempts at political mobilisation from above fuelled by an individual party's short-term political interests, which were accompanied by more spontaneous actions by dissatisfied citizens. Neither of the two kinds of attempts to mobilise citizens politically can be directly linked to any 'EU factor'.

Although political participation in Slovenia was a little higher in 2006 than in 2002, any conclusion about the EU's impact on participation is the same as for the other two countries. Nonetheless, it is interesting to observe that participation in individualised political activities dropped significantly in 2003. Perhaps this turning away from party politics can be explained to some extent by the excessive use of the institution of the national referendum – as many as five were organised in 2003 (but mainly attracted low turnouts). In 2004 participation started to rise, chiefly because of a one-hour strike by 120,000 workers. In 2005 Slovenia recorded a sharp increase in individualised political participation – this was the year when trade unions organised a major protest against the government's proposal to introduce a flat-rate tax and demanded that the established procedures of social dialogue should be respected.

To conclude, comparisons of participation characteristics and their predictors in the three countries in the 2002–6 period indicate two trends apparently caused by domestic political factors: (a) a level of political participation negatively related to conflictual, corrupt and incompetent behaviour of political party elites; and (b) growing detachment from party-related political participation, which can be explained by the dynamics of the elite–voter relations seen in national parties.

Conclusions

According to our research, the characteristics of the post-communist countries' political participation pattern detected at the start of the 1990s persisted until 2006. Institutional participation (associated with party-related activities) remains the dominant mode in these countries, although qualified by the post-communist idiosyncrasy of a deep distrust of political institutions – including parties. Non-institutional, individualised forms of participation remain weakly developed and (according to the ESS data for Poland, Hungary and Slovenia in the 2002–6 period) seems to be increasingly detached from party identification. Nevertheless, in all the young democracies (according to the analysis of the 2006 ESS data), the most active overall were also those who expressed most trust in parties. It remains to be seen if this suggestion of a tendency towards a clearer distinction between (institutional) party politics and civil society activities will be supported by long-term evidence.

Within this deep pattern of participation, variations can be seen among the post-socialist countries as well as within the same country over time. A preliminary insight into these variations in three countries (Poland, Hungary and Slovenia) suggests possible domestic factors which may cause them. All in all, it is domestic social and political developments in accession countries and not EU membership itself that apparently continue to be the most important long-term factors co-determining political participation patterns.

Our findings are in line with the theses presented at the beginning of the chapter, although they suggest a correction to Newton and Montero's (2007) thesis on three country families. In fact, in terms of patterns of political participation there are basically only two main groups of EU members: old democracies (older EC/EU members) and the third wave of transition countries (both South Mediterranean as well as post-communist members). This finding supports the thesis that patterns of participation develop over long periods and are not radically transformed by EU membership.

Europeanising party politics

Appendix

Table 4.A1 Political participation – proportion of individuals taking part in various activities (in %)

	Work in a party (%)	Work in other organisations (%)	Contact a politician (%)	Worn a campaign badge (%)	Signing a petition (%)	Taking part in a demonstration (%)	Boycotting products (%)	Voted at the last elections (%)
Cyprus	10.7	8.6	20.6	6.3	10.3	2.5	4.6	92.9
Austria	9.2	26.4	22.3	7.8	21.1	4.1	19.4	87.8
Norway	6.2	27.4	21.7	23.8	37.2	8.1	25.8	85.6
Switzerland	6.2	13.7	13.7	5.9	36.5	7.3	29.0	66.9
Belgium	5.8	25.7	19.2	9.5	30.5	7.7	10.6	92.9
Spain	5.2	14.1	12.2	7.7	22.8	18.0	10.2	79.6
Finland	5.0	34.2	19.2	15.1	32.2	2.1	28.2	83.6
Sweden	4.9	27.2	15.2	16.0	44.5	4.7	31.0	89.2
Denmark	4.3	25.5	19.2	8.9	35.8	7.0	25.2	93.3
Ukraine	4.2	1.3	8.7	5.3	5.2	7.1	1.0	91.8
Netherlands	4.0	24.5	14.4	3.7	20.7	3.1	9.4	84.3
Germany	3.9	20.3	12.5	4.5	27.8	7.1	23.7	79.7
Ireland	3.9	12.5	23.3	7.2	24.8	5.1	12.4	75.6
Slovenia	3.8	2.5	15.7	3.3	14.0	3.8	5.1	77.6
Bulgaria	3.5	0.7	3.2	1.9	5.1	2.1	2.0	69.1
France	3.5	15.3	15.5	12.0	33.9	15.5	26.1	78.4
Russia	3.0	4.8	9.3	2.8	6.6	5.0	3.3	66.3
Slovakia	2.9	8.4	9.5	3.8	19.0	2.9	10.1	68.7
Estonia	2.7	4.4	10.6	3.2	6.8	2.3	4.9	58.6
Great Britain	2.6	9.3	17.2	9.1	41.1	4.5	24.2	72.3
Hungary	2.5	1.3	13.3	2.8	5.5	3.8	4.5	77.7
Portugal	1.8	4.1	8.5	4.6	4.9	3.1	2.3	76.4
Poland	1.7	4.4	6.5	2.5	5.5	1.3	3.9	67.3

Source: ESS 2006.

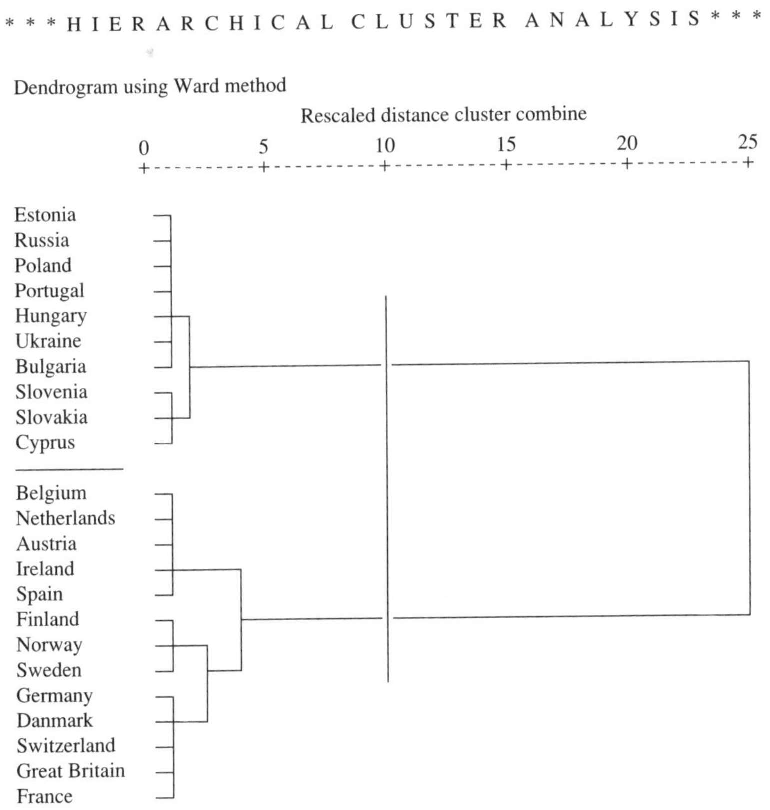

* * * H I E R A R C H I C A L   C L U S T E R   A N A L Y S I S * * *

Dendrogram using Ward method

Rescaled distance cluster combine

```
        0           5          10          15          20          25
        +----------+----------+----------+----------+----------+

Estonia        ┐
Russia         ┤
Poland         ┤
Portugal       ┤
Hungary        ┤
Ukraine        ┤
Bulgaria       ┘
Slovenia       ┐
Slovakia       ┤
Cyprus         ┘

Belgium        ┐
Netherlands    ┤
Austria        ┤
Ireland        ┤
Spain          ┘
Finland        ┐
Norway         ┤
Sweden         ┘
Germany        ┐
Danmark        ┤
Switzerland    ┤
Great Britain  ┤
France         ┘
```

Figure 4.A1 Classification of European countries by level of participation in different forms of political activity (contacting a politician, working in a political party, working in other organisations, wearing a campaign badge, signing a petition, taking part in a lawful demonstration, boycotting certain products)
Source: ESS 2006.

Table 4.A2 Predictors of political participation – results of linear regression analysis

	Hungary			Poland			Slovenia		
	2002	*2004*	*2006*	*2002*	*2004*	*2006*	*2002*	*2004*	*2006*
Trust in national parliament	−0.047	**−0.115	−0.063	−0.047	0.009	0.038	0.022	−0.008	0.000
Trust in EP	−0.058	−0.041	*0.064	0.049	−0.028	0.005	−0.007	−0.002	**0.112
Generalised trust	0.044	**0.084	−0.046	0.040	*0.066	−0.009	−0.036	0.033	−0.022
Subjective competence	**0.141	**0.096	**0.152	**0.172	**0.126	**0.123	**0.157	**0.138	0.169
Religiosity	**0.099	**0.106	**0.173	−0.006	−0.054	−0.009	0.053	−0.016	−0.019
Gender-m (binary)	0.014	−0.004	0.025	0.015	0.048	0.029	0.047	0.057	0.049
Age	−0.047	0.033	−0.031	**0.096	*0.076	0.059	−0.010	0.058	**−0.092
Education (years)	**0.100	**0.136	**0.157	**0.241	**0.219	**0.235	**0.127	**0.183	**0.140
Rural (binary)	−0.044	−0.012	−0.017	0.016	−0.007	−0.016	−0.055	0.002	0.047
Weighted N	1112	1149	1170	1359	1223	1311	1178	1091	1156
Adj. R^2	0.048	0.051	0.083	0.108	0.083	0.078	0.058	0.066	0.095

* Sig. < 0.05 ** sig. < 0.01.

Note: Dependent variable: number of different political activities in which respondents have taken part in the last twelve months (maximum 7).
Source: ESS 2002–2006 (Hungary, Poland and Slovenia; standardised regression coefficients beta).

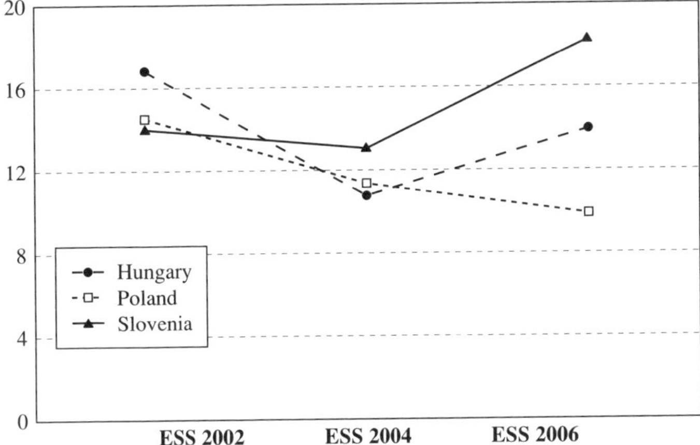

Figure 4.A2 Levels of institutionalised political activity in Hungary, Poland
and Slovenia, 2002–6 (proportion of citizens taking part in at least one of
the three activities included in the index, in %)
Source: ESS 2002, 2004 and 2006.

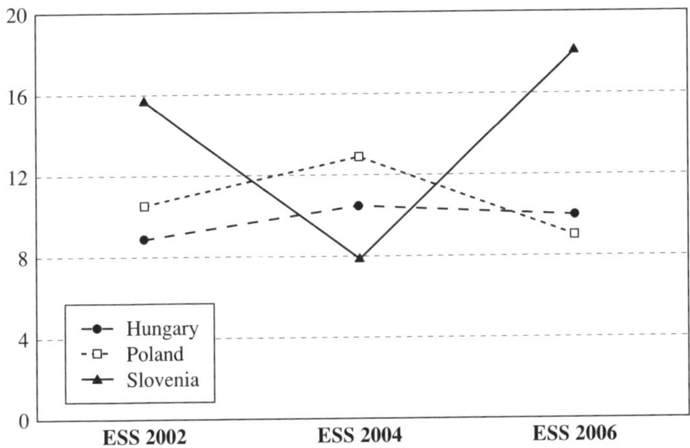

Figure 4.A3 Levels of individualised political activity in Hungary, Poland
and Slovenia, 2002–6 (proportion of citizens taking part in at least one of
the three activities included in the index, in %)
Source: ESS 2002, 2004 and 2006.

Notes

1 Bulgaria became a full EU member in January 2007.
2 We used data from the first three rounds of the ESS (2002, 2004 and 2006).
  ESS data are archived and distributed by the Norwegian Social Science Data

Services (Bergen, Norway) (NSD). For more, see the ESS web pages: www. europeansocialsurvey.org.
3 The data include information on politically relevant events just before the start of each ESS survey in each country covered and during the survey period.
4 The seven forms of activities included in ESS Round 3 were: contacting a politician, government or local government official; work in a political party or action group; work in another organisation or association; wearing or displaying a campaign badge/sticker; signing a petition; taking part in a lawful public demonstration; boycotting certain products (Jowell and Central Co-ordinating Team 2007).
5 For analytical purposes, each form of participation was coded as a binary variable ($1 = $ done; $0 = $ not done). We applied principal component analysis using an oblimin rotation of components. A criterion for a decision on the number of components was an eigenvalue higher than 1.
6 The following twenty-three countries were included in the analysis: Austria, Belgium, Bulgaria, Cyprus, Denmark, Estonia, Finland, France, Germany, Great Britain, Hungary, Ireland, Netherlands, Norway, Poland, Portugal, Russia, Slovakia, Slovenia, Spain, Sweden, Switzerland, Ukraine.
7 Based on an analysis of the ESS data for Slovenia (Round 1: 17 October 2002–30 November 2002; Round 2: 18 October 2004–30 November 2004; Round 3: 18 October 2006–4 December 2006), Hungary (Round 1: 29 October 2002–26 November 2002; Round 2: 2 April 2005–31 May 2005; Round 3: 21 November 2006–28 January 2007) and Poland (Round 1: 30 September 2002–19 December 2002; Round 2: 10. October 2004–22 December 2004; Round 3: 2. October 2006–13 December 2006).
8 As an indicator of party identification we used the following question from the ESS (Round 1, Round 2 and Round 3): 'Is there a particular party you feel closer to than all other parties?' There were only two possible answers: yes or no (ESS Final Source Questionnaire, p. 10; at www.europeansocialsurvey.org/index.php? option=com_content&view=article&id=63&Itemid=356 (accessed 22 November 2009).

References

Barnes, S. (2004), 'Political participation in post-communist Central and Eastern Europe', Center for the Study of Democracy, paper No. 04'10, available at http:// repositories.cdlib.org/cgi/viewcontent.cgi?article=1040&context=csd, accessed 31 October 2005.

Barnes, S. H., M. Kaase, K. R. Allerbek, B. G. Farah, F. Heunks, R. Inglehart, M. K. Jennings, H. D. Klingemann, A. Marsh and L. Rosenmayr (1979), *Political Action. Mass Participation in Five Western Democracies* (Beverly Hills, London: Sage Publications).

Beck, U. and E. Beck-Gernsheim (2002), *Individualization: Institutionalized Individualism and its Social and Political Consequence* (London, Thousand Oaks, New Delhi: Sage).

Dalton, R. J. (1996), 'Democracy and its citizens: patterns of political change', available at www.democ.uci.edu/publications/papersseriespre2001/dalton.htm, accessed 31 October 2005.

Dalton, R. J. and A. van Sickle (2005), 'The resource, structural and cultural bases of protest', available at http://repositories.cdlib.org/cgi/viewcontent.cgi?article=1066&context=csd, accessed 31 October 2005.

Deželan, T., D. Fink-Hafner, M. Hafner-Fink and S. Uhan (2007), *Državljanstvo brez meja?* (Ljubljana: Založba FDV).

European Journal of Political Research Political Data Yearbook (2003–2007).

Fink-Hafner, D. and S. Kropivnik (2006), 'Politična udeležba v posocializmu: med deformirano modernostjo, novo modernizacijo in postmodernostjo', *Družboslovne razprave* 22, pp. 55–72.

Haughton, T. and D. Malová (2007), 'Emerging patterns of EU membership: drawing lessons from Slovakia's first two years as a member state', *Politics* 27, pp. 69–75.

Jowell, R. and the Central Co-ordinating Team (2003), *European Social Survey 2002/2003: Technical Report* (London: Centre for Comparative Social Surveys, City University).

Jowell, R. and the Central Co-ordinating Team (2005), *European Social Survey 2004/2005: Technical Report* (London: Centre for Comparative Social Surveys, City University).

Jowell, R. and the Central Co-ordinating Team (2007), *European Social Survey 2006/2007: Technical Report* (London: Centre for Comparative Social Surveys, City University).

Kluegel, J. R., and D. S. Mason (1999), 'Political involvement in transition. Who participates in Central and Eastern Europe?', *International Journal of Comparative Sociology* 40, pp. 41–60.

Kostelecky, T. (2002), *Political Parties after Communism: Developments in East-Central Europe* (Washington, DC and Baltimore, MD: Woodrow Wilson Centre/ Johns Hopkins University).

Lane, J.-E. and S. Ersson (2003), *Democracy. A Comparative Approach* (London: Routledge).

Lewis, P. G. (2000), *Political Parties in Post-Communist Eastern Europe* (London: Routledge).

Lewis, P. G. (ed.) (2001), *Party Development and Democratic Change in Post-Communist Europe* (London: Frank Cass).

McClosky, H. (1968), 'Political Participation', in D. L. Sills (ed.), *International Encyclopedia of the Social Sciences*, vol. 12 (New York: The Macmillan Company and The Free Press), pp. 252–65.

Merriam, C. E. and H. F. Gosnell (1924), *Non-voting* (Chicago: University of Chicago Press).

Newton, K. and J. R. Montero (2007), 'Patterns of political and social participation in Europe', in R. Jowell, C. Roberts, R. Fitzgerald and E. Gillian E. (eds), *Measuring Attitudes Cross-Nationally. Lessons from the European Social Survey*, European Social Survey (Los Angeles, London, New Delhi, Singapore: Sage), pp. 205–37.

Rybář, M. (2005), 'From isolation to integration: internal and external factors of democratic change in Slovakia', in T. Flackhart (ed.), *Socializing Democratic Norms* (Palgrave, Macmillan), pp. 169–89.

Schwartz, S. H. (2007), 'Value orientations: measurement, antecedents and consequences across nations', in R. Jowell, C. Roberts, R. Fitzgerald and E. Gillian (eds), *Measuring Attitudes Cross-Nationally. Lessons from the European Social Survey, European Social Survey* (Los Angeles, London, New Delhi, Singapore: Sage), pp. 169–203.

van Biezen, I. (2003), *Political Parties in New Democracies: Party Organization in Southern and East Central Europe* (Houndmills: Palgrave Macmillan).

Vandenberg, A. (ed.) (2000), *Citizenship and Democracy in a Global Era* (New York: St. Martin's Press).

Verba, S., K. Lehman Schlozman and H. E. Brady (1995), *Voice and Equality: Civic Voluntarism in American Politics* (Cambridge, MA, London: Harvard University Press).

Weiner, M. (1971), 'Political participation: crisis of the political process', in L. Binder *et al.* (eds), *Crises and Sequences in Political Development* (Princeton, NJ: Princeton University Press), pp. 159–204.

5

Voter turnout and electoral success of pro-European parties in post-communist Europe

Mikołaj Cześnik

Introduction

There are two major features of voter turnout in Central and East European (CEE) post-communist countries. Firstly, it is relatively low. Mean voter turnout in the region (for the ten CEE democracies which are now members of the European Union (EU) – fifty elections) in the 1990–2007 period is 67 per cent (70 per cent if Poland is excluded), while for instance in Western Europe it equates to 77 per cent since 1945. Mean voter turnout in the new century is even lower – 59 per cent (eighteen elections).

Secondly, and more importantly, voter turnout in CEE has been steadily decreasing from the very beginning of the transition to democracy. Figure 5.1 shows this trend: in the years 1990–2007 voter turnout in the ten CEE countries has on average been falling by 1.43 per cent each year. If Poland – a 'deviant' case where from the beginning of the transition period voter turnout was low and has not been decreasing during the period discussed – is omitted from the analysis (Figure 5.2), the trend is even stronger (voter turnout has been falling by 1.59 per cent a year on average).

It is interesting that EU enlargement has not influenced this trend. However, it is worth mentioning that in two countries (the Czech Republic, Estonia) voter turnout in the first parliamentary elections held after joining the EU increased (by approximately 3 per cent in Estonia and 7 per cent in the Czech Republic). It is difficult to estimate whether this was due to any sort of 'European factor', but the fact itself is noteworthy.

A great deal has been said about the decline of voter turnout in the region. First of all, it has been argued that falling voter turnout constitutes a threat to democracy; many have perceived this process as harmful for democratic legitimacy and the stability of the democratic system, etc. Moreover, given the history of the CEE region, it is a great challenge to explain why

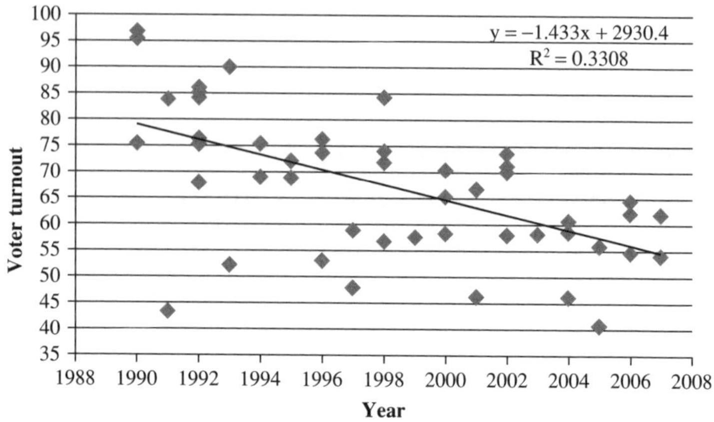

Figure 5.1 Voter turnout dynamics in CEE in the post-communist period
Source: Author's calculations based on IDEA data.

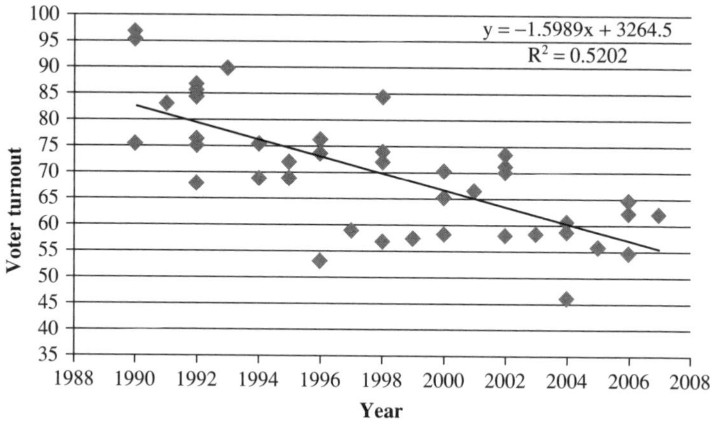

Figure 5.2 Voter turnout dynamics in CEE in the post-communist period, excluding Poland
Source: Author's calculations based on IDEA data.

'post-communist' citizens refrain from voting and participating in the most fundamental democratic procedure, which was for so many years unavailable to them. On the other hand, little has yet been done to explain this phenomenon. The problem is often discussed, but we lack solid, academic analyses that address this issue. There is little doubt that falling voter turnout, especially if accompanied by both falling legitimacy and growing socio-political inequalities (unfortunately a decline in voter turnout usually implies these two processes – cf. Lijphart, 1997), is of fundamental importance for the whole political system. It usually has an impact on parties, party systems, patterns of voting behaviour, party manifestos, election campaigns, competition between parties, electoral volatility and many other aspects of the political system. Therefore any analysis of post-communist politics cannot ignore this process and any research project on CEE democracies has to confront the issue.

Theoretical background

If voter turnout is low and/or decreasing, concerns increase about the functioning of democracy. Low voter turnout – a situation where many citizens do not participate in the most basic democratic procedure – is often perceived as a problem for the democratic regime. Arend Lijphart calls low voter turnout democracy's 'unresolved dilemma' (1997), pointing to the fact that low (usually unequal) participation spells unequal representation and unequal political influence. In such situations equality, one of the most fundamental democratic ideals, is seriously jeopardised. More specifically, Lijphart (1997) argues that there are three particular reasons why low voter turnout is a serious democratic problem in our time. Firstly, low voter turnout is usually unequal (biased against the poorer, less educated etc.) and thus systematically disadvantages lower social strata. Secondly, unequal voter turnout means unequal representation and unequal political influence (this notion is strongly based on the assumption that in contemporary democracies voting is the only vehicle for exercising political influence). Thirdly, voter turnout seems to be declining everywhere at the present time.

However, low voter turnout is not per se a threat to democracy. In fact, it matters in two specific situations (McManus-Czubinska *et al.*, 2004). Firstly, low voter turnout matters when it signifies the delegitimation of a regime. In this situation, non-voting 'carries the message' of dissatisfaction, distrust, lack of support. Dissatisfied citizens are 'left outside' the political system. This process undermines the democratic regime because dissatisfaction cannot be mediated through 'standard' procedures of electoral politics. Instead of being diminished, it grows, fostering populist and anti-democratic attitudes and behaviours. Secondly, low voter turnout matters when it overlaps with social and political inequalities. In this situation, non-voting leads to unequal representation and unequal political influence – parties which the electorate would otherwise have supported lose elections, and consequently their policies (which usually favour under-represented social strata) are not implemented. This in turn implies inequality as far as policies are concerned: non-voter interests and needs are ignored. Citizens whose demands are disregarded gradually become dissatisfied with the way democracy works. Often these two situations occur simultaneously, which is not surprising, since inequality usually leads to and correlates with the delegitimation of a regime. Citizens who are not represented (and thus unable to influence the course of political affairs) become dissatisfied; this process decreases diffuse political support (cf. Easton, 1975) and thus weakens the legitimacy of a democratic regime.

But low voter turnout can also be discussed from a different perspective. It can be considered either as a potential effect (correlate) of democratic crisis, or as its cause. Its status (as an effect or cause) differs, depending on whether it concerns the first previously mentioned situation (when voter turnout is correlated with satisfaction with democracy), or the second situation (when voter turnout is correlated with socio-political inequalities). If voter turnout falls because of increasing dissatisfaction with democracy (falling legitimacy, weakening diffuse political support), and dissatisfied citizens do not vote (there is a correlation between voting and satisfaction with democracy), then a drop in voter turnout is a clear sign (effect) of crisis of democracy. However, this situation also has an impact on democracy: dissatisfied citizens 'exclude' themselves from democratic politics (elections are its core), which can only deepen their dissatisfaction and frustration.

The situation is somewhat different as far as inequality of participation between social groups is concerned. If voter turnout falls because particular social groups (for instance women) refrain from voting, it may be perceived as a negative phenomenon in itself (especially from the point of view of many normative theories of democracy), but it has first and foremost 'prospective' implications in the context of policy which is to be implemented after elections. Members of under-represented groups have fewer chances than members of well-represented groups for their expectations to be met, their goals to be achieved, and their interests to be secured. 'Unequally' elected parliaments may (though not necessarily) implement policies which will disadvantage some social groups while favouring others.

It is an empirical question whether or not low voter turnout is in fact dangerous (or at least dysfunctional) for democracy. Even if we observe differences either in satisfaction with democracy between voters and non-voters, or in participation between different social strata, we cannot at once claim that these facts have any negative impact on democracy – evaluation of democratic performance is a much more complex task. However, if we assume that equality is one of the crucial democratic ideals (a widespread notion in the contemporary theory of democracy – cf. Dahl, 1989), then such results undoubtedly mean that something wrong is happening within the particular democratic regime we are concerned with. As voter turnout in many countries has been in decline for the decade since 2000 or even longer, the empirical study of the consequences of low and falling voter turnout has become a priority topic for political scientists. Nowadays, these analyses constitute the mainstream of the discipline, and our understanding of the problem has improved significantly. A great deal of data has been collected concerning different countries, different institutional settings and different elections. The conclusions that can be drawn, however, are not unambiguous.

On the one hand, some studies show that low as well as falling voter turnout matters a great deal. These studies demonstrate that those who vote and those who abstain have an impact on who gets elected, who governs and which policies are implemented (c.f. Lijphart, 1997). Many studies assess the relationship between low and/or falling voter turnout and support for left-wing parties, demonstrating that the success of the left is strongly associated with higher voter turnout (Pacek and Radcliff, 1995). Some studies go a step further, showing that inequalities in voter turnout, resulting in the particular structure of a parliament, influence tax and welfare policies and favour privileged citizens over those less so (Hicks and Swank, 1992).

On the other hand, there are studies (Lutz and Marsh, 2007: 539) which show that low voter turnout does not matter a great deal. Almost all the research papers published in *Electoral Studies* (vol. 26, 2007), in a special colloquium on the consequences of low voter turnout, suggest the minimal effects of low or falling voter turnout. Despite using different approaches, referring to different elections, looking at different institutional systems, they find no (or a very weak) relationship between voter turnout and the results of elections. In addition, an important contribution to these analyses is the distinction between the direct and indirect effects of voter turnout: 'Direct effects occur when higher, or lower, turnout would lead to an election outcome different than that with the current level of turnout. Indirect effects happen when elites lean their policies towards the voters and ignore the needs of the non-voters' (Lutz and Marsh, 2007: 541).

The latter analyses, showing the minimal effect of low voter turnout, suffer from two inadequacies. Firstly, their authors focus mostly on estimating the results of elections if everyone had voted. Such a research design, good as it may be, ignores other important aspects of low or falling voter turnout. Thus, it is difficult to assess the relationships between decreasing voter turnout and legitimacy, and between decreasing voter turnout and socio-political inequalities, which are, according to the previously mentioned theoretical arguments, of primary importance as far as a drop in voter turnout is concerned.

Secondly, these analyses, though rigorous and methodologically advanced, refer solely to Western democracies. There are many plausible reasons to argue that Western democracies are significantly different from CEE democracies in many regards – perhaps also to the extent that the consequences of low voter turnout are concerned. Hence, these analyses seem to be of limited value for students of post-communist politics, since it is extremely difficult to extrapolate their results to the context of CEE democracies.

There is, however, a counter-argument to this notion. The ongoing process of the Europeanisation of CEE party systems (Grabbe, 2006; Ladrech, 2008; Lewis, 2008), which results *inter alia* in the homogenisation of voting patterns, can make the above-mentioned analyses of low voter turnout highly relevant in the context of CEE democracies: as politics in these systems is 'Europeanised' (i.e. reshaped in ways that reflect patterns observed in the EU and Western Europe), the findings reported above, which show the minimal effects of low or falling voter turnout on democracy, become more valid in the CEE context. It is an empirical question whether and to what extent CEE party systems have in recent times been undergoing Europeanisation (in fact a major aim of this book is to answer this question). After the eastward enlargement of the EU, it is plausible to expect this process to intensify, accelerate and deepen. As a result, low voter turnout should become less of a problem in the region, in accordance with what some earlier analyses of Western politics have suggested.

Research question

In light of these arguments it seems crucial for students of post-communist politics to analyse in detail the consequences of falling voter turnout in CEE countries. This decrease has probably had many different consequences in post-communist citizenries. It has influenced the democratic regime, its stability, political culture, economy, civil society etc. Furthermore, it has possibly had an effect on policies. From a European perspective, it may be particularly interesting to investigate the impact of falling voter turnout on the EU enlargement process. If policies depend on voter turnout, then it is plausible to expect that there is an association between the drop in voter turnout in the region and policy outcomes (which of course have had an impact on the enlargement process).

This chapter, therefore, addresses a particular research question: *What is the impact of falling voter turnout on the electoral success of pro-European parties in the CEE countries?* Before elaborating, a more general question arises concerning possible links between falling voter turnout in CEE countries and EU enlargement. Becoming a member of the European Union was from the very beginning of the democratic transition a leading, if not the main, objective of almost all post-communist democracies (although in the early 1990s, when accession was a less likely scenario, party stances related more to a vague 'return to Europe') . For various, but primarily historical and strategic reasons, joining the EU was a major *raison d'etat* for each CEE country. However, becoming a member of the EU is a long and complex process. The European Council (Copenhagen 1993) emphasised this aspect of the enlargement process: 'Accession will take place as soon as an associated country is able to assume the obligations of membership by satisfying the economic and political conditions required.' The membership criteria for CEE countries were defined as early as 1993 ('the Copenhagen criteria').

Membership criteria require the candidate country to achieve certain goals. Firstly, the country must have achieved specific political goals, such as the stability of institutions guaranteeing democracy, the rule of law, human rights and respect for and protection of minorities (in other words, it can be assumed that the candidate countries must have launched the process of Europeanisation within their party systems). Secondly, the country must have achieved particular economic goals: the existence of a functioning market economy and the capacity to cope with competitive pressure and market forces within the EU. Thirdly, it must have achieved the ability to take on the obligations of membership, including adherence to the aims of political, economic and monetary union.

Under-developed and democratising CEE countries required a large number of fundamental reforms in order to meet the membership criteria. In democratic regimes such transformations are implemented through the legislative process, which is closely linked to elections: the policies and laws implemented are (more or less direct) outcomes of election results. As CEE countries are not unique in this regard (they are democracies, where the laws and policies implemented are a function of election outcomes), it is plausible to expect that decreasing voter turnout in CEE countries has been somewhat associated with election results and subsequent policy outcomes.

Hypotheses

What sort of association between (falling) voter turnout and policies do we expect? Our expectations about the relationship between (falling) voter turnout and (EU linked) policies are not 'accidental' or 'random'. We can hypothesise a particular connection between them. According to what we know about post-communist citizens and citizenries, it is plausible to expect that falling voter turnout has been associated with increasing support for pro-European parties (or the more broadly defined pro-European camp). There are several arguments that strengthen this line of reasoning.

Firstly, we know that post-communist citizenries have not been homogeneous as far as support for and attitudes towards European integration are concerned. Many studies show that joining the EU, though vastly supported in CEE countries, has also had many opponents (cf. Taggart and Szczerbiak, 2004). Accession referendum results reflect a similar pattern (cf. Tverdova and Anderson, 2004; Markowski and Tucker, 2005; Szczerbiak and Taggart, 2005) – in each country we find a large group of citizens who either voted against accession or abstained (abstention can be perceived as a 'softer' expression of opposition to accession).

Secondly, we know that (broadly defined) support for the EU is correlated with voting. We lack the comprehensive, solid empirical evidence for each election under scrutiny, but partial, limited and incomplete results show that there is a clear connection between the two variables. European Election Survey data presented below (Table 5.1) show this relationship: those with a higher propensity to vote are also more pro-European.

Therefore our hypothesis is that the lower the voter turnout in CEE democracies, the more successful pro-European parties are, and thus the more pro-European the policies implemented. The following logic lies behind our hypothesis: if voter turnout is falling, there are increasingly fewer anti-European citizens among voters (i.e. the voting segment of the electorate); this process in turn results in higher support for pro-European parties; higher support for pro-European parties affects the policies imple-mented (pro-European parties win elections and implement pro-European policies, or at least are strong enough to promote and advocate pro-European policies).

The hypothesis proposed has paradoxical and controversial implications. It can be assumed, in opposition to what most students of post-communist politics argue, that a drop in voter turnout in the CEE has been, paradoxically, functional for the development of democracy in the region[1] (it is assumed here that joining the EU gives democracy a major boost). No matter how con-troversial it may appear, it is plausible to argue that declining voter turnout in the region has facilitated EU enlargement. The whole process would have been much more complicated and longer if voter turnout had been higher and all citizens had voted (the anti-European camps would probably have been much stronger).

Research design

How to test the proposed hypothesis? Firstly, the unit of analysis must be identified. In the following analyses we focus on the aggregate level. A single election is the unit of analysis. In order to test the hypothesis we need to estimate for each election the values of two variables: voter turnout and support for pro-European parties. An additional challenge is the classification of all the political parties competing in all elections in the period studied and placing them on a 'pro-European vs anti-European' continuum.

Table 5.1 Relation between support for the EU and voter turnout

Country	*Generally speaking, do you think that [country's] membership of the European Union is a good thing, a bad thing, or neither good nor bad?*	*Did voter turn out for national election?*	
		No	*Yes*
Czech	Good thing	20.9% (64)	79.1% (242)
Republic	Bad thing	29.1% (108)	70.9% (263)
	Neither	35.2% (43)	64.8% (79)
	Total	26.9% (215)	73.1% (584)
Estonia	Good thing	16.5% (68)	83.5% (343)
	Bad thing	46.3% (38)	53.7% (44)
	Neither	27.3% (96)	72.7% (256)
	Total	23.9% (202)	76.1% (643)
Hungary	Good thing	17.9% (91)	82.1% (417)
	Bad thing	41.2% (28)	58.8% (40)
	Neither	26.3% (72)	73.7% (202)
	Total	22.5% (191)	77.5% (659)
Latvia	Good thing	17.9% (59)	82.1% (270)
	Bad thing	28.8% (30)	71.2% (74)
	Neither	26.7% (96)	73.3% (263)
	Total	23.4% (185)	76.6% (607)
Poland	Good thing	24.1% (84)	75.9% (264)
	Bad thing	39.7% (27)	60.3% (41)
	Neither	38.9% (107)	61.1% (168)
	Total	31.5% (218)	68.5% (473)
Slovakia	Good thing	12.5% (44)	87.5% (307)
	Bad thing	27.4% (17)	72.6% (45)
	Neither	26.6% (109)	73.4% (301)
	Total	20.7% (170)	79.3% (653)
Slovenia	Good thing	17.5% (80)	82.5% (378)
	Bad thing	39.1% (25)	60.9% (39)
	Neither	28.4% (33)	71.6% (83)
	Total	21.6% (138)	78.4% (500)

Note: In all countries the relationship is statistically significant (Chi-square test p < .01).
Source: European Election Study 2004.

Secondly, the data used below must be discussed. Empirical tests of the proposed hypothesis require different data: both aggregate-level and individual-level data are necessary. In general, as our hypothesis pertains to the aggregate level, such data are crucial: for each election aggregate-level measures (levels of voter turnout and support for pro-European parties) must be obtained. However, the use of individual-level data would be advantageous as well.

Limiting an analysis to the aggregate level brings about the danger of committing an ecological fallacy. Negative correlation observed on the aggregate level between voter turnout and support for pro-European parties does not imply any association between voting and supporting EU on an individual level. Indeed, a drop in voter turnout can be caused by citizens who are very pro-European and who switched from voting to non-voting for entirely different reasons. The same is relevant for an increase in support for pro-European parties – their success can have very different causes than their pro-European or anti-European profile. Thus, finding a negative correlation between voter turnout and support for pro-European parties on the aggregate level cannot be a definitive confirmation of the hypothesis tested. Nonetheless, such an observation would be an important result, reinforcing the probability that a hypothesised relationship exists (especially in light of the knowledge we have about the relationship on the individual level between voting and supporting Europe).

Thus, an 'ideal' empirical test of the proposed hypothesis would also require individual-level data, which could show that non-voters (in particular elections) are more anti-European than voters. If we could estimate non-voters' policy preferences and, more importantly, their party preferences, it would be possible to estimate the results of the election, had everyone voted (had non-voters participated in the election and had they voted according to their preferences expressed during an interview). Then we could show what would have been the impact of increased voter turnout on election results (and the policies implemented as a consequence of election results).

The best data for these purposes would be a National Election Study (NES) (for each election), which usually includes the best estimates of voter turnout and political attitudes of a given citizenry in the election period.[2] Studies which are not fielded in the election period suffer from many deficiencies (e.g. higher over-reporting of voter turnout) and as such are less useful for analyses of voting behaviour and political attitudes (and relationships between them).

We lack such data for all the elections under scrutiny, so we cannot estimate either non-voters' policy preferences or their party preferences for each election. As a result we cannot assess the relationship between voting and being pro-European, which is crucial for testing our hypothesis (only if we know there is such a relationship can we then argue that in particular elections an increase in voter turnout would have resulted in a decrease in support for pro-European parties). However, the partial evidence mentioned above shows a fairly clear pattern: voting is positively associated with pro-European attitudes at the individual level. Thus we are compelled to make a significant assumption (which is relatively well supported, at least for several elections) that, in each election, a decrease in voter turnout is caused by the transition of certain citizens from voting to abstention, which implies an increase in the number of pro-Europeans in the (active) electorate.

A crucial element of the analysis is a comparison of voter turnout and support for pro-European parties. These data are relatively easy to collect. Once they have been collected, the relationship between the two variables must be investigated. Regression analysis is employed for this purpose: we estimate the effect of a drop in voter turnout in support of pro-European parties.

More problematic is the estimation of support for pro-European parties. Policy positioning and locating parties in the political space has for a long time been one of the major challenges students of politics have faced. Indeed, in most political systems it is rather difficult to tell where a particular party is located on a certain issue – parties are often heterogeneous in this regard (factions), their voters can differ from the party elite, electoral manifestos tend to be at odds with what parties really intend to do etc. Thus, it is difficult to provide a comprehensive and at the same time unquestionable classification of the position of parties in the political space. This also pertains to parties' positions on EU-related issues in post-communist democracies.

How can we estimate parties' positions in the political space (or on a particular issue)? Spatial theories of politics propose various ways of estimating policy positions. Some students of politics rely on survey data (mean position of voters or the party elite), others employ expert techniques (expert judgements), yet others study their budget structure (Klingemann *et al.*, 1994). One interesting line of research refers to electoral platforms and manifestos (Klingemann *et al.*, 2006). In this study, this method of estimating the policy positions of parties is employed. Using a data set produced by the Manifestos Research Group project (MRG) we estimate how pro-European and anti-European a particular party is. Unfortunately, we must limit ourselves to electorally successful parties – the project only coded the manifestos of those parties that won seats in parliament.

For each electoral manifesto all quasi-sentences that constitute the document are ascribed to one and only one category of the coding scheme. There are fifty-six categories (plus an extra category: 'no category applies'). There are two categories related to Europe and European integration: categories 108 (positive references to Europe and European integration) and 110 (negative references to Europe and European integration). For each manifesto the values of these two variables can be obtained. Thus, on this basis each party can be classified as pro- or anti-European – the only question is how to do this technically.

The authors of the MRG/CMP (Comparative Manifestos Project) data set estimate for each party an indicator of being pro-European (EUROP – category 110 subtracted from category 108). In our analyses each party that is more pro-European than the average (that has a value of EUROP above its mean) is coded as pro-European. Then the percentage of votes cast for all these parties is calculated; this is the value of the 'support for pro-European parties' variable (which is estimated for each election). One could argue that it would be more appropriate to define as pro-European all parties that have positive values of EUROP (category 110 subtracted from category 108). However, then almost all the parties studied would have been coded as pro-European and there would not be any variance (there are only 8 parties out of 310 which are anti-European, i.e. with a negative EUROP value).

Empirical test

In order to test the hypothesis one must compare voter turnout with support for pro-European parties. Both variables have now been conceptualised and operationalised. Firstly, the distributions of both variables must be investigated. Voter turnout dynamics in the post-communist period have already been discussed (see Introduction). However, what has the support been for pro-European parties in the ten new EU member states during the post-communist period? Has it been stable? Have there been any cross-country differences? Figure 5.3 shows the dynamics of support for pro-European parties in the ten new EU member states in the years 1990–2003.

Support for pro-European parties in the ten new EU post-communist member states has been steadily increasing in the years 1990–2003, as the results of the analysis presented in Figure 5.3 show. In some elections in the early 1990s support for pro-European parties was around zero. On the eve of

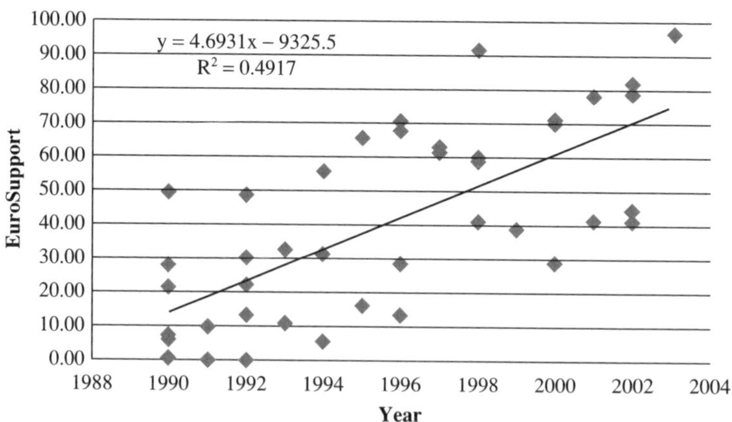

Figure 5.3 Support for pro-European parties in the post-communist period
Source: Author's calculations based on MRG/CMP data.

Table 5.2 Support for pro-European parties in CEE countries

Country	N (elections)	Minimum	Maximum	Mean	Standard deviation
Bulgaria	5	0.00	78.07	30.44	36.93
Czech Republic	5	40.91	70.50	50.76	11.54
Estonia	4	16.19	95.09	43.05	36.01
Hungary	4	21.40	91.48	46.35	31.14
Latvia	4	32.41	78.80	59.18	19.52
Lithuania	3	0.00	67.39	32.11	33.81
Poland	4	9.52	61.35	30.82	25.09
Romania	4	0.00	69.93	24.72	32.93
Slovakia	5	27.87	81.81	50.82	22.39
Slovenia	4	7.39	70.87	26.24	29.88

Source: Author's calculations based on MRG/CMP data.

enlargement it was way higher, ranging from 40–50 per cent to 80–90 per cent. On average, during the period studied, support for pro-European parties has been increasing by more than 4 per cent per year. Correlation between the variables is strong (Pearson's R equals 0.70) and statistically significant.

Though the pattern observed is very clear, there are significant differences between elections – even those held in the same year (Table 5.2). Moreover, there is significant cross-country variance: some party systems are more pro-European (the Czech Republic, Latvia), while others are less so (Romania, Slovenia); within some party systems the differences (between elections) are higher (Bulgaria, Estonia), while elsewhere they are more moderate (the Czech Republic, Latvia).

These findings are in line with our hypothesis. We hypothesise that there is a negative correlation between voter turnout and support for pro-European parties. As we find a strong correlation between time and both voter turnout (negative) and support for pro-European parties (positive), we can expect to find that both variables are closely correlated. In fact the relationship is weaker than expected.

Figure 5.4 shows the relationship between voter turnout and support for pro-European parties in the ten new EU member states in the years 1990–2003. The X-axis represents voter turnout, while the Y-axis represents support for pro-European parties (as defined earlier). As can be seen, the correlation between these two variables is negative (Pearson's R equals −0.28), and is almost statistically significant (p = 0.068). According to this basic OLS model,[3] a 1 per cent increase in voter turnout signifies a drop in support for pro-European parties of 0.6 per cent.

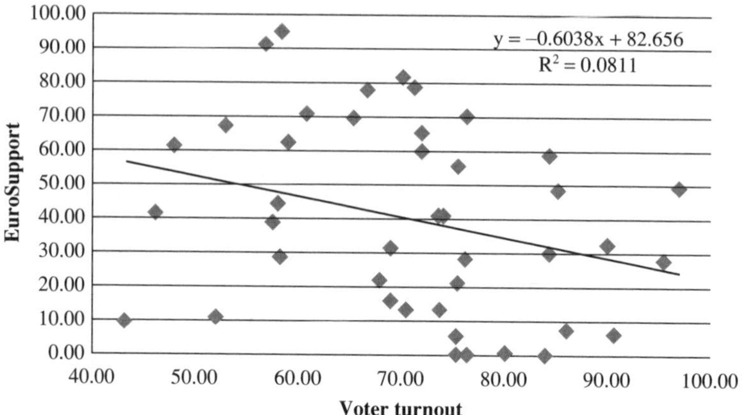

Figure 5.4 Voter turnout and support for pro-European parties
Source: Author's calculations based on MRG/CMP and IDEA data.

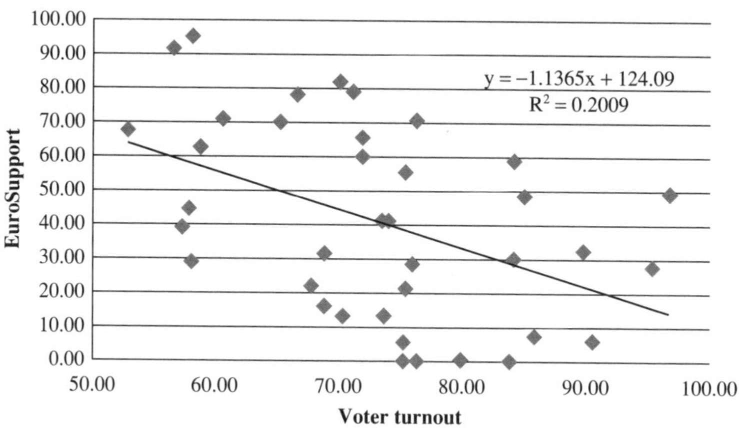

Figure 5.5 Voter turnout and support for pro-European parties, excluding Poland
Source: Author's calculations based on MRG/CMP and IDEA data.

As it was argued earlier, Poland is a deviant case as far as voter turnout is concerned. While in other CEE countries it has been gradually falling during the post-communist period, in Poland it has been relatively stable. Thus it is plausible to omit Poland from this analysis. Figure 5.5 shows the results. If Poland is omitted, the correlation is stronger (Pearson's R equals −0.45) and is statistically significant. The model suggests that a 1 per cent increase in voter turnout signifies a 1.14 per cent drop in support for pro-European parties.

There is one more deviant case – the Czech Republic (see Table 5.1). If this country is also omitted from the analysis, the model fit increases to

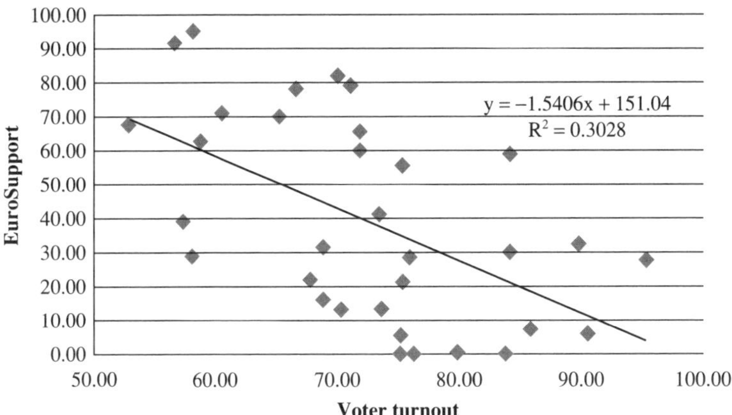

Figure 5.6 Voter turnout and support for pro-European parties, excluding Poland and the Czech Republic
Source: Author's calculations based on MRG/CMP and IDEA data.

more than 30 per cent. Therefore, if we do not include in our analysis two exceptional, deviant cases (Poland and the Czech Republic – Figure 5.6), the pattern is much more evident and stronger (Pearson's R equals −0.55 and is significant at the level of 0.01). According to this model, a 1 per cent increase in voter turnout signifies a drop in support for pro-European parties of 1.5 per cent.

These analyses imply a negative relationship between voter turnout and support for pro-European parties. However, is there a link between voter turnout and the policies implemented? Using the MRG/CMP data it is possible to estimate not only support for pro-European parties, but also the programmatic profile of the government formed after each election.[4] A government's policy position is the weighted mean score of the parties in government (estimated on the basis of their programmes) on an EU scale. Weights are the proportions of parliamentary seats held by each party in government.

What are the results? Firstly, there is a clear positive relationship (Pearson's R equals 0.6) between support for pro-European parties and a pro-European profile of government. Figure 5.7 shows this pattern. This means that the representation mechanism in CEE countries works effectively (at least as far as Europe-related issues and policies are concerned): higher support for pro-European parties in particular elections indicates a more pro-European profile of the government formed as a result of the election.

Poland and the Czech Republic are outliers, as seen above. Therefore, it is also possible to omit them from the analysis. Indeed, if they are removed from the analysis (Figure 5.8), the correlation is stronger (Pearson's R equals 0.8) and the model fit is much better (the model explains more than 65 per cent of

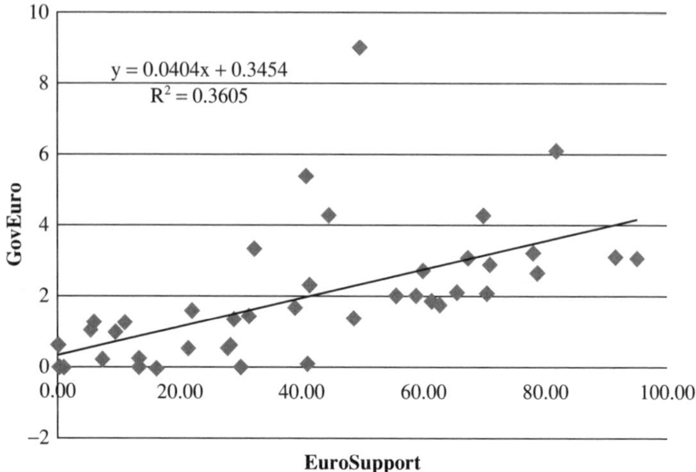

Figure 5.7 Support for pro-European parties and the European profile
of the government
Source: Author's calculations based on MRG/CMP data.

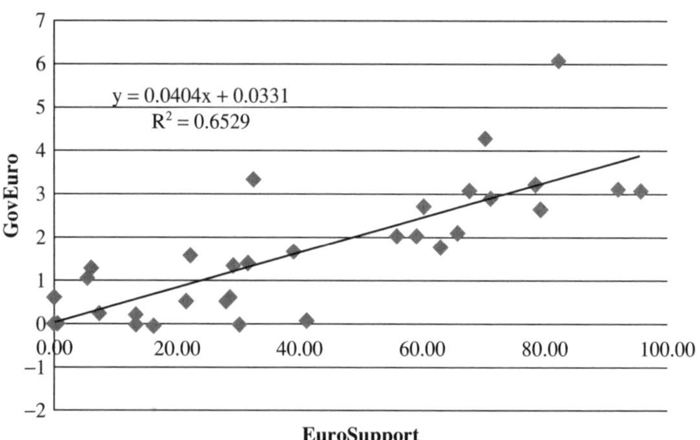

Figure 5.8 Support for pro-European parties and the European profile of
governments, excluding Poland and the Czech Republic
Source: Author's calculations based on MRG/CMP data.

the variance observed). There is a clear linear relationship between electoral
support for pro-European parties and the programmatic profile of the governments formed (at least to the extent that European issues are concerned): the
higher the support, the more pro-European the government. This is a very
important finding as far as representation and responsiveness mechanisms in
CEE countries are concerned.

Conclusion

One of the chief questions in contemporary political science is what the consequences are of (falling) voter turnout. Some students of voting behaviour downplay its role, while others perceive it as the main threat to democracy. The key aim of this paper has been to discuss the effect of falling voter turnout on election results in CEE countries in the years 1990–2003. More specifically, the relationship between voter turnout and support for pro-European parties (and its effects) has been scrutinised. Our findings highlight several important points about voter turnout and election outcomes.

Firstly, empirical results confirm that voter turnout matters for election results. Its decline in the CEE region in the period 1990–2003 greatly affected election results (which doubtless had an impact on policies). There is evidence that support for pro-European parties was gradually increasing (in most CEE countries) as voter turnout was falling. However, there are substantial differences among countries as far as the relationship under scrutiny is concerned. In some countries the pattern is very clear: election by election, voter turnout was falling and, simultaneously, support for pro-European parties was rising. In others, especially in the Czech Republic and Poland, there is almost no relationship between voter turnout and support for pro-European parties. Further, empirical results show also that governments formed as a result of the elections examined were becoming more pro-European. This (indirectly) implies that the policies implemented were increasingly more pro-European, which was 'functional' from the point of view of EU accession enthusiasts: a more pro-European government profile and more pro-European policies implemented facilitated the accession process, and/or in some cases even made it possible.

These facts are important for a discussion on representation mechanisms in CEE countries. We find strong evidence that there is a close link between election results, government profiles and the policies implemented afterwards (as a result of a particular election): as support for pro-European parties in CEE countries has been increasing, governments have been becoming increasingly more pro-European (which probably resulted in more pro-European policies being implemented).

Our findings shed new light on falling voter turnout in CEE. It has often been argued that this process has only negative consequences. Our findings show a somewhat different picture: decreasing voter turnout is associated with increasing support for pro-European parties, which most probably eased the progress of the enlargement process, and in this way enhanced and strengthened democracy in the region. Thus one can advance the following notion: successful EU enlargement and the accession of ten new member states were possible not despite falling voter turnout but actually because of this very process. If voter turnout had not been decreasing, more citizens would have participated in elections (including opponents of accession), election results would have been different, anti-European parties would have been stronger and thus the whole process of accession would have been much more complex and difficult to achieve (or would, maybe, have even been unsuccessful).

These facts are crucial for a discussion of the Europeanisation of party systems in CEE. It is evident that anti-European parties, though visible and relatively strong in the pre-accession period in the region, atrophied due to falling voter turnout. Hence, there is little doubt that this process had, in turn, a crucial effect on the Europeanisation (and also democratisation) of CEE party systems: higher voter turnout would have strengthened anti-European camps, which at the same time would have been less democratic, more populist, xenophobic, chauvinistic and intolerant.

Finally, the whole process described above can be perceived, from a more general perspective, as an important development in democratisation and, as such, a clear sign of the Europeanisation of CEE party systems. Through a democratic process, CEE citizenries have made an important decision regarding their future. As in Western Europe, the preferences of citizens have been structured, mediated, aggregated and transmitted into specific policies. Democratic institutions function properly and effectively: parties have reacted to the demands and preferences of citizens. Through electoral processes certain parliamentary majorities (and governments) have been formed, implementing policies desired by (the majority of) citizens. In addition, minorities (losers) accepted the decisions made, or at least did not oppose them in any illegal or violent manner. This is an apparent sign of the democratisation and Europeanisation of decision-making processes in CEE party systems.

Notes

1 I would like to thank Zsolt Enyedi for highlighting this point.
2 It should be borne in mind that studies in other periods that ask questions about voting and elections provide information that is at odds with reality. This is due to the fact that respondents do not remember their behaviour, thoughts and attitudes. For this reason post-election surveys (like NES) are the most appropriate data sources for analyses of voting behaviour.
3 Analyses which control for autocorrelation and heteroscedascity (i.e. linear regression with panel-corrected standard errors) reveal a quite similar effect.
4 It is important to remember that 'Estimates of government preferences calculated along these lines should not be confused with the estimates for actual government policy declarations [. . .] These were based on a coding of separate documents – the government's publicly stated programme at its investiture debate' (Klingemann *et al.*, 2006: 125). Unfortunately, these data are not available for CEE countries in the period 1990–2003.

References

Dahl, R. (1989), *Democracy and Its Critics* (New Haven, CT: Yale University Press).

Easton, D. (1975), 'A re-assessment of the concept of political support', *British Journal of Political Science* 5, pp. 435–57.

Grabbe, H. (2006), *The EU's Transformative Power: Europeanization through Conditionality in Central and Eastern Europe* (Houndmills: Palgrave Macmillan).

Hicks, A. and D. Swank (1992), 'Politics, institutions, and welfare spending in industrialized democracies, 1960–82', *American Political Science Review* 86, pp. 658–74.

Klingemann, H.-D., R. Hofferbert and I. Budge (1994), *Parties, Policies, and Democracy* (Boulder, CO: Westview Press).

Klingemann, H.-D., A. Volkens, I. Budge, J. Bara and M. McDonald (2006), *Mapping Policy Preferences II* (Oxford: Oxford University Press).

Ladrech, R. (2008), 'Europeanization and the variable influence of the EU: national parties and party systems in Western and Eastern Europe', *Journal of Southern Europe and the Balkans* 10, pp. 139–50.

Lewis, P. (2008), 'Changes in the party politics of the new EU member states in Central Europe: patterns of Europeanization and democratization', *Journal of Southern Europe and the Balkans* 10, pp. 151–66.

Lijphart, A. (1997), 'Unequal participation: democracy's unresolved dilemma', *American Political Science Review* 91, pp. 1–14.

Lutz, G. and M. Marsh (2007), 'Introduction: consequences of low turnout', *Electoral Studies* 26, pp. 539–47.

McManus-Czubinska, C., W. L. Miller, R. Markowski and J. Wasilewski (2004), 'When does turnout matter? The case of Poland', *Europe-Asia Studies* 56, pp. 401–20.

Markowski, R. and J. Tucker (2005), 'Pocketbooks, politics, and parties: a macro and micro analysis of the June 2003 Polish referendum on EU membership', *Electoral Studies* 24, pp. 409–33.

Pacek, A. and B. Radcliff (1995), 'Turnout and the vote for left-of-centre parties: a cross-national analysis', *British Journal of Political Science* 25, pp. 137–43.

Szczerbiak, A. and P. Taggart (2005), *EU Enlargement and Referendums* (London: Routledge).

Taggart, P. and A. Szczerbiak (2004), 'Contemporary Euroscepticism in the party systems of the European Union candidate states of Central and Eastern Europe', *European Journal of Political Research* 43, pp. 1–27.

Tverdova, Y. and C. Anderson (2004), 'Choosing the West? Referendum choices on EU membership in East-Central Europe', *Electoral Studies* 23, pp. 185–208.

6

Patterns of party competition (1990–2009)[1]

Zsolt Enyedi and Fernando Casal Bértoa

Introduction

Almost two decades have passed since the 'Third Wave' of democratisation brought new democracies into being in Central and Eastern Europe (CEE). In their constitutional order and economic regime the ten new member states have followed largely Western European patterns. Many feared the development of hybrid, semi-authoritarian regimes but the countries of the region are by now (at least) as liberal in terms of economic policy and the regulation of individual rights as Western Europe. Yet, in terms of the fluidity of party systems the differences between post-communist and Western countries have remained conspicuous (Mair, 1997; Toole, 2000: 442; Millard, 2004; Enyedi, 2006; Lewis, 2006; O'Dywer, 2006: 43; Webb and White, 2007).

Close cooperation with Western political institutions within the European Union (EU) provides stimuli for both stabilisation and destabilisation (Enyedi, 2007). The mechanisms of transnational cooperation, imitation, diffusion and socialisation may reduce the prevalence of idiosyncratic party ideologies and conflict patterns, and foster the standardisation of political discourse, party identities and coalition strategies. Such processes not only bring West and East closer to each other but are also likely to provide the new member states with more temporal continuity and a more transparent and simple structure of political competition. But the introduction of new arenas of contestation (European parliamentary election, selection of EU commissioners, etc.) has in fact caused considerable turbulence in the respective countries (Enyedi and Lewis, 2006).

As of the autumn of 2009, the ten new EU states had held at least five free and fair parliamentary elections. This time span allows us to synthesise the fundamental characteristics of their political configuration and assess the trends of change. While doing so, we also attempt to advance the understanding of party systems in general and suggest a set of criteria around which the analysis of party systems should be structured. The chapter proceeds as follows. First, we outline briefly the concepts employed and the way they are operationalised. Then we report data that show both the direction of temporal change and the differences across the ten countries, averaged for the post-communist period. Finally we examine the relationships between the various features of the party systems.

The analysis will show that in terms of the configuration of competition the party systems analysed do not converge to a single pattern, half of them adjusting to a bipolar structure with the other half moving to a multipolar one. The coalition-building strategies of parties show signs of path-dependency: most of the countries can be easily classified as having either open or closed governmental arenas. The groupings based on the closure of the governmental arena and on the stability and relevance of alliance structures largely coincide with the division into polarised and non-polarised countries. The fragmentation of parliaments is also related to the previous dimensions, but so far as fragmentation is concerned there has been a marked decline across the region during the decade since 2000, with the notable exception of Lithuania and Bulgaria.

While in terms of electoral volatility the region is characterised by rather trendless fluctuation, it is still possible to distinguish the notoriously unstable countries from more stable ones. This division, however, diverges somewhat from the grouping of countries based on the previously noted variables. It is therefore possible to differentiate countries where the progress towards institutionalisation is driven primarily by elite behaviour from those where it is, rather, the electorate that shows signs of consolidation. On average, however, the different dimensions of party systems are closely intertwined.

Conceptualising the party system

The lack of consensus concerning the conceptualisation of party systems has been lamented by many students of the field (Sartori, 1976: 297; Daalder, 1983: 27; Ware, 1996; etc.). But there seems to be a convergence around Sartori's (1976: 44) classical definition of party system as 'the system of interactions resulting from inter-party competition'. We also take this definition as the starting point of our conceptualisation and operational-isation, but complement it with the observation that 'how parties compete with one another at one level of the polity may well be different from how they compete at another level' (Bardi and Mair, 2008: 161). Therefore we suggest that the profiles of the party systems should be drawn by observing the parties' behaviour in all three major political terrains (Smith, 1990: 195): the electoral, parliamentary and governmental arenas.

A number of researchers, most importantly Mair (2001), consider the competition for government as the core of the party systems. More precisely, in his view the regularity and predictability of coalition making determines the closure of party systems. Closure is relevant not only because it captures an important aspect of elite strategy but also because it has the potential to influence the behaviour of voters. We take openness *versus* closure as one of the principal dimensions of party systems.

No matter how important it is, the governmental level is only one of the arenas where parties interact. Looking only at government coalitions, for example, we learn little about the opposition parties, although the functioning of the party systems and the stability of the governments are inevitably related to the character of the opposition. Therefore a proper description of party systems should contain variables that describe the mechanics of party politics outside the government as well. Three such variables are based on routinely applied criteria: ideological polarisation, fragmentation and electoral volatility. *Fragmentation* tends to have a significant impact on the stabilisation of party politics, determining the number of possible interactions and reflecting on the balance of power. The amount of electoral *volatility*, although more a feature of the voting population than of the parties, captures that aspect of electoral behaviour which is most relevant for party system stability and consolidation. Finally, the lack of *polarisation* is expected to facilitate coalition making, promote policy continuity and reduce the stakes and decisiveness of elections. Polarisation, as demonstrated recently (Enyedi and Todosijevic, 2008), is also a major factor behind party identification in both Eastern and Western Europe. Polarisation, understood as hostility between parties, may be a more relevant phenomenon in the region than the spread of programmatic positions. But since we have information only on the latter and since the comparative politics literature also focuses on ideological-programmatic differences, polarisation will henceforth be equated with ideological distance between parties.

The four dimensions discussed so far typically appear in the form of continuous variables in party system analyses (see below, the section on operationalisation). They allow the development of standardised instruments of measurement, facilitating the comparison of a large number of countries. By relying exclusively on these aspects, however, one risks downgrading national peculiarities and treating differences in quality as differences of quantity.

In order to get a realistic picture of the structure of party politics in a particular country, one should also describe the principal electoral alternatives and the most important blocs of the party systems: their ideological character, the leading (or core) party (if there is one), their stability and weight (relevance) within the political system. A cluster of parties is regarded as forming a bloc, or a principal alternative, if parties within the cluster have cooperative internal relations, claim some common ideological identity and aim to determine who is prime minister. The latter clause means that the blocs analysed should also be considered electoral alternatives. While party system change can be conceptualised in various ways, for the actors involved the change in principal alternatives, in their ideological character and in the leading party is perhaps the most visible and most consequential development. In comparative work the configuration of these factors is often neglected, partly because of their qualitative character and partly because of the concomitant danger of subjective judgement on the part of the analysts. When a party or a group of parties is distinct and strong enough to count as an alternative is, for example, a difficult question to tackle. We think, on the other hand, that shying away from qualitative assessment is no less problematic than just coming up with tentative decisions. Therefore, we suggest the *relevance of party-blocs* and *bloc-pattern stability* as the fifth and sixth dimensions of the party system.

Dimensions of the party system

To measure fragmentation we use a commonly employed indicator, Laakso and Taagepera's (1979) 'effective number of parties' (ENP), applied to parliaments (ENP = $1/\Sigma s_i^2$, where s_i is the proportion of seats of the ith party.). The measurement of polarisation is inevitably more controversial, since this field lacks a formula that would be as universally accepted as ENP. In this chapter we use the standard deviation of the parties' left–right position. For the party position we rely on multiple (i.e., four) data sources, in order to arrive at an unbiased assessment. The data come from two expert surveys (Hooghe *et al.*, 2008 and Benoit and Laver, 2006) and from the EES 2004 survey. The European Election Study (EES) allows for the calculation of both the party electorates' mean self-placement and the respondents' assessment of party position (unfortunately Lithuania, Bulgaria and Romania were not covered by EES). The overall ranking of the countries on polarisation will be determined by taking into account all information that is available. For electoral volatility we use a widely established, though not uncontroversial formula, the Pedersen index of total electoral volatility (TEV = $\Sigma |v_{i,t-1} - v_{i,t}|/2$, where, $v_{i,t}$ is the vote share for a party $_i$ at a given election $_t$, Pedersen, 1979). This measure reflects both the amount of vote switching and stability in the supply of parties, but in our model it represents primarily the electoral aspect of party system consolidation.

The identification of blocs inevitably carries with it some degree of uncertainty. Our classifications have been informed by analysis of ideological similarities, membership of international party federations, public gestures – friendly and hostile – of politicians, expert opinion of observers, and both pre-electoral[2] and post-electoral coalitions. We need to go beyond actual coalitions because they are often due to idiosyncratic short-term considerations. For example, parties may stay out of a government not because of policy differences or hostile relationships with government parties but just, for example, to avoid the negative incumbency effect.

The major blocs form the principal guidelines on the mental map of the voters. This means that, following a Sartorian logic, electoral support is an important criterion, but not the only one. An extremist party, for example, that receives 10 per cent is more likely to have a prominent role in shaping the political discourse and dynamics than a 20 per cent-strong niche party that represents an ethnic minority or professional group. The latter may be a more stable component of the party system, but it is unlikely to represent one of the fundamental directions the country can take and therefore should not be counted as a principal alternative.

We describe the party blocs using labels that go beyond the restricted terminology of left and right but still travel across a range of countries: nationalism, populism, conservatism, liberalism, socialism and communism. Blocs that have their leaders as the fundamental appeal will be marked as 'charismatic'. In some instances this feature only complements the established ideological profile, but in others it forms the very essence of the party's identity. Countries in which the coalitional alternatives can be predicted from historical and ideological patterns rank high on the bloc relevance dimension. Position on the bloc stability dimension is defined by the frequency of cases when alliance structures change, whether in opposition or government.

The operationalisation of closure is the most complicated. Mair (1996, 2007) identifies three components. *Alternation in government* can take the forms of wholesale alternation, partial change and non-alternation. In the first case, the incumbent government leaves office in its entirety and is replaced by a wholly different party or group of parties. In the second case the new cabinet contains both incumbents and new parties. The third option is marked by a complete absence of alternation, as the same party or parties remain in exclusive control of government over an extended period of time. The second component is *innovation* or *familiarity of the governing formula*: whether there are stable groups of parties that tend to govern together (familiarity) or whether there is a tendency towards previously unseen forms of party combination (innovation). The third and final component, *access to government*, simply indicates whether all parties have a chance to join the executive or whether some parties are permanently excluded from participation in office. Party systems are considered to be closed if (1) alternations of governments are either total or none (2) governing alternatives are stable over a long period of time, and (3) some parties ('outsiders') are permanently excluded from participation in national government. They are open when there are (1) partial alternations of government (2) no stable combinations of governing alternatives and (3) access to government has been granted to all relevant parties.

In the numeric representation of the above characteristics 0 stands for openness, 1 for closure. If, in case of a change of government, the composition of the cabinet did not change at all or changed in its entirety (meaning that all parties have been replaced), then that change receives a value of 1 on *alternation*. If no new party joined the government and the party composition of the government was not altered either, then our score will have a 1 on *access* and *formula* as well. Being open on one account (e.g. partial alternation) but closed on the other two variables (no new party and no unfamiliar coalition) results in 66.6 per cent on the overall indicator of closure. The values of individual government changes are added up and divided by the number of government changes experienced in the period under study.

We need counting rules to establish the number of governments and their partisan composition in order to determine which parties actually have governing status, taking into consideration only parties that are directly represented in the executive by their members and/or nominees.[3] As for distinguishing between governments, in accordance with the literature on party government in Western democracies, *changes of government* are recorded when (1) there is a change in the partisan composition of the government coalition (i.e. when the representatives of one or more parties leave the coalition government or join it); (2) the prime minister leaves office; and (3) parliamentary elections are held, even in cases when there is no change in the partisan composition of the cabinet (Müller and Strøm, 2000: 12). Caretaker ('technocratic') governments, if they are in office for a short time to bridge the period until the next election, are excluded from the analysis. Since non-partisan government represents a radical break with the usual patterns of government formation, they receive by default a 0 on all three variables. Exceptions are made in cases when support for specific parties is clearly discernable behind a formally non-partisan process.

Innovative governments are considered to be all those that have never previously existed in that form during the post-authoritarian period. Thus, a party coming to office for the first time in the form of a single-party government is innovative, even if it has previously governed as part of a coalition (Mair, 2007: 140). On the other hand, and building on Sikk (2005: 399), *genuinely new governing parties* are considered to be all those which, having a novel name and structure, are not successors to any previous government party. In order to count a party as 'new', we apply the following rules (this is also relevant for categorising the 'governing formula'):

1. If two parties merge into one, the new party is counted as old.
2. If one party splits and one of the splinter parties can be clearly considered as a successor, then we consider that party as an old party. Otherwise all splinter groups are counted as new formations.

We also needed to determine when the first democratic government was invested. This is a difficult issue. As Müller-Rommel *et al.* (2004: 870) have put it:

> In some countries, the first democratic government was formed after the first free election but before the country became independent [. . . In others . . .] an interim 'Constituent Assembly' together with an interim government was mainly responsible for drafting a new constitution. Once the constitution was approved by parliament (or by a referendum), new elections took place, and the interim democratic government resigned, being replaced by a fully responsible party government

In order to allow for a systematic comparison, we define *founding government* as the one created after 'founding elections' are held. Reich (2001: 1239–40) defines founding elections as the 'first competitive, multiparty elections occurring during a transition to democracy after (a) at least ten years of authoritarian rule and (b) following reforms that allow for the formation of multiple political parties independent of the state and free from state repression'. In this sense, founding governments are defined as those created by the first free election taking place in a country after regime collapse, independence, or after a revised constitution is approved by an interim constituent assembly (Table 6.1).[4]

Party system profiles: patterns and trends

The configuration of party systems: blocs, core parties and ideological divides

None of the countries can be characterised by one single pattern for its entire post-communist period, but some did spend most of the two decades from 1990 under one particular structure of alternatives. The condensed review below captures the most relevant changes in the configuration of the principal alternatives in the ten countries analysed.

The Slovenian party system started off fragmented, with a rapidly emerging pivotal party. The liberals (LDS), although left of centre in their ideological orientation, occupied a position that was similar to the status of Christian Democrats in a number of West European countries. The left- and right-wing parties played a secondary role in government coalitions dominated by the liberal centre. The relational and ideological structuration of the party system remained low, but this loose form of structure proved to be stable, lasting

Table 6.1 Regime transition in new Central and East European democracies

Country	Independence date	Breakaway elections	Founding elections	Founding government
Bulgaria	–	10 June 1990[b]	13 October 1991	8 November 1991
Czech Republic	1 January 1993	8–9 June 1990[a]	5–6 June 1992	1 January 1993
Estonia	6 September 1991	–	20 September 1992	21 December 1992
Hungary	–	–	3 May 1990	23 May 1990
Latvia	6 September 1991	–	5–6 June 1993	4 August 1993
Lithuania	6 September 1991	–	25 October 1992	2 December 1992
Poland	–	4 June 1989[c]	27 October 1991	23 December 1991
Romania	–	20 May 1990[b]	27 September 1992	13 November 1992
Slovakia	1 January 1993	8–9 June 1990[a]	5–6 June 1992	12 January 1993
Slovenia	25 June 1991	–	6 December 1992	12 January 1993

Notes: [a] Czechoslovak Federal Assembly.
[b] Elections to the Constituent Assembly.
[c] Only one-third of the seats were freely contested.
Source: Adapted from Müller-Rommel *et al.* (2004: 871).

until the collapse of the Liberal Democrats in 2004. The second phase is characterised by a more bipolar logic (pitting conservatives against social democrats, SDS and SD), although the style of competition remained pragmatic.

The tripolar pattern had a much shorter life span in Hungary, and barely lasted until 1994. Even during this period, when the socialists (MSZP), conservatives (led by MDF) and the liberals (led by SZDSZ) offered distinct ideological alternatives, the discourse and the political preferences tended to be structured in a bipolar way: during the first months evolving around the communist vs anti-communist divide, after that around the cultural differences splitting conservatives and (social) liberals. From 1994 until the end of the period analysed a two-bloc pattern prevailed: the left (led by MSZP) and the right (led by Fidesz) commanded similar levels of support, and they jointly received close to 90 per cent of the vote. The particularly aggressive, uncompromising attitude of the blocs towards each other engendered a centrifugal pattern of competition.

In the Czech Republic the first period was characterised by the opposition between the communists and the gradually fragmenting anti-communist bloc. In this regard the pattern was fairly similar to that in many of the neighbouring countries (with the exception that instead of a large, social-democratising ex-communist party and a few hardliners, in the Czech Republic there was a medium-sized hardliner party). As the social democrats (CSSD) grew in size the political arena became dominated by the rivalry of centre-left and centre-right forces. The small parties in the middle played an important role in government building, but in terms both of ideology and of electoral strength the communists (KSCM) were the third relevant force. Given, however, their irrelevance from the point of view of government building, the Czech party system is best described as a two-and-a-half party system, with the social democrats and the conservative ODS as the principal alternatives. The bipolar logic has become particularly crystallised during the last years of our period.

The Estonian party system can be less easily captured with ideological labels, since Estonian politics is less ideological in general. The original competition unfolded between moderate and technocratic reformers, on the one hand, and nationalist (but also pro-West) anti-communists, on the other. The second pattern, the one that is still in place, is a multipolar one, with a particular relevance of three forces: conservatives (led by Isamaa), liberal technocrats (led by Reform) advocating right-wing economic policies, and the Centre Party (Keskerakond). The last alternative is ideologically the most ambiguous component of the system, but perhaps it is best described as a leftish and moderately populist force which happens to occupy the pro-Russian minority corner of the party system, and which bases its electoral appeal, to a large extent, on its leader. The Estonian parties have realigned with considerable frequency in the past, although conservatives and liberals often consider each other as natural allies.

The trajectory of the Romanian party system is divided into three phases. The first configuration was bipolar, pitting the post-communist socialists against a cluster of parties that was dominated by conservatives and liberals. Between the two blocs operated the small but significant social-liberal Democrats and on the right flank of the system the nationalists, who cooperated during the 1990s with the socialists but maintained a distinct ideological appeal. In the second formula the nationalists lost, while the Democrats gained significance. But the two major alternatives remained the same (except that the right-wing alternative became dominated by the liberals, PNL, after the collapse of the conservatives, PNTCD). The third formula reflects the further ascendance and transformation of Democrats who, under a charismatic leadership, became a major pole of party competition. They have a vague ideological profile, combining populist and centre-right elements. The three parties (PDS, PNL and PDL, together with a few minor satellites) form an almost perfect triangle, leaving open the possibility of cooperation on all fronts.

The first Slovak party system was anchored by the presence of a sizable nationalist force (HZDS) that was opposed by the colourful bloc of liberals, conservatives and social democrats. By the dawn of the new millennium the pivotal role of nationalists vanished, but the bipolar logic survived and continues to structure the second configuration as well. In both configurations liberal conservatives (recently led by SDKÚ) faced a populist opponent led by a charismatic leader. Perhaps the only significant difference between the two patterns was that in the second socio-economic left-right issues divided the two blocs more evidently and Smer, the leader of the populist-bloc, is more pragmatic (and therefore more open to alternative coalitions) than HZDS used to be.

Latvia is characterised by high degree of fragmentation in terms of both individual parties and clusters of parties. During the 1990s a partly ethnic (Russian) and partly ideologically (leftist) defined bloc (led by Harmony) faced two right-wing clusters, a more liberal one (led by LC) and a more nationalist/conservative one (led by LNNK). As a result of the decline of LC the system became less centre based, the right-wing parties regrouped around the conservative TP and the style of competition became more confrontational. The second pattern resembles the first, to the extent that it maintains high fragmentation, high volatility and the exclusion of leftist parties from government.

Lithuania started with a clear two-bloc competition, dominated by the attitude towards the communist heritage, pitting LDDP against Homeland Union. This simple logic was disturbed at the end of the century by the emergence of liberals, represented by NS. The third phase continued to be based on a tripolar logic, but at this time populists, represented by a number of consecutive charismatic politicians, form the non-socialist and non-conservative pole.

In its first phase the Polish system was tripolar, but the position of liberals (led by UD, later UW), situated between socialists (led by SLD) and conservatives (whose most important party at that time was ZChN), weakened rapidly. Some of them left politics, others joined the conservatives, transforming the configuration of competition into a two-bloc pattern. The last phase is somewhat more difficult to summarise and is definitely more unusual. Socialist groups survive, but are relegated to a marginal position. Conservatives (PiS) and liberals (PO) form the only viable electoral alternatives, and while ideologically these two groups used to be relatively close, by now the difference between them is clear both in economy (conservatives being more statist), in culture (liberals being more permissive) and anti-communism (conservatives being more intransigent).

Finally, the Bulgarian party system, as with many other countries in our sample, was also originally structured by the anti-communist cleavage. The two-bloc structure (socialists, led by BSP, and conservatives, led by SDS) lasted almost a decade, producing a centrifugal and bipolar structure. This transparent logic was complicated by the emergence of a centrist, liberal force (NDSV) which, however, based its appeal more on its leader than on its ideology and which turned out to be more open to cooperation with the socialists than with the conservatives. While the socialists continue to form a principal electoral alternative in the third phase, the liberal bloc contracted, and under the leadership of GERB a new, conservative-populist bloc was formed. Radical right-wing nationalists have been present in both of the last two patterns, but only on the margins of the system.

The patterns in Table 6.2 capture with a great degree of simplification the principal developments in the configuration of the ten party systems analysed. The ideological character of the blocs is signalled by abbreviations explained in the note below the table. Wherever possible, we describe blocs as being either socialist, conservative or liberal (in some cases conservative liberal or liberal conservative). Adjectives like nationalist or populist typically appear as secondary features (in brackets), fine-tuning the ideological profile of the parties, together with references to the parties' charismatic nature, communist origin or economic and cultural policies. But in some instances these adjectives refer to the very essence of the parties' ideological appeal, and therefore they are used as the principal labels describing the party's profile.

Table 6.2 shows that the party systems of the region do not converge to a single pattern of competition. Some countries have always had a fundamentally bipolar structure (Czech Republic, Slovakia), or drifted in that direction after a tripolar beginning (Hungary, Poland, Slovenia), while in other countries the configuration became multipolar in the second stage (Romania, Estonia, Lithuania, Bulgaria) or has always been fragmented (Latvia). The discussion above also suggests that the countries analysed do not completely lack structure and stability. It has been possible, after all, to summarise almost two decades of – turbulent – party politics by distinguishing only two or three patterns. Note, however, that these patterns do not have the same relevance for each country. In those countries where the alliance structures change often and where coalitions are not based on ideological traditions, there is less mileage to be gained from noting similarities and friendships among parties. Table 6.3 contains an assessment concerning the overall stability and relevance of blocs. Stability and relevance are closely related, with some notable exceptions. In the Czech Republic the ideological configuration is stable, but parties do cross over bloc borders from time to time in order to provide the country with a governing majority. In Hungary intra-bloc loyalty is a more serious factor, but the alliance structures went through a fundamental reconfiguration in 1994. At the other end of the scale, in Latvia only the ethnic divide represents a solid line of demarcation, while in Estonia virtually no coalition can be excluded. But in Estonia there is more continuity in the (weak) underlying structure than in Latvia, to a large extent because new parties appear more frequently in the latter country.

Table 6.2 Patterns of party relations: number, identity and leaders of the major party blocs

Country	Period	No.	Ideological character of principal alternatives	Bloc leaders	Cause of the change in bloc pattern
Bulgaria 1	1990–2001	2	Soc Conslib	BSP SDS	The king's movement creates a strong liberal centre, the system moves towards multipolarity.
Bulgaria 2	2001–7	3.5	Soc (CP) Lib (CH) Conslib (Nationalists)	BSP NDSV SDS (Ataka)	Collapse of NDSV and SDS, emergence of GERB.
Bulgaria 3	2007–	2.5	Soc (CP) Cons (CH, P) (Nationalists)	BSP GERB (Ataka)	
Czech Republic 1	1992–95	2	Com Libcons	KSCM ODS	Social Democrats become the left-wing alternative, the system becomes bipolar.
Czech Republic 2	1995–	2.5	Soc Libcons (Com)	CSSD ODS (KSCM)	
Estonia 1	1992–99	2	Soft reformers Libcons (N, RE)	Koond Isamaa	Kesk and Reform emerge as principal alternatives.
Estonia 2	1999–	3	Pro-minority populists (CH) Lib (RE) Cons (N, RE)	Kesk Reform Isamaa	
Hungary 1	1990–94	3	Soc (CP) Lib Cons (N)	MSZP SZDSZ MDF	Fidesz joins the right, SZDSZ joins the Socialist government, the system becomes bipolar.

Table 6.2 *Continued*

Country	Period	No.	Ideological character of principal alternatives	Bloc leaders	Cause of the change in bloc pattern
Hungary 2	1995–	2	Soc (RE, LC, CP) Cons (N, LE)	MSZP Fidesz	
Latvia 1	1993–2002	3	Soc/Russian Lib Cons(N)	Harmony LC LNNK	LC declines, TP becomes the main party of the right-wing cluster.
Latvia 2	2002–	3	Soc/Russian Lib and cons and green	Harmony TP	
Lithuania 1	1990–2000	2	Soc (CP) Cons	LDDP Homeland (TS/LK)	Liberals emerge as a principal alternative.
Lithuania 2	2000–4	3	Soc (CP) Lib (CH) Cons	LSDP NS Homeland (TS/LK)	Populists emerge as a powerful force.
Lithuania 3	2004–	3	Soc (CP) Populists (CH) Cons	LSDP No stable leader Homeland (TS/LK)	
Poland 1	1991–2001	3	Soc (CP) Lib Cons (N)	SLD UD ZCHN	Left liberals decline, liberal conservatives emerge.
Poland 2	2001–5	2	Soc (CP) Libcons (RC)	SLD PO	Socialists become a minor party, the moderate and populist wings of the right separate.
Poland 3	2005–	2	Libcons Cons (RC)	PO PiS	

Romania 1	1992–2003	2, 5	Soc (CP, N) Conslib (Nat, CH)	PDSR/PSD PNTCD/PNL (PRM)	Democrats turn populist and enter alliance with Liberals, Nationalists decline.
Romania 2	2003–7	2, 5	Soc (CP) Lib Populists (CH, RE)	PSD PNL (PD)	Liberals and Democrats split. Democrats eliminate statutory clause of non-coalition with the PSD.
Romania 3	2007–	3	Soc (CP) Populists (CH) Lib	PSD PDL PNL	
Slovakia 1	1992–2002	2	Nationalists (P, CP) Libcons and Soc	HZDS KDH	The populist left reorganizes under the leadership of Smer.
Slovakia 2	2002–	2	Soc and Nat (P, CP) Libcons (RE)	Smer SDKÚ	
Slovenia 1	1990–2004	3	Soc (CP) Lib (CP) Cons	ZSLD LDS SLS	Centre declines, SDS becomes the main right-wing party.
Slovenia 2	2005–	2	Soc Cons	SD (ZSLD) SDS	

Notes: Column 3 contains number of principal alternatives.
Acronyms: soc (socialists), con (conservatives), lib (liberals), N (nationalist), P (populist), RE (right-wing economic), LE (left-wing economic), RC (right-wing cultural), (LC) (left-wing cultural), CH (charismatic), CP (communist past).

Table 6.3 Relevance and stability of blocs

Country	Relevance of blocs	Bloc pattern stability
Slovenia	Very low	High
Hungary	Very high	Very high
Czech Republic	High	Very high
Estonia	Very low	Low
Romania	Low	Low
Slovakia	High	Low
Latvia	Very low	Very low
Lithuania	High	High
Poland	High	Low
Bulgaria	Low	Low

Governmental arena: closure patterns

Figure 6.1 shows how the character of competition for government changed in the new EU member states during the last two decades. The data indicate that there is some tendency towards convergence across the ten countries, and also that countries tend to cluster into distinct groups. The difference between Bulgaria, Slovakia, Slovenia and Latvia, on the one hand, and Hungary, the Czech Republic and, to a lesser extent, Romania and Lithuania, on the other, is constant and clear: after the third election the lines of 'very high/high' and 'very low' countries do not cross. The 'very high/high' countries never fall below 50 per cent of closure, while the 'very low' countries almost never reach above 35 per cent (Slovakia being the only exception in 1994 and 1998). At the same time the 'very low' countries gradually increase their level of closure, and therefore the distance between the different groups has decreased. The Czech Republic, Lithuania and Estonia started out with a relatively high level of predictability, but the first two countries deviated from this pattern already during the early 1990s, while Estonia lost its 'high' status gradually, and by now all three belong to the group of countries with medium closure. Bulgaria is the only country whose level of closure has not fluctuated (33.3 per cent).

Table 6.4 contains the averaged summary index of closure for the ten countries. In terms of its mean, Hungary stands out as the country with the most closed governmental arena. Then, after a large gap, there is a group of countries with mid levels of closure: the Czech Republic, Romania and Lithuania. This group is followed by Poland and Estonia. Finally, and after a large gap, at the open end of the scale we find Slovakia, Bulgaria, Slovenia and Latvia.

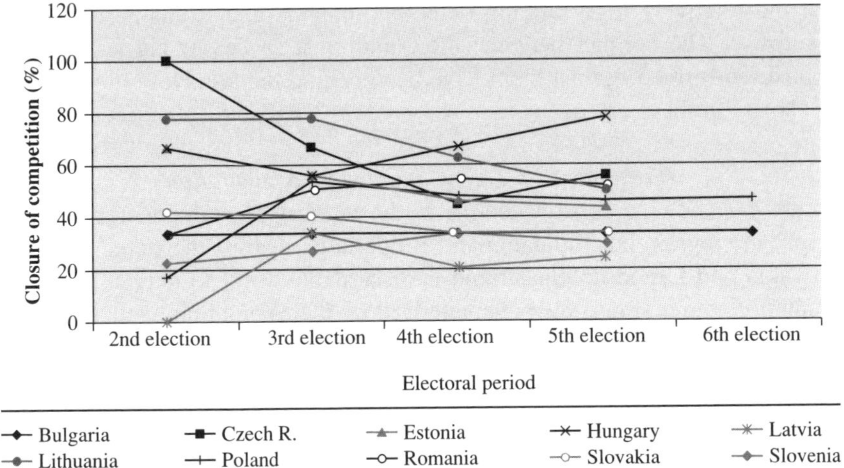

Figure 6.1 Closure of competition for government, 1990–2009

Table 6.4 Closure averages by government

Country	*Closure (%)*
Hungary	75.0
Czech Republic	55.6
Romania	51.5
Lithuania	50.0
Poland	46.7
Estonia	42.4
Slovakia	33.3
Bulgaria	33.3
Slovenia	29.6
Latvia	27.1

Source: All data on government formation and stability are based on Müller-Rommel *et al.* (2004), but cross-checked with information provided by the *European Journal of Political Research Political Data Yearbooks*, and by country experts and sources on the World Wide Web.

It follows from these results that, at the level of government, fluidity prevails over predictability. According to data analysed by Casal Bértoa and Mair (2009), the party systems of Western and Southern Europe showed considerably more closure in the decades following democratisation. The other conclusion must be that there is a large variance within the region. The countries at the extremes of the scale are the ones that have been reported by other scholars as being over- and under-achievers in terms of institutionalisation.

But the relatively high ranking of both Lithuania and Romania comes as a surprise. The conflict between the communist successor parties and the opposition formed against them have been behind the relatively high degree of closure in these cases.

Parliamentary arena: degree of fragmentation

Figure 6.2 shows a general decline in the number of parliamentary parties across the region, but Lithuania and Bulgaria go against the trend, while in Slovakia and Latvia no clear trend is discernable. Next to decreasing fragmentation, the region is also characterised by increasing homogeneity in the number of parties, because extreme results (cf. first Polish or second Latvian election) do not occur any more.

Table 6.5 confirms, however, that the last two decades of post-communist politics have been characterised by a high level of multipartism. The majority of post-communist countries have an average ENP above 4, which is the cut-off point used in a number of classifications of party systems (Mainwaring and Scully, 1995: 31–2; Siaroff, 2000: 72). Countries that are subject to the most intense competition in terms of the average number of political actors are Slovenia and Latvia, followed by Slovakia, Poland, Lithuania and Estonia. At the opposite end Hungary and Bulgaria exhibit the lowest average ENP, and Romania and the Czech Republic follow this group relatively closely. Most likely the confrontational and bipolar competition between BSP and SDS and between MSZP and Fidesz has limited the number of entrants into the political contest in these two countries.

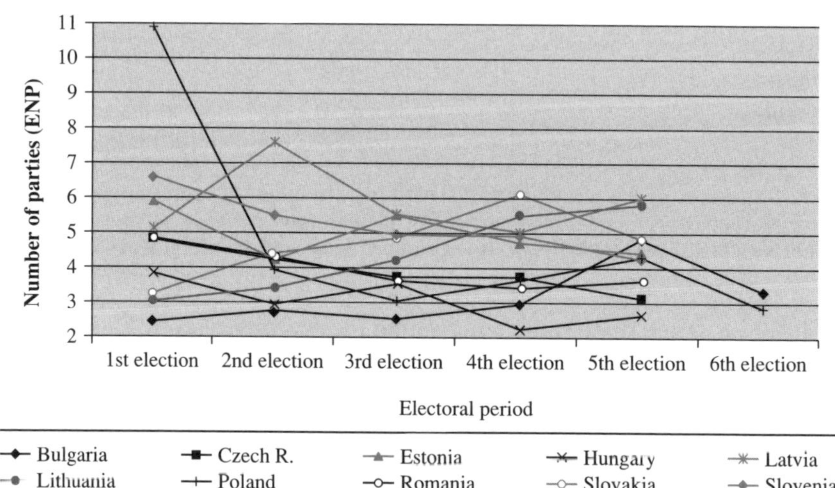

Figure 6.2 Effective number of parties in the parliaments, 1990–2009

Table 6.5 Effective number of parties (ENP): parliamentary averages

Country	ENP
Hungary	3.0
Bulgaria	3.1
Czech Republic	3.9
Romania	3.9
Lithuania	4.4
Slovakia	4.7
Poland	4.8
Estonia	4.9
Slovenia	5.2
Latvia	5.8

Sources: Gallagher (2009). Data from 2006 to 2009 are from our own calculations.

Electoral arena: levels of volatility

Figure 6.3 indicates that in terms of volatility there is larger variance between elections than between countries. In Bulgaria, for example, volatility increased from 19.1 to 44.0 per cent between 1993 and 2005, while in Hungary it decreased from 32 to 8 per cent between 1998 and 2006. This means that volatility is less systemic than the dimensions examined previously: it is more exposed to factors outside of the political institutional framework (economic crises, scandals etc.). Only the Czech Republic, and to a lesser extent Lithuania, appear to have rather constant levels of volatility. Slovakia, Bulgaria and Slovenia have experienced their most volatile elections during the last years, while Hungary and, less unambiguously, Estonia, Latvia, Romania and Poland saw a trend towards greater electoral stability.

Table 6.6 contains the averaged volatility figures for the ten countries. These figures must be treated with caution, however, because, as we have seen above, the volatility figures for most countries change rather erratically from election to election. The region as a whole exhibits more than twice as much volatility as the West does (28.2 vs 13 per cent), and more than three times more than the West did between 1945 and 1965 at 10 per cent (Bartolini and Mair, 1990). The figure exceeds the Southern European average of 13.4 per cent (Gunther and Montero, 2001: 90) and even the Latin American figures – for the 1970 to 1993 period Mainwaring and Scully (1995: 8) reported 24.3 per cent. The Czech Republic, Hungary and Romania are the most stable countries in the region as far as vote shifts are concerned, followed by Estonia, Slovakia and Slovenia. Bulgaria and Poland are markedly more volatile, while the extreme positions (by any standards) are occupied by Latvia and Lithuania.

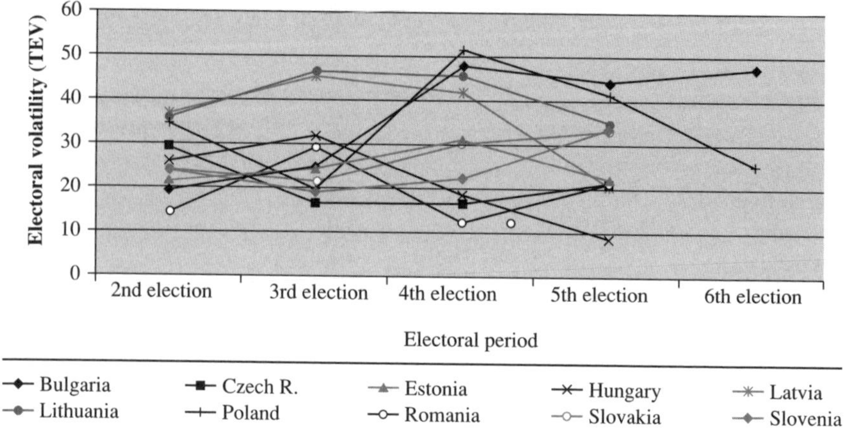

Figure 6.3 Electoral volatility, 1990–2009

Table 6.6 Total electoral volatility: country averages

Country	*TEV (%)*
Romania	19.1
Czech Republic	20.8
Hungary	21.0
Estonia	24.6
Slovenia	24.7
Slovakia	27.0
Poland	34.3
Bulgaria	34.8
Latvia	36.0
Lithuania	40.7

Sources: Sitter (2005), Tóka and Henjak (2007). Data from 2006 are from our own calculations.

Polarisation

So far as left–right polarisation is concerned, we must refrain from commenting on temporal trends, as we have comparable information only on the 2002–2004 period. This period is, however, highly relevant, since this is the time when the majority of the countries examined joined the EU. The diverse indicators included in Table 6.7 do not give identical rankings, but by comparing and averaging the indicators we find the Czech Republic, Hungary and Slovakia among the most polarised party systems, followed by Lithuania and Poland. Then, after a gap, come Estonia, Bulgaria and Latvia, and finally, at the opposite end one finds Slovenia and Romania.

Table 6.7 Polarisation figures, 2002–4

Country	EES party electorates (2004)	EES party positions (2004)	Marks et al. party positions (2002)	Benoit and Laver party positions (2003–4)
Slovenia	1.58152	1.84116	1.54157	4.28333
Slovakia	1.68371	2.32246	2.50570	5.22860
Latvia	1.17355	1.58762	2.26163	5.46281
Hungary	2.10153	2.291035	2.36712	5.69129
Estonia	0.64848	1.18976	n.a.	4.92185
Czech rep.	2.05163	2.69802	2.55925	5.01439
Poland	1.51638	1.90992	2.02728	5.93345
Romania	n.a.	n.a.	1.70716	2.45868
Bulgaria	n.a.	n.a.	1.79070	4.05816
Lithuania	n.a.	n.a.	2.63201	3.55596

Relations between the party system dimensions

As the final step of the analysis we have examined the relationships among the different dimensions of party systems. Table 6.8 presents the rough (four-degree) ranking of the countries on the principal dimensions.

The six dimensions are related to each other in various ways: mechanically, causally, through third variables etc. The task of the present analysis is not to examine the causes of the relations but to simply find out which are the most marginal and which the most central variables of the entire 'package'. Based on the literature, positive correlations could be expected between closure, polarisation, stability and the relevance of blocs, low fragmentation and low volatility. All these variables are related, more or less directly, to the overall institutionalisation of the party systems. If one converts the category 'very low' into 1, 'low' into 2, 'high' into 3 and 'very high' into 4, then it becomes possible to analyse the data in a more quantitative fashion (in the case of fragmentation and volatility, the ranking has to be reversed, as high volatility and fragmentation are expected to indicate low levels of institutionalisation). We have checked whether the countries are similarly ranked on the various dimensions or there are substantial (that is, more than one position) differences between the rankings and we have also examined Spearman correlations and Cronbach alphas. Given the low number of cases and the large amount of noise in the data, the conclusions can be, of course, only tentative.

The analysis of the covariances indicated that volatility is most marginal to the overall 'package'. The Cronbach alpha (.85) of the six variables would somewhat decrease if any of the items were to be deleted, with the exception

Table 6.8 Dimensions of inter-party competition in Central and Eastern Europe

Country	Relevance of blocs	Bloc pattern stability	Closure by government	Fragmentation	Volatility	Polarisation
Hungary	Very high	Very high	Very high	Very low	Very low	Very high
Czech Republic	High	Very high	High	Low	Very low	Very high
Romania	Low	Low	High	Low	Very low	Very low
Lithuania	High	High	High	High	Very high	High
Estonia	Very low	Low	Low	High	Low	Low
Poland	High	Low	Low	High	High	High
Slovakia	High	Low	Very low	High	Low	Very high
Bulgaria	Low	Low	Very low	Very low	High	Low
Slovenia	Very low	High	Very low	Very high	Low	Very low
Latvia	Very low	Very low	Very low	Very high	Very high	Low

Notes: Closure categories: very low (0–35), low (35–50), high (50–65), very high (65–100); Fragmentation categories: very low (0–3.5), low (3.5–4), high (4–4.5), very high (5–); Volatility categories: very low (0–23), low (23–30), high (30–35), very high (35–100). Polarisation categories were determined by judgements on the four indicators displayed, while bloc-politics was categorised on the basis of the qualitative description of party systems.

of volatility. Governmental closure, bloc politics and polarisation appear as more central. Given the low number of cases, correlation figures (Spearman) are not completely satisfactory indicators of the robustness of the ties between the variables, but it is indicative that the three relationships that reach the level of 95 or 96 per cent significance are: closure and the relevance of blocs (.61), closure and stability (.63) of blocs,[5] and the relevance of blocs and polarisation (.84). Loyalty to friends and opposition to enemies seem to be at the heart of institutionalisation.

In order to summarise the binary relationships between variables, we shall first examine the linkages between the three classical dimensions: volatility, fragmentation and polarisation. Based on the literature on Western countries (e.g. Bartolini and Mair, 1990; Lane, 2008), a particularly close covariance was expected between party system fragmentation and volatility. Most of the results are in accordance with this expectation, although Slovenia has many parties and relatively low volatility, while Bulgaria has a volatile electorate that supports relatively few parties. Fragmentation and polarisation also seem to go together, but in Romania and Bulgaria there are more parties than expected based on the polarisation figures, while Slovakia is surprisingly polarised for its relatively few parties. Most party systems that are volatile are also less polarised, although Slovenia and Romania are simultaneously relatively stable in terms of vote shifts and depolarised, while the Lithuanian voters keep moving between the parties in spite of the relatively high level of polarisation.

As the next step let us examine the behaviour of less standard but apparently more crucial variables: bloc politics and closure. The two characteristics of bloc politics are very closely related, and Slovenia is the only country where the alliance structures are relatively stable in spite of the low relevance of ideology in the choice of governmental coalition partners. In general parties tend to be loyal to their bloc partners in countries where the electoral volatility is low. Partial exceptions are Lithuania, where the relatively stable alliances failed to produce stable electoral loyalties, and Romania, where voters are more predictable than the politicians. In Romania blocs are not only volatile but also of secondary relevance when it comes to coalition making, similarly to Slovenia, although electoral volatility is relatively low in both countries. The latter country is deviant also in the sense that it is the only one that disturbs the otherwise close covariation between bloc stability and governmental closure.

In fragmented party systems blocs tend to be unstable and inconsequential, although they play a relatively marginal role in the concentrated Bulgarian system as well, and the fragmented Slovenian system should have had even more promiscuous parties. As noted above, alliances are most consequential in highly polarised party systems, the relationship between these two variables having no exception. The stability of alliances is also closely related to polarisation, with the partial exceptions of Slovakia (where the stability of blocs is relatively low) and of Slovenia (which has a depolarised system with relatively stable alliance structures).

The review of the relationships above already indicates the strategic status of government closure. Closed governmental arenas go together with low electoral volatility, although in the Lithuanian system government closure coincides with a relatively high level of electoral volatility, while the Slovaks and the Slovenes managed to keep electoral volatility low in spite of the relatively open governmental arena. Fragmentation and closure would be almost perfectly related were it not for Bulgaria, which is on the extremes of both party system concentration and government openness. So far as closure and polarisation are concerned, there are two deviant countries: Romania, with its low polarisation, and, more importantly, Slovakia, where the openness of governmental interactions coincides with very high polarisation. As mentioned above, with the partial exception of Slovenia and Romania, bloc stability and relevance seem to be closely related to governmental closure. This should not come as a surprise, since the two variables tap to a large extent the same phenomenon: fidelity in inter-party relations.

There is a high degree of covariation across the six variables examined. In only three instances is there a large divergence between the variables: the levels of polarisation and volatility in Romania, of closure and polarisation in Slovakia and of fragmentation and closure in Bulgaria, which indicate different levels of institutionalisation.

Putting all the dimensions together, there is a clear and sharp difference between Hungary and the Czech Republic, on the one hand, and Slovenia, Estonia, Bulgaria and Latvia, on the other. In the case of Slovenia, nevertheless, the stability of the blocs does suggest the seeds of institutionalisation, while in Bulgaria the low level of fragmentation could be seen as promising for institutionalisation, were it not a heritage of the past rather than a reflection of novel trends. So far as the remaining four countries are concerned, Romania is perhaps the closest to the institutionalised group by having a high level of closure, low fragmentation and low electoral volatility, at least compared to the volatile regional environment. Poland, Slovakia and Lithuania all share a relatively high level of polarisation and disciplined bloc politics, but only the last of these managed to achieve a high level of government closure and all three are fragmented, with volatile electorates.

In the case of Poland it is the ideological constraints on alliances that give some degree of structure to the system. The Lithuanian system is institutionalised on many accounts, but far too fragmented and particularly volatile. Slovakia is a mixed bag: on the one hand highly polarised, with a relatively high bloc relevance and low volatility, but the stability of blocs, the relatively high level of fragmentation and the lack of closure point to an open, amorphous pattern of competition. Romania is closer to the institutionalised group: electoral behaviour, as well as the behaviour of parties in government formation, is relatively predictable and the number of parties in parliament is low. But the level of polarisation is also low, there are shifting alliances among parties and ideological constraints are often disregarded. In three of the cases the ambiguity is to a large extent due to temporal change, as Romania and Lithuania were originally more polarised, with stricter bloc boundaries, and they have opened up only in the second part of the period.

To conclude, the different facets of party systems tend to be intertwined in CEE. Volatility is the least integrated aspect of party systems. It is particularly loosely related to the relevance of blocs and to polarisation. This is not surprising, however, since volatility is the aspect of the party systems that is least controlled by the parties themselves. Institutionalisation and Europeanisation processes are closely related, but not identical. The conspicuous symptoms of de-institutionalisation in many West European party systems underscore this observation. At the same time predictability in party relations based on the logic of classic party families is a pattern that would satisfy both criteria. The present chapter has demonstrated that countries of the region vary considerably in their proximity to this model. However, it is not cultural closeness to the West or integration with the EU that are the principal driving forces behind stability, but rather, domestic institutional factors and the choices of domestic elites.

Notes

1 We would like to express our gratitude to Marina Popescu, Vello Pettai, Alenka Krasovec, Daniel Bochsler, Kristin Nickel and Sean Hanley for their expert opinions. All responsibility for the final classifications is ours.

2 Whether coalitional preferences are made public before the election is relevant both for the decisiveness of elections and for the predictability of party systems (Strøm and Müller, 1999; Powell, 2000; Martin and Stevenson, 2001; Golder, 2006; Carroll and Cox, 2007).

3 All those cabinets formed by so-called 'independents' or non-partisan members have been excluded.

4 Focusing only on 'founding elections' in Eastern Europe, rather than on 'breakaway elections' (i.e. the ones held immediately after the collapse of communist rule) as a point of departure is also justified because the latter 'were often merely referenda on communist rule rather than true expressions of political preferences' (Ishiyama, 1997: 309; Jasiewicz, 2003). Hungary is the only exception to this general rule.

5 There is some overlap in the definition and operationalisation of closure and bloc politics (although the latter covers oppositions as well), and therefore these covariations were expected.

References

Bardi, L. and P. Mair (2008), 'The parameters of party systems', *Party Politics* 14, pp. 147–66.

Bartolini, S. and P. Mair (1990), *Identity, Competition, and Electoral Availability: the Stabilization of European Electorates 1885–1985* (Cambridge: Cambridge University Press).

Benoit, K. and M. Laver (2006), *Party Policy in Modern Democracies* (London: Routledge).

Carroll, R. and G. W. Cox (2007), 'The logic of Gamson's Law: pre-election coalitions and portfolio allocations', *American Journal of Political Science* 51, pp. 300–13.

Casal Bértoa, F. and P. Mair (2009), 'Two decades on: how institutionalized are post-communist party systems?', paper presented at the ECPR Joint Sessions (Lisbon, 14–19 April).

Daalder, H. (1983), 'The comparative study of European parties and party systems: an overview', in H. Daalder and P. Mair (eds), *Western European Party Systems – Continuity and Change* (London: Sage).

Enyedi, Z. (2006), 'Party politics in post-communist transition', in W. Crotty and R. Katz (eds), *Handbook of Political Parties* (London: Sage), pp. 228–38.

Enyedi, Z. (2007), 'The "Europeanisation" of Eastern Central European party systems', *EpsNet Kiosk Plus* 5, pp. 65–74.

Enyedi, Z. and P. G. Lewis (2006), 'The impact of the European Union on party politics in Central and Eastern Europe', in P. G. Lewis and Z. Mansfeldová (eds), *The European Union and Party Politics in East Central Europe* (Houndmills: Palgrave Macmillan), pp. 247–68.

Enyedi, Z. and B. Todosijevic (2008), 'Adversarial politics, civic virtues and party identification in Eastern and Western Europe', in J. Bartle and P. Bellucci (eds), *Political Parties and Partisanship: Social identity and Individual Attitudes* (London: Routledge).

Gallagher, M. (2009), 'Electoral Systems' website, www.tcd.ie/Political_Science/Staff/Michael.Gallaguer/ElSystems/, accessed September 2009.

Golder, S. (2006), 'Pre-electoral coalition formation in parliamentary democracies', *British Journal of Political Science* 36, pp. 193–212.

Gunther, R. and J. R. Montero (2001), 'The anchors of partisanship: a comparative analysis of voting behaviour in four Southern European democracies', in P. N. Diamandouros and R. Gunther (eds), *Parties, Politics and Democracy in the New Southern Europe* (London: Johns Hopkins University Press).

Hooghe, L., R. Bakker, A. Brigevich, C. de Vries, E. Edwards, G. Marks, J. Rovny, and M. Steenbergen (2008), 'Reliability and validity of measuring party positions: the Chapel Hill Expert Surveys of 2002 and 2006', unpublished manuscript.

Ishiyama, J. T. (1997), 'The sickle or the rose?', *Comparative Political Studies* 30, pp. 299–330.

Jasiewicz, K. (2003), 'Elections and voting behaviour', in S. White, J. Batt and P. G. Lewis (eds), *Developments in Central and Eastern European Politics* (Durham, NC: Duke University Press).

Laakso, M. and R. Taagepera (1979), ' "Effective" number of parties. A measure with application to West Europe', *Comparative Political Studies* 12, pp. 3–27.

Lane, J.-E. (2008), *Comparative Politics: The Principal–Agent Perspective* (London, New York: Routledge).

Lewis, P. G. (2006), 'Party systems in post-communist Central Europe: patterns of stability and consolidation', *Democratization* 13, pp. 562–83.

Mainwaring, S. and T. Scully (1995), *Building Democratic Institutions: Party Systems in Latin America* (Stanford, CA: Stanford University Press).

Mair, P. (1996), 'Comparing party systems', in L. LeDuc, R. G. Niemi and P. Norris (eds), *Comparing Democracies: Elections and Voting in Global Perspectives* (London: Sage).

Mair, P. (1997), *Party System Change. Approaches and Interpretations* (Oxford: Clarendon Press).

Mair, P. (2001), 'The freezing hypothesis: an evaluation', in L. Karvonen and S. Kuhnle (eds), *Party Systems and Voter Alignments Revisited* (London: Routledge).

Mair, P. (2007), 'Party systems and alternation in government, 1950–2000: innovation and institutionalization', in S. Gloppen and L. Rakner (eds), *Globalisation and Democratisation: Challenges for Political Parties* (Bergen: Fagbokforlaget).

Martin, L. and R. T. Stevenson (2001), 'Cabinet formation in parliamentary democracies', *American Journal of Political Science* 45, pp. 33–50.

Millard, F. (2004), *Elections, Parties, and Representation in Post-communist Europe* (Houndmills: Palgrave Macmillan).

Müller, W. C. and K. Strøm (eds) (2000), *Coalition Governments in Western Europe* (New York: Oxford University Press).

Müller-Rommel, F., F. Katja and P. Harfst (2004), 'Party government in Central Eastern European democracies: a data collection (1990–2003)', *European Journal of Political Research* 43, 869–93.

O'Dwyer, C. (2006), *Runaway State-Building: Patronage Politics and Democratic Development* (Baltimore, MD: Johns Hopkins University Press).

Pedersen, M. (1979), 'The dynamics of European party systems: changing patterns of electoral volatility', *European Journal of Political Research* 7, pp. 1–26.

Powell, G. B. Jr. (2000), *Elections as Instruments of Democracy: Majoritarian and Proportional Visions* (New Haven, CT: Yale University Press).

Reich, G. M. (2001), 'Coordinating party choice in founding elections: why timing matters', *Comparative Political Studies* 34, pp. 1237–63.

Sartori, G. (1976), *Parties and Party Systems. A Framework for Analysis, Volume I.* (Cambridge: Cambridge University Press).

Siaroff, A. (2000), *Comparative European Party Systems. An Analysis of Parliamentary Elections since 1945* (New York and London: Garland Publishing).

Sikk, A. (2005), 'How unstable? Volatility and the genuinely new parties in Eastern Europe', *European Journal of Political Research* 44, pp. 391–412.

Smith, G. (1990), 'Core persistence, system change and the "People's Party" ', in P. Mair and G. Smith (eds), *Understanding Party System Change in Western Europe* (London: Palgrave).

Strøm, K. and W. C. Müller (1999), 'Political Parties and Hard Choices', in W. C. Müller and K. Strøm (eds), *Policy, Office, or Votes? How Political Parties in Western Europe Make Hard Decisions* (Cambridge: Cambridge University Press), pp. 1–35.

Tóka, G. and A. Henjak (2007), 'Party systems and voting behaviour in the Visegrad countries 15 years after the transition', in P. Šaradín and E. Bradová (eds), *Visegrad Votes: Parliamentary Elections 2005–2006* (Olomouc: Palacky University Press), pp. 210–44.

Toole, J. (2000), 'Government formation and party system stabilization in East Central Europe', *Party Politics* 6, pp. 441–61.

Ware, A. (1996), *Political Parties and Party Systems* (Oxford: Oxford University Press).

Webb, P. and S. White (eds) (2007), *Party Politics in New Democracies* (Oxford: Oxford University Press).

7

The radical right and its nearby competitors: evidence from Eastern Europe

Lenka Bustikova and Herbert Kitschelt

Introduction

The beginning of the twenty-first century and the aftermath of European Union (EU) accession were coterminous with a rise in nationalist and intolerant political appeals across Central and Eastern Europe (CEE).[1] Examination of these appeals speaks directly to three fundamental yet unresolved questions; first, whether EU accession fulfilled the 'great expectations' of citizens in CEE (Grzymala-Busse and Innes, 2003); second, whether the EU moderated extremist voices in domestic politics and third, whether the social and economic agenda outlined in the EU accession process became entrenched as a focal point of domestic party competition.

It is too early to assess the long-term effects of EU enlargement, but we can advance the debate by outlining a general analytical framework that will enable us to understand the sources of variation in support for radical-right demands in electoral politics, and particular radical right-wing parties across and within countries, over time. Though we are aware of excellent case study-oriented research on right-wing political currents in many CEE polities, the literature, we believe, lacks a theoretical map that frames variation in radical-right mobilisation across countries and over time.[2]

In order to fill this gap in the literature, it is first necessary to theorise the link between the process of Europeanisation, domestic party politics and the radical right. We concur with Lewis (2009) that nationalist politics has been mild in CEE Europe thus far, but if the process of welfare retrenchment that we describe in the chapter continues, it may create a large reservoir of dissatisfied voters available for radical party mobilisation. In line with other scholars, we highlight the absence of significant differentiation among parties on the issue of EU accession and on the core economic decisions associated with the transition, especially until 2004 (for an overview, see Lewis's introductory chapter).

We argue that the process of EU accession has, in effect, narrowed the policy options of domestic governments, as suggested in Ladrech (2002) and Mair (2006). The effect of EU conditionality on narrowing the menu of policy choices was most intense during the accession period. After the enlargement, post-communist countries have diverged in their adoption of second-generation reforms, such as tax reduction and social programme cuts (O'Dwyer and Kovalčík, 2007; Fisher *et al.*, 2007).

The Maastricht criteria, such as caps on budget deficits and inflation, are a set of non-negotiable policies that reduce the economic manoeuvring space for executives in the long run. This has led to the perception that 'there is no choice' in economic policy making (Rupnik, 2007: 22; Greskovits, 2007). Despite the fact that the new EU members are obliged to comply with the conditionality of Maastricht, some countries have dragged their feet by not complying, while others have complied and already adopted the euro. The timing of adopting the euro has turned into a contentious domestic political issue (Johnson, 2008). It stands to reason that the uncertain future of the euro in the wake of the Greek bailout will fuel further divergence in countries' economic trajectories. The Bulgarian prime minister's statement implies a source of endogenous variation in the timing of euro adoption: 'Everybody in the EU feels rather scared by the events in Greece. That is why this is not the best time to raise the question of Bulgaria's accession to the ERM II.'[3] Despite divergence in economic policies during the post-accession phase, Maastricht has generally narrowed down the economic choices available to countries, since countries can determine the pace of compliance and therefore adoption, but do not have the option of opting out of the euro entirely. This decision about whether to delay compliance is ultimately a policy choice that directly impinges upon party competition.

We argue that the process of EU accession has contributed to the narrowing of the economic policy-making options for post-communist political elites. This has an impact both on the demand side and on the supply side of right-wing politics. On the demand side, Europeanisation has accelerated fiscal stabilisation policies that may have hurt employment, particularly in the public or non-profit sectors, such as social services. Europeanisation forces governments to respond to EU strictures. Under conditions of government alternation, sooner rather than later all major parties will have served in government and endorsed EU-compatible economic policies. This convergence of partisan politics through EU membership, in conjunction with government alternation, may encourage disgruntled citizens to opt for new right-wing partisan alternatives.

On both the demand and the supply sides, economic policies and partisan competition are 'proximate' causes of radical-right mobilisation. They are in part conditioned by deeper, durable causes that affect the differential potential for right-wing politics across the post-communist region. If we had the space, we would focus on two major mechanisms. *On the demand side* we would home in on whatever ethno-cultural division has gained salience in a country. Politicians who strive to capture an electoral constituency among the most numerous ethnicities may decide to politicise ethnic relations, contingent upon the costs and benefits of such a strategy. For reasons we will not engage in this chapter, this cost-benefit balance for ethno-cultural polarisation often may be most conducive to mobilisation by the dominant group when the minority constitutes a fraction of the total population too small to become a fundamental threat to the major ethnic group, but still sufficiently visible in size to attract that majority's attention and crystallise the suspicions of some of its members. The critical minority size may range from 5 per cent to 20 per cent of the population.

On the supply side, legacies of pre-communist and communist rule are important in patterning the proximate cause for right-wing supply-side partisan politics, the convergence of major political parties on economic liberalism. This programmatic partisan convergence is least likely where regime legacies and post-communist transitions have left behind hardcore intransigent communist parties that scavenge the population for voters willing to oppose market liberalisation and, often enough, also political democracy. Whether as direct successors of former ruling communist parties or not, such parties tend to develop a 'red-brown' anti-market and socio-culturally authoritarian and exclusionary appeal. In other strands of communist legacy that resulted in the social democratic transformation of former ruling parties, by contrast, it is more likely that the radical-right elements in politics congeal around new parties or are at least partially incorporated into the field of centre-right parties emerging from the opposition to communism.

Mediated by the initial ideological distribution of post-communist political parties, legacies thus may also affect the political construction of salient ethnicities and their relations of conflict. Moreover, such legacies have a more or less strong influence on EU accession and, via this very causal path but also directly through the ever-changing partisan stripes of national government executives, on the extent to which the initial cohort of newly founded or renewed parties in a post-communist polity converge in their positions on salient, visible policy conflicts.

EU integration is an intervening mechanism in more senses than one. Configurations of salient ethno-cultural conflict are likely to lower a country's chances of entering the EU or to delay entry into the EU. But EU membership, in turn, may have a direct effect beneficial to the containment of inter-ethnic hostilities (Kelley, 2004). This may dampen ethno-cultural strife to a certain extent, but may make it reappear through the consequences of macro-economic and social welfare retrenchment policies as well as the convergence

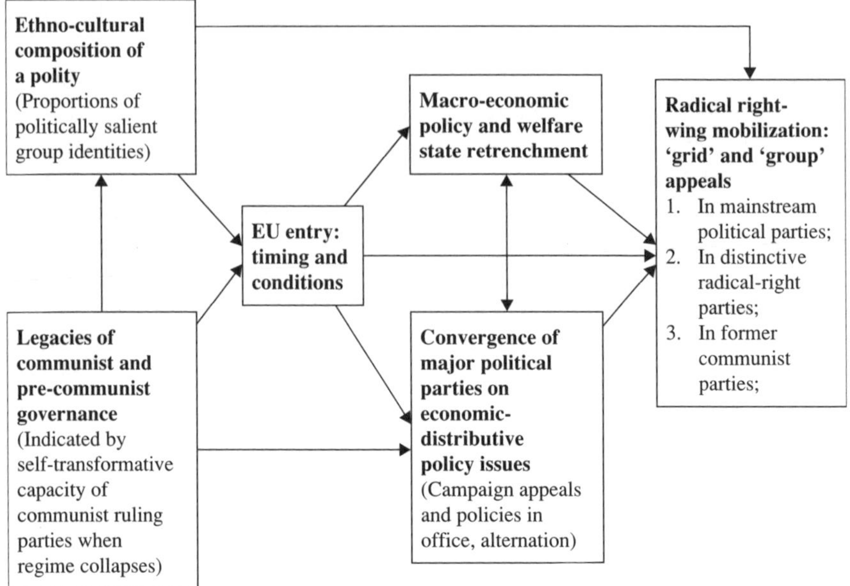

Figure 7.1 Causal mechanisms explaining radical-right politics
in post-communism

of all major parties in their positions on issues of economic redistribution and liberalisation. These are the themes we will examine in more detail in this chapter. Consider Figure 7.1 our effort to clarify in simplistic fashion the causal relations involved in our narrative in the preceding paragraphs. Our chapter will primarily confine itself to the proximate mechanisms of macro-economic policy and the partisan convergence. At the same time, we affirm that a 'deeper' analysis of the proximate mechanisms is called for which we cannot deliver in our current chapter.

We distinguish constellations of party convergence and the extent to which they encourage either the rise of new radical right-wing parties or the turn of 'conventional' moderately conservative parties to radical right-wing appeals. With regard to fiscal retrenchment and the welfare state, we discuss not these policies themselves, but one implication that we derive from this dynamics for the field of democratic party competition under post-communism, *namely that citizens' losses in incomes, jobs and hence also self-respect and quality of life satisfaction are widely dispersed throughout the social structure and therefore support a socio-economically and demographically diffuse profile of radical right-wing party supporters.* Much less so than in Western Europe or the United States, radical-right support does not crystallise around distinctive sociological categories of actors, be they occupation or education.

Our chapter is divided into three sections. We begin by differentiating two fundamental types of identity-based appeals, based on grid/group theory – appeals that are associated with (1) norms and regulatory provisions and (2) appeals that address group boundaries. On the basis of these two dimensions, we create a typology of radical-right parties. We then account for variation in support for identity-based appeals in post-communist Europe and political competition associated with radical-right party mobilisation. We focus on two mechanisms associated with party competition to explain the strength of radical-right parties in post-communist Europe: (1) the convergence of major parties on economic issues and (2) patterns of party system polarisation resulting from communist legacies and EU pressures. We also search for evidence documenting the diffuse character of radical-right voters.

Conception of the radical right

How do we define the radical right? We are not trying to reinvent the wheel here, given the tremendous discussion that has surrounded the concept of radical right and associated conceptions of the 'right with attributes' (Mudde, 2007). It is critical to recognise that in addition to economic issues of income and wealth distribution, political parties may compete on identity-based issues, which take two ideal forms: exclusionary appeals based on ethnicity (nationality) or group affiliation ('group') and socio-cultural appeals that seek to regulate the web of social relationships ('grid') and impose regulations on sexual behaviour, social conduct or life-style decisions. We take the grid/group distinction from the work of the anthropologist Mary Douglas, as communicated into political science especially by Aaron Wildavsky's *Cultural Theory* (Wildavsky *et al.*, 1990).

We define radical-right politics as the combination of an exclusionary definition of membership ('group') that erects high walls between those who are in and those who are out in society and a hermetic conception of group obligations that decisively subordinates the individual under the group ('grid'). This leads to a situation where the individual can neither voice protest and go against the group nor enter or exit a group to choose an arrangement consistent with personal preferences. Douglas refers to this combination as a *hierarchical conception of society* with little tolerance for difference and individual expression.

The grid-group definitions designate a delineation of group inclusion (membership) and attitudes towards authoritarianism. They do not define cleavage structures. We do not investigate the origins of particular grid-group ordering principles and how they relate to historical transformative processes. Political parties differ in their grid-group definitions of polities. We are interested in this variation and the way political parties define societal boundaries.

Empirically, the identification of radical-right political parties – as the organised effort of political entrepreneurs to win political office with an explicitly hierarchist programmatic appeal – thus turns on questions concerning the definition of friend and foe ('groupness') and subordination of the individual under collective norms ('gridness'). With respect to the former, appeals to the nation and the significance of national collective identity are one indicator. The acceptance of immigrants into the community is a related indicator. With respect to the latter, hierarchists embrace traditional social conceptions of authority in the family and gender relations, as well as more generally a uniform civilisational conception of the good life in which they leave little room for multiculturalism among sub-groups or for individual non-conformism. As a further conceptual convention, let us refer to as 'radical rightists' those politicians who pursue authoritarian objectives within the confines of a democratic political order, and as 'extreme rightists' those who want to replace the democratic order itself with an authoritarian regime. In this sense, most of the political undertakings this chapter examines are 'radical rightist', whereas a few also exhibit tendencies to embrace 'extreme rightism'.

As the object of analysis, let us here offer an inventory of parties in post-communist politics that have taken on 'radical right' grid-group appeals and their relative electoral support at different points in time. We confine ourselves to post-communist countries that displayed at least a modicum of democratic politics in the sense of permitting open competition among rival coalitions of political entrepreneurs for legislative and executive office safeguarded by a modicum of civil and political rights. This rules out the Caucasus region and Central Asia.

There have been a number of studies that have explored the appeal of radical right-wing forces in the post-communist region and generated highly nuanced judgements (Minkenberg, 2002; Mudde, 2005 and 2007). Here we draw on the Benoit and Laver (2006) expert survey of political parties. National panels of political scientists were asked to rate political parties on scales ranging from 1 to 20 on a variety of issues. While the scores are not directly comparable across countries, we are looking here for the extreme positions in each party system on relevant operationalisations of 'grid' and 'group' concepts. Generally, these are scores above 15.0 or below 5.0 on the 20-point scale. We also include 'nearby' parties that also reach the relevant threshold values on the issue dimensions or at least come very close to it.

We found three issues in the Benoit/Laver study that most directly grasp the grid/group distinctions (Table 7.2). For external boundary drawing, a question is suitable that asks experts to rate the extent to which parties promote a *national rather than a cosmopolitan* consciousness of history and culture ('nationalism'). A second, minor item invites experts to rate the extent to which parties oppose the right of foreigners to buy domestic land and real estate. For the grid dimension, we take an item that concerns 'social' *liberal policies* on matters of abortion, sexual preference and euthanasia (social liberalism).

We added three other items that we do not expect to relate to these grid-group distinctions in a perfectly consistent way, but which often may line up with them. The first item is the treatment of former communists implicated in the authoritarian regimes that preceded post-communist democracy. While authoritarians coming from the anti-communist opposition advocate the harshest possible treatment of former communists, 'red-brown' politicians steeped in the communist organisational pillar obviously take exactly the opposite position. Another item concerns the propensity of parties to support joining the EU. While there may be a general tendency among exclusionary/ authoritarian hierarchists to reject membership in the EU, pragmatic concerns might override this aversion in post-communist party systems even on the radical Right or Left.[4]

The third item is a placement of the parties on the left–right scale. It is not always the case that 'radical right' parties in the grid/group sense actually situate themselves on the extreme of a formal left–right scale, as they might combine their grid/group beliefs with more 'leftist' notions of economic redistribution. Summary (self-)placements of politicians and parties may take both grid/group and distributive policy issues into account (Kitschelt *et al.*, 1999: 249–55). Radical right (brown) parties often take the most extreme positions on identity-based issues; although identity-based appeals can be observed on the nationalistic extreme left as well (red-brown). Consider the Czech communists, who are extremely left on redistribution, libertarian on certain social issues (gay and Roma rights, for example), opposed to anti-Semitism, but also strongly nationalist and xenophobic. Russia's communists would differ from their Czech counterparts by showing more cultural author-itarianism on grid issues, but agree with their nationalist group stance and their redistributive economic policy preferences. Finally, a large number of post-communist parties combine mixed, or mildly redistributive economic issue stances with radical-right grid and group positions. Examples would be Vladimir Zhirinovsky's oddly labelled 'Liberal Democrats' in Russia, the Slovak National Party, the League of Polish Families or the Hungarian Justice and Life Party.

Table 7.1 Strength of identity-based parties: radical right (RR) (Brown) and nationalist successor communist parties (Red-Brown)

Party system features		1990s	2000s
RR > 20% average	Brown CP > 5% av.	Serbia	Serbia
	Brown CP < 5% av. or n.a.	No case	No case
RR 5–20% average	Brown CP > 5% av.	Czech Republic Romania Russia	Russia
	Brown CP < 5% av. or n.a.	Estonia Latvia Slovakia Slovenia Ukraine	Poland Romania Slovakia Slovenia
RR < 5% average	Brown CP > 5% av.	Bulgaria	Czech Republic
	Brown CP < 5% av. or n.a.	Albania Croatia Hungary Lithuania Macedonia Poland	Albania Bulgaria Croatia Estonia Hungary Latvia Lithuania Macedonia Ukraine

Source: Based on Bustikova (2009).

Let us list parties here according to their brown and red-brown predilections. Caveats are in order. Party systems and individual party labels are still quite fluid in some instances (Baltic states, Poland) and some parties obviously compete not only on policy platforms, but also on the ability to deliver selective inducements targeted at specific constituents ('clientelism') or the personality of their leader ('charisma' of party founder).

Despite these necessary qualifications, Table 7.1 exhibits important variation in identity-based appeals across the region and over time. We partition the strength of the radical-right parties (in terms of their grid/group appeals and general placement on the left–right spectrum) into three categories: strong, moderate and weak. A moderate appeal is when the party received between 5 to 20 per cent of the popular vote in national elections on average in a given time period. The time period is split into two segments: the 1990s and 2000s. We consider the average popular vote obtained in elections to lower assemblies if a country has a two-tier parliament/assembly. Referendums, local, regional, presidential and European elections are not included.[5]

Table 7.2 shows parties' positions on the various items in the Benoit-Laver expert survey for the most 'radical right' parties and for 'nearby' parties that approximate meeting the criteria for inclusion. Table 7.2 shows a remarkable association between grid and group scores of parties' programmatic position taking. Those parties that scored high on the nationalism measure also end up supporting less individual freedom in choosing each citizen's way of life and social norms. The table also reveals a tendency of nationalist-exclusionary and authoritarian, socially conservative parties to demand punishment and elimination of communists from public life, but this tendency is not expressed uniformly. The same applies to the EU question. Many right-wing parties actually support entrance into the EU, but some have major second thoughts about this strategy of international alliance building and integration.

Table 7.1 suggests that the strength of radical-right parties varies quite substantially across countries and temporally from the 1990s to the new millennium. This will now become the object of further probing and empirical explanation in this chapter. In some countries, genuine radical right-wing parties appear to have hardly any impact at all. But in a number of countries such formations have gained considerable strength. Our general working hypothesis is that where moderate right-wing parties also make some nod to exclusionary group/authoritarian grid themes, the success of radical-right parties is lower. If we traced the causal mechanisms further back historically, we would find that this is likely under certain communist legacy conditions, particularly countries where the communists had little grounding in an industrial working class and mobilised in a by-and-large agrarian society against authoritarian regimes with a weak associational protective belt. Also certain configurations of salient socio-cultural markers make radical right-wing mobilisation by majority group parties more likely, especially when the minority group is sufficiently large to make it salient for citizens to compute group-based chances for individual income or public goods but the minority group is sufficiently small to pose no fundamental threat to the persistence of the dominant group.

Theory: proximate causes of radical-right partisan crystallisation

It is one thing to have restrictive and exclusionary radical-right grid/group appeals represented in the competitive politics of a democracy, e.g. by low-key incorporation at the fringes of a moderately conservative party. It is quite another thing to see the emergence and electoral success of specialised radical right-wing parties, let alone the partial or whole conversion of previously moderately conservative parties to radical right-wing grid/group rhetoric. There may always be a substantial general reservoir of voters that has a vague 'demand' for radical-right grid/group positions in contemporary polities.This

Table 7.2 Positioning of radical-right parties on issue dimensions (2001–4)

The parties		Core issues			Contingent correlates			
Party coverage	Party labels: RR membership (RR) or 'nearby' competition?	% of electoral support in the last two elections (average after 2000)?	Value of national autonomy (= 20)	Foreign land ownership (against = 20)	Social conservatism (= 20)	Treatment of former communists (20 = punish)	Joining EU? (yes = 20)	Left-right positions (left = 1; right = 20)
Albania	None	n.a.	n.a.	n.a.	n.a.	n.a.	n.a.	n.a.
Bulgaria	National Union Attack (RR)	8.9 (only 2005)	No data	No data	No data	No data	No data	No data
Croatia	HSP (RR)	4.9	19.0	16.0	15.0	18.0	7.3	17.7
	HDZ (nearby)	14.5	17.7	12.2	14.2	12.2	14.5	14.5
Czech Republic	KSCM (nearby)	15.7	16.6	16.6	6.6	1.6	4.9	2.6
	RMS+NS	1.3	19.2	18.6	15.9	16.5	4.4	15.3
Estonia	ISAMAA (nearby)	7.3 (2003)	19.1	7.4	14.6	17.9	17.0	14,1
	RL (nearby)	10.0	17.6	16.8	16.0	5.0	14.9	10.4
Hungary	MIÉP (RR)	3.3	19.8	19.0	19.8	18.9	2.5	19.1
	Fidesz (nearby)	38.6	16.2	15.8	15.1	15.0	12.9	15.1
Latvia	TB/LNNK	22.9	19.3	17.3	14.5	17.1	15.6	16.3
Lithuania	LKD (RR)	1.7	15.9	13.3	18.4	n.d.	15.6	15.3
	TS (nearby)	11.6	14.8	6.8	15.8	n.d.	18.7	15.7
Macedonia	VMRO-DPMNE (nearby)	20.8 and 32.5 (in coalition)	17.5	14.8	17.3	14.8	17.4	15.2

Moldova	PPCD	9.4	13.4	8.5	10.4	14.5	16.1	14.4
Poland	LPR (RR)	4.6	19.0	19.3	19.1	17.3	1.5	16.4
	PiS (nearby)	30.0	14.7	14.7	15.1	17.6	12.5	12.5
	S (nearby)	5.8	16.1	18.5	13.1	6.6	3.0	5.5
Romania	PRM (RR)	17.2	19.6	19.6	18.2	2.8	11.0	11.5
	PNG (RR)	28.3	No data	No data	No data	No data	No data	No data
Russia	LDPR (RR)	9.8	17.5	15.7	14.1	12.4	n.d.	13.9
	KPRF (nearby)	12.2	16.3	18.0	14.3	2.0	n.d.	4.8
Serbia	SRS (RR)	28.2	18.7	19.3	16.8	11.0	4.5	19.0
	SPO (nearby)	5.0	13.5	11.0	13.8	15.0	15.3	15.3
Slovakia	SNS (RR)	7.5	19.4	19.5	19.7	17.4	8.5	17.1
	KDH (nearby)	8.3	15.7	9.7	16.1	11.4	15.9	15.1
	HZDS (nearby)	13.9	13.8	13.9	9.5	7.1	14.9	10.9
Slovenia	SNS (RR)	5.4	17.1	17.4	11.7	9.3	6.8	10.1
	NSi (nearby)	8.8	15.1	10.4	17.3	18.1	16.9	17.0
Ukraine	NU (nearby)	18.6	17.0	10.5	11.8	14.3	18.4	15.6
	KUN (no data)	No data	No data	No data	No data	No data	No data	No data

Note: Questions posed:

Nationalism: *Strongly promotes a cosmopolitan rather than a national consciousness, history and culture* (1). *Strongly promotes a national rather than a cosmopolitan consciousness, history and culture* (20).

Foreign land ownership: *Supports unrestricted rights of foreigners to purchase and own land* (1). *Opposes any rights of foreigners to purchase and own land* (20).

Social policy: *Favours liberal policies on matters such as abortion, homosexuality, and euthanasia* (1). *Opposes liberal policies on matters such as abortion, homosexuality, and euthanasia* (20).

Former communists: *Former communist party officials should have the same right and opportunities as other citizens to participate in public life* (1). *Former communist party officials should be kept out of public life as far as possible* (20).

EU Joining: *Opposes joining the European Union* (1). *Favours joining the European Union* (20).

Left-Right: the general Left-Right dimension *Please locate each party on a general left-right dimension, taking all aspects of party policy into account*, Left (1) Right (20).

Source: Expert Survey, Benoit and Laver (2006).

radical-right 'demand' may vary a bit, contingent upon socio-cultural and political-economic conditions. But we need to account for the varying intensity of such demands, combined with strategic conditions in the party system that give political entrepreneurs the incentives to invoke radical-right appeals with the prospect of winning political office and influence over policy making.

Demand conditions for radical right politics in post-communism: economic reforms and identity-based appeals

It is well known that lack of educational sophistication is a common individual-level trait disposing voters to fear societal diversity and become intolerant to socio-cultural 'otherness' (Hainmueller and Hiscox, 2007). In order to prime these dispositions and make them salient for party competition, however, critical events and experiences will be needed, such as a state breakdown against the backdrop of which issues of ethnic diversity tend to become politicised or novel types of economic failure and material deprivations emerge that do not appear to lend themselves to simple solutions of economic redistribution in favour of the less well-off, in terms of individual or household-based (rather than group-based) welfare payoffs.

Several conditions favour the mobilisation of group demands. Citizens obtain scarce resources and access to the political decision-making process contingent not only upon their individual assets and capacities, but also because of group markers that award advantages or disadvantages in the distribution of material resources, political rights or cultural autonomy. Particularly in times of deep economic and political crises, when established pre-existing group-based divisions of labour and the institutionalised governance of economic institutions break down, group-based anxieties intensify. It is not simply an ethnic division of labour and division of political clout, but *uncertainty* about such division of labour and the prospects of belonging to groups of winners or losers resulting from such crises that may create the pool of political demand that enables strategic politicians to invoke ethno-regional sentiments (Olzak, 1992).

Particularly when the communist 'lid' blows off many CEE and Central Asian states, a period of heightened anxiety about group benefits creates an environment favourable to the strategic mobilisation of ethnic difference by vote-seeking political entrepreneurs. But there may be no simple linear relationship between ethno-political mobilisation and the size of minority groups or the value of ethnic fractionalisation indices, as we argue elsewhere (Bustikova and Kitschelt, 2009). Politicians must be able *to make potential group losses credible to large electoral constituencies*. This is particularly plausible in polities that pit an overwhelming ethno-cultural majority against small but distinctive and visible ethno-cultural minorities. They are threatening either because they are more affluent and/or politically connected than the ethno-cultural majority or much poorer than the majority, just harbouring an intensive drive for redistribution of resources. At the same time, politicians also must suggest to citizens that pursuit of group advantages involves relatively limited risks to make costly mistakes, particularly the risk of civil war. The desirable cost-benefit balance appears most plausible in cases where the ethno-cultural minority group(s) are not too powerful already to inflict severe damage on their adversaries.

Beyond ethno-cultural considerations of group power and status, it is *particularly political-economic conditions* that may directly or indirectly fuel radical-right mobilisation. It is a common explanatory template in the study of radical-right politics in affluent, highly institutionalised Western democracies to construct a connection between economic deprivation (through 'globalisation' or technologically induced devaluation of professional skills etc.), on the one hand, and the rise of exclusionary group and authoritarian grid sentiments, on the other. People adopting such sentiments blame a subversive socio-cultural 'other' to cause economic misery and cultural dissent. As remedial action, grid/group authoritarians therefore seek to victimise cultural non-conformists and minorities, particularly immigrants.

But there are complications to this story when it is examined closely. Sophisticated empirical studies have shown that it is really the lack of cultural resources and capabilities (such as low education), *not* the rational calculation of personal economic loss, due to competition from non-conformists, immigrants or foreign goods, that drives people's grid/group views (see, e.g. Hainmueller and Hiscox, 2007). There is only a *correlation* between the experience of economic and social loss (unemployment, falling wages, high divorce rates etc.) and radical-right grid/group views, but *not a direct causal relation*. The causal chain in fact goes from cultural resources and cognitive capabilities to political preferences, with general economic circumstances – and configurations of party competition (see below) – possibly acting as catalysts to prime people's mobilisation of authoritarian dispositions. Economically deprived and uneducated voters with nationalistic and authoritarian views may vote for radical parties, even if radical parties do not support redistribution towards the poor. Voting for the radical right is mediated by low levels of education, which contribute both to poverty and to authoritarian, xenophobic attitudes. The indirect link between poverty and authoritarianism explains why low-educated, less well-off voters may vote against their economic interests. Nevertheless, broadly spread economic crisis may still be likely to create a general political climate that activates right-wing grid/group dispositions more intensively among those who carry them anyway, more so than a vibrant economy.

What are the implications of these different causal relations between citizens' market opportunities and political-preference mobilisation for post-communist polities? Let us first lay out a straightforward *economic interest-based argument* that essentially hypothesises the emergence of a very large socio-economically amorphous pool of voters dissatisfied with the government policies of whichever parties hold political office. The existence of this pool, however, by itself does not explain the collective mobilisation of a radical-rightist grid/group bias. Only by examining the supply side of politics under conditions of democratic competition does it become intelligible why radical right-wing partisan appeals could benefit from a widespread sense of economic deprivation in post-communist polities. Moreover, whereas in affluent established capitalist democracies radical rightists might vote *against* their direct economic interests in favour of redistribution by supporting radical-right parties that often enough buy into market liberalism, albeit with limitations on free trade, under post-communism it turns out to be more likely that radical right-wing parties, consistent with the predilections of many grid/group authoritarians, endorse more populist-social protectionist economic and social policies.

Let us first set out the *economic argument*. Economic reform trajectories in post-communist countries proceeded in two major stages. The first stage involved stabilisation, liberalisation, privatisation and building of core market institutions throughout the 1990s. With the exception of building institutions of market oversight, all of the post-communist electoral democracies successfully completed the first stage of reforms. The real divergence emerges not only from variation in the quality of the 'rule of law', but from different trajectories of welfare state dismantlement and subsequent levels of inequality. In particular, most of the CEE democracies left their old communist welfare state relatively intact from the early 1990s onwards, whereas the fission products of the former Soviet Union and some South-East European countries quickly dismantled them and, together with the predominant techniques of privatisation in that region, saw levels of inequality and poverty rise quickly throughout the 1990s.

The main reason for the difference was that effective party competition in functioning electoral democracies with civic and political rights prevented vote-seeking politicians from dismantling social protections that clearly were popular with the median voter. Instead, they reformed and even extended social protection at a time of rising unemployment. Competition helps social protection. By contrast, in hybrid regimes with lop-sided, stunted or distorted political competition, existing social programmes decayed and politicians made little effort to rejuvenate them. But a perpetuation of socialist welfare states in CEE proved to be difficult beyond the first stage of reforms in the 1990s. Socialist economies suffered from over-staffed, but underpaid social services in healthcare and education. State pensions were low, but employees became eligible at an early age (Vanhuysse, 2006).

As the first stage reforms bore fruit and private sector wages began to rise, it became increasingly difficult to fund inefficient welfare states, as social service providers and pensioners demanded to participate in the recovery through higher wages and pensions, while consumers insisted on the preservation of cheap and comprehensive social services. At the same time, however, private employers and employees were already paying extremely burdensome payroll taxes to finance these systems that could not be further increased. This predicament forced upon the agenda of politicians consideration of a second stage of reform in which governments embark on major retrenchment of social benefits and services, including social service employment, and an increase in charges and fees for the remaining services. Sooner or later, stage-one reforms result in fiscal tensions and imperatives of retrenchment that set post-communist governments on a collision course with the social service providers and service consumers, which are the vast majority of each country's electorates. *Social policy reform retrenchment in universalist, comprehensive insurance and service systems hurts just about everyone and benefits very few people in an obvious and subjectively perceived sense.* Social policy reform thus has a highly incendiary potential for political conflict. The economic argument thus identifies an almost universal outcry against social policy retrenchment. This political challenge has particular intensity in those post-communist countries where social protection had not been dismantled right after the collapse of the old regimes.

Economic developments by themselves, however, cannot provide a rationale demonstrating why actors turned to radical-right grid/group appeals and political entrepreneurs featuring such politics in their electoral campaigns. What the economic argument does suggest is that citizens upset about social retrenchment will opt against market liberalism for economic redistribution. In order to understand how the second-stage fiscal crisis of the post-communist welfare state boosts radical-right grid/group appeals, it is necessary to turn to the political supply side of democratic party competition. What were the political alignments of party competition that made radical-right appeals attractive to vote-seeking politicians and actually rewarded them with substantial shares of electoral support? Why did voters, faced with social policy retrenchment, not turn simply to politicians with a leftist economic-redistributive appeal?

Supply conditions for radical-right politics in post-communism
Our basic premise is that, in aggregate, voters support parties in a spatial manner by opting for the party alternatives closest to their own ideal points, but possibly subject to strategic voting (avoidance of wasted votes). Most voters do not rationally deliberate about the relationship between their personal issue preferences and the competing parties' policy appeals before

choosing among the alternatives, but the minority that do create a central tendency at the aggregate population level that makes it appear as if all voters choose the party that matches their preference profile. Our second premise is that when parties are seen as being very close to each other in political appeal on issues that voters find most salient, then voters become indifferent about them. Voters either abstain or vote on a secondary-issue dimension, provided that parties offer more meaningful alternatives on it. One might call this the 'directional' element of our presumed model of voter choice. It can be formulated as a *lexicographical ordering principle*: First, vote for the party closest to you on the policy dimension most salient to you. Second, if there is little difference between alternatives on the most salient dimension, choose among parties based on their meaningful differences on the next most salient dimension. Third, abstain from voting (or vote on personality, party identity etc.) if there are no salient policy differences between parties, or risk voting for a new entrant into the competition without reputation and track record.

A modicum of divergence of issue positions, however, may not always help established parties to pre-empt the entrance of a new contender. The preventive effect comes about only if established parties martial some *credibility* for their divergence, as revealed by past action. If established parties politicise the salience of issues on which they have no credible track record – whether this is protecting the environment or enforcing an ethno-cultural line between friends and foes – their activities may not deter, but rather, may encourage new party entry and support.[6]

In this chapter we elect to accept the 'facts' of convergence or divergence of the first cohort of parties in the post-communist party system as the exogenous descriptive starting points of our analysis and offer our thoughts on a spatial-lexicographical framework for the proximate causes of radical-right wing partisan mobilisation for future research. We plan to highlight only the proximate causes of radical right-wing party performance without probing into the preceding 'deeper' causes of parties' strategic choice. We will not try to explain these differences in the origins of strategic position taking by established parties here.

The critical claim in this chapter is that citizens disgruntled by economic developments will find different menu options to vent their anger by voting among partisan alternatives, contingent upon the party system into which they are inserted. Sometimes they may simply opt for a new redistributive populist-social protectionist alternative. On other occasions, a party that has embraced the mainstream of market-liberal reform in economics may diverge from the status quo and embrace authoritarian exclusionary grid/group appeals, support for which may serve as signal of dissatisfaction with the status quo. In a third configuration, old 'red-brown' communist successor parties may bundle anti-capitalist, authoritarian and xenophobic appeals against liberal-democratic reform parties.

In the empirical section of our chapter, we therefore now try to probe into only two claims. First, to what extent is the spatial-lexicographic argument borne out in accounting for the fortunes of extreme rightist parties? Is there a trade-off between radical-right and 'nearby' parties, such that the emergence of distinctly radical-right parties coincides with the weakness of 'nearby' parties, indicated by an unwillingness (strategic inability?) of conventional mainstream parties to embrace the themes of the radical right in an environment of welfare state retrenchment? Second, we want to probe into the socio-demographic distinctiveness of the radical-right electorate. If our argument about the broadly based nature of welfare state challenges in the second reform stage in post-communism after the turn of the millennium is correct, then radical-right electorates should have a very diffuse, indistinctive socio-demographic support pattern in the population.

Before we proceed to the empirical testing of our hypothesis, let us outline implications of our spatial-lexicographical framework for the proximate causes of radical-right wing partisan mobilisation in post-communist democracies worthy of future investigation.

1. Where, in the first decade, the major vote-getting parties *converge* on the issues of primary salience in most post-communist polities – economic reform and the introduction of inequality-enhancing market exchange – at the aggregate level voters will distinguish between parties based on policy dimensions of secondary salience, such as normative social order (grid) and ethno-cultural diversity (group).
2. Where established parties can meaningfully differentiate their grid/group appeals under conditions of economic policy convergence, they can hold the rise of new parties specialised in these issues at bay, particularly if the established contenders have some credibility as proponents of their grid/group positions.
3. Where established parties converge on economics and do not (credibly) diverge on grid/group issues, new radical-right parties have a good chance to thrive in elections, possibly together with other entrants that differentiate their appeal from the mainstream centre. Opportunities for new-party success in general, and radical-right party success in particular, are greater when the government performance of the (converged) major parties on salient policy issues – such as economic recovery/growth creating new employment and containing inflation – is widely perceived as unsatisfactory.

A spatial-lexicographic theory of party competition thus implies a trade-off between support for a radical-right grid/group party and for a 'nearby' more mainstream party that adopts elements of the exclusionary group and/or authoritarian grid agenda. If one type is strong, the other must be weak. The political space is not sufficiently crowded to let two major parties – a radical-right party and a 'nearby' party – coexist. Of course, the sum of support for radical-right and more moderate 'nearby' parties is not entirely fixed, but it cannot be infinitely expanded.

The spatial-lexicographic argument raises several important issues. First, how do we recognise convergence of parties on an issue dimension? At least two empirical signals come into play. Parties advocate policies in their programmatic statements that are highly similar to those of their competitors. But such pronouncements, by themselves, could be mere lip-service. As another signal, therefore, it may be important to examine the history of coalition building and alternation in the government executives. Where parties join coalitions and/or where parties alternate in office while maintaining a continuity of salient policies, they either reveal the credibility of their rhetorical convergence or discredit their rhetorical polarisation.

Next, if convergence of parties' policies in programmatic rhetoric, and especially in executive policy practice, has serious downsides, such as massive voter abstention in elections or the support of new maverick parties with polarising appeals, why do established parties ever adopt converging stances? Would not this conduct be blatantly irrational and politically suicidal? At least two considerations that are mutually compatible, if not complementary, can be invoked that account for contingent convergence among political parties. The first derives from a loose application of Downs's median voter theorem. Parties may be not only policy seeking, but also office seeking, for the sake of office itself. If that requires them to capture the median voter, either alone as a unified party or in a coalition of parties, they may have incentives to move their issue appeals closer to those of the median voter.

Next, parties may consider conditions of reputation building over a long period of time. Even if short-term polarisation might enhance vote-getting and office-winning capacities in the current round of elections, political-economic and/or cultural constraints may be such that victorious parties cannot redeem their pre-election promises in post-election policies, because the medium-term consequences of such policies would be too negative, even in the eyes of their own supporters, to be worth pursuing. Radical populist policies of fiscal expansion, for example, may generate strong bursts of monetary instability (capital flight, inflation etc.) that undermine the reputation of the incumbent. Conversely, after having made populist-expansionary economic policy promises, an incumbent party may renege on pre-election promises ('policy switching'), but then may have to pay a heavy electoral price for reneging on its promises in the next election. Policy convergence through policy switching may be the lesser evil for a governing party's re-election prospects than steadfast 'responsible partisan government' with disastrous institutional failures.

Finally, where does political entrepreneurs' differential capacity and drive to promote convergence come from, given that not all politicians engage in convergence and that parties and politicians do not always choose the most 'efficient' trajectory between polarisation and convergence? These are questions worthy of future exploration. As a second objective beyond this chapter, it should be explored to what extent different trajectories and challenges in social policy reform since the early 1990s coincide with different fortunes of radical-right parties, contingent upon the competitive strategic appeals and the actual policy responsiveness of conventional parties in government.

Spaces of partisan competition in post-communist democracies

Let us now examine where radical-right parties in post-communist democracies place themselves relative to other political parties. Based on the data set of expert judgements of political party positions collected by Benoit and Laver (2006), Table 7.2 above depicted the issue positions of radical-right and 'nearby' parties in 2003–4 on core group/grid issues as well as a few issues that are 'contingent correlates'. We do not need to assume now that the scores experts award to parties are cross-nationally comparable, as we are interested in the relative electoral strength of radical-right and 'nearby' parties relative to each other *within each country*. According to our spatial-lexicographical argument, new radical-right parties 'make it' only where their conventional competitors fail to assimilate at least some authoritarian-exclusionary grid/group positions. Conversely, where conventional parties have strong authoritarian-exclusionary grid/group credentials, separate radical-right parties should remain weak.

Table 7.3 places the post-communist countries' party configurations in a table with nine cells, contingent upon each country's averaged relative strength of radical right-wing parties and 'nearby' conventional mainstream parties in legislative elections from 2000 to 2008. The cells that would indicate that both radical-right parties are rather strong (greater 5 than per cent or greater than 10 per cent average electoral support) *and* nearby parties are strong as well (greater than 10 per cent or even more than 20 per cent) are empty, with the partial exception of Slovakia, which has both a rather strong nationalist party, the SNS obtaining an average of almost 8 per cent of the vote after 2000, as well as two 'nearby' parties that garner on average 22 per cent of the vote together (KDH and HZDS). In all other instances, either radical right-wing parties are strong but nearby parties weak or non-existent (e.g. Romania, Serbia), or the other way round (Croatia, Estonia,

Table 7.3 Radical right-wing parties and 'nearby' competitors of
the conventional right

		Electoral strength of 'nearby' electoral competitor of the conventional right (average support in legislative elections, 2000 and after)		
		>20%	*10–20%*	*<10%*
Electoral strength of radical right-wing party (average support in legislative elections, 2000 and after)	>10%		**Slovakia**	*Serbia* *Romania*
	5–10%		*Russia*	*Bulgaria* **Slovenia**
	<5%	**Croatia** Estonia **Hungary** Poland *Macedonia*	Czech Republic **Lithuania** *Ukraine*	*Albania* Latvia *Moldova*

Note: **Bold**: countries with 'optimally' sized ethnic minorities (5–20% of the population) for radical right mobilisation; *italics:* Orthodox Christian countries in South-Eastern Europe and the former Soviet Union.

Hungary, Macedonia, Poland). Then, there are some countries in between these poles, as well as countries in which neither 'nearby' nor radical right-wing parties matter electorally.

Countries in which 'nearby' mainstream parties with selective radical-right grid/group appeals have become strong in the new millennium are almost all located in East-Central Europe and are almost all members of the European Union: Czech Republic, Estonia, Hungary, Lithuania, Poland and Slovakia, with the major exception being Macedonia and the less clear-cut exceptions of Russia and Ukraine. The two most recent and contentious EU members, however, show the opposite configuration, namely (moderately) strong radical-right parties, but no nearby allies (Bulgaria, Romania).

Authoritarian-exclusionary grid-group themes appear to resonate in the East-Central European countries particularly well. It is in these countries that convergence on economic-distributive issues has been practised since the 1990s. As their strong ties to the West and EU integration make it inconceivable that any party could take a staunchly anti-capitalist stance, they thus prevent polarisation on the economic dimension of party competition and enable polarised politics over grid-group issues. For the established parties to differentiate themselves, grid-group issues thus offer a convenient opportunity to develop a distinctive appeal. Of course, this is an incomplete explanation, as one would also have to highlight why such themes 'resonate' with the population and the demand side.

The countries where neither 'nearby' nor explicit radical-right parties politicise grid-group issues all share one thing in common: they are concerned about very large ethnic minorities, either internally (Latvia, Moldova, Ukraine) or in an external irredentist region, now constituted as a sovereign state (Albania/Kosovo). Politicians and citizens know that politicising ethnic boundaries may mean internal and possibly international war (Kosovo). Countries with names in bold type, by contrast, all offer the 'optimal' configuration for mobilising exclusionary ethnic appeals from the perspective of majority ethnic group entrepreneurs. They can target visible, yet harmless and defenceless small ethno-cultural minorities and/or draw attention to the country's immigration potential in order to collect support for their parties.

Convergence of established parties on economic issues

So far, we have talked only about relative party strength, taking parties' non-economic issue positions into account. But is there a relationship between *convergence of established parties on economic issues* and support for the radical right (Kitschelt and McGann, 1995)? We hypothesise that the convergence of mainstream parties opens up a second dimension of party competition, may lead to the entrance of new parties and creates incentives for mainstream parties to shift to grid-group divisions. If mainstream parties converge on economic policy, the grid/group issue dimension becomes more salient.

What are the possible determinants of convergence? The process of economic reforms and restructuring at the beginning of the 1990s and later the technocratic nature of the EU accession process narrowed the policy options of governing political elites in the new EU member states. It is difficult to impose nation-blind directives on minority issues, due to their non-technocratic nature, however.[7] While radical parties are not perceived as especially competent on economic issues, particularly when compared to mainstream parties, they do hold credible and distinct positions on identity matters.

Figure 7.2 shows evidence that convergence of mainstream parties (or two strongest parties in the political system, aside from the radical-right party) is associated with the strength of the radical right. We plotted the square root of average vote shares for radical right-parties in the 2000s and economic policy distance between two parties that received the largest share of votes

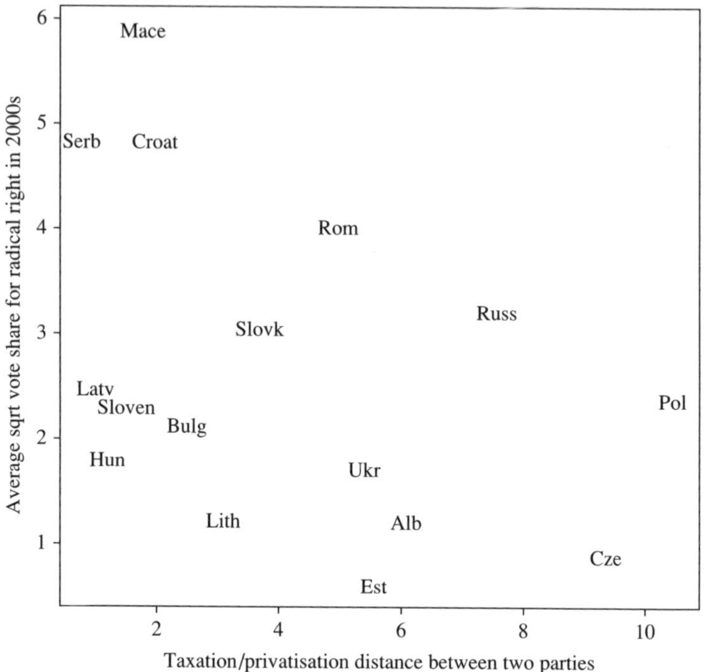

Figure 7.2 Support for radical right and policy convergence
Note: Taxation/privatisation distance based on Benoit and Laver (2006), Table 5.7b
(to determine whether privatisation or factor score is stronger); Taxation versus spending/
privatisation positions of parties based on Benoit and Laver (2006), Appendix B.

(from 2000 to 2004 as reported in Benoit and Laver, 2006). In cases where the radical-right party was the strongest or the second-strongest party in the political system, we took into account the position of the third-strongest party.

There are two major economic policy issues in the post-communist party competition: (1) privatisation and (2) taxation versus spending. We were guided by the dimensional analysis in Benoit and Laver (2006) and took the distance between parties on the economic issue, with the stronger factor loading on the economic axis. Then we took the absolute value of the policy distance between two parties. We consider all post-communist countries that are electoral democracies for which data were available. When we expand our sample beyond Central Europe, most of the countries fall into the category of states with high inequalities and fast dismantlement of welfare states. What differentiates post-communist countries is their diverse ethnic composition and the position of parties on major policy issues.

There are two clusters of countries following a linear pattern. The first cluster of countries, with a strong radical right, composed of Russia, Romania, Croatia, Serbia, Macedonia, Slovakia (and Poland), is aligned parallel to the second cluster with low shares of radical-right support (and a lower intercept). The second cluster, with weak radical-right parties in the 2000s, is comprised of the Czech Republic, Estonia, Albania, Ukraine, Lithuania, Bulgaria, Hungary, Slovenia and Latvia. The first group of countries is comprised mostly of countries with patrimonial legacies and/or with substantial minorities. Ukraine and Albania do not fit the pattern, due to their extreme scores on ethnic composition. According to the 1989 census, Albanians are at least 95 per cent of the population. Ukraine, on the contrary, is comprised of at least 22 per cent of Russians, according to the 2001 census.[8] Fears of ethnic escalation, being part of Russia's 'near abroad' and the regional character of major electoral blocks suppress explicit grid-group specialisation of parties. In general, *the presence of issue convergence on economic issues is associated with larger shares for radical-right parties.*

Individual-level profile of radical-right voters

If radical-right parties emerge in a broad fiscal crisis of the post-communist welfare state and also signal voters' displeasure with a 'cartel' of converging parties on the most salient dimension of party competition (economic-distributive issues), then we probably should encounter a socio-demographically rather diffuse electorate of the radical right, where strategic configurations give such parties a chance.

Can we identify any profiles of radical-right voters? Are they concentrated in any of the income groups, do they have any specific socio-demographic characteristics? We investigate these questions using a representative Euro-barometer Survey (2003: 3) taken just before the first wave of enlargement. This survey has socio-demographic profiles of respondents, their vote preferences and attitudes reflecting exclusionary views on economic, national and cultural minorities. It includes questions about immigration, asylum seekers, attitudes towards the EU and the provision of welfare (social) benefits to outsiders.[9]

Do their cultural resources or their position on the labour market characterise radical-right voters? To examine voting for radical-right parties, we use a rare events logistic regression (Imai *et al.*, 2007) with a rare events bias correction since some of the radical-right parties are very small. We pool eight post-communist countries together, since we are interested in general, cross-national, description of the radical-right voters. The dependent variable of the model is whether the respondent voted for a radical-right party (1 = vote for RR) or otherwise (= 0).

Table 7.4 summarises the results or rare events logit. If we were to focus only on the occupational profiles of the respondents, we would find that manual workers, self-employed, unemployed and housekeepers are more likely to vote for radical-right parties (Model 0). However, once we control for the age of a respondent and the age at which voters completed their education, the effect of occupational groups disappears (Model 1.1). When age and its square and age at which respondents completed their education and its square are added to the model (M1.1, M1.2 and M1.3), the coefficients become significant. The estimate on age becomes positive and the estimate on age at completion becomes negative, suggesting that support for the radical right increases as people get older, and decreases as people stay longer in school. Nevertheless, the square terms of both age and age at completion of education point in the opposite direction and are significant as well. This suggests a non-linear relationship. Twenty-five per cent of the respondents in the survey completed their education at age 18, which is both the median and modal category. By age 20, 75 per cent of respondents are done with their schooling. There are respondents that left school at age 7 and, on the other extreme, at age 50. The non-linear relationship suggests that there is a plateau effect of education, once a respondent is relatively well schooled; it does not matter if he or she stays one more year in school.

The effect of education is the strongest predictor of the vote for the radical right, it is the most robust estimate that remains stable when we include controls such as income, place of residence, citizen status, religiosity, marriage status and employment in the public sector. The result is robust to different transformation and to the use of different weights in the survey.

The effect of education dominates different attitudinal measures in the survey as well. Attitudes about social benefits for foreigners, future of the EU, criminality, corruption and EU social rights are insignificant. We included a measure of anti-immigrant attitudes[10] in Model 1.3 in Table 7.4.[11] While a t-test with unequal variances suggests that the index captures a difference between radical-right voters and the others when it comes to anti-immigrant attitudes, once we control for education, the effect disappears. Some of the models suggest that gender may play a role and that men are more prone to vote for the radical right. But these findings are very sensitive to model specifications and we conclude that, aside from a modest effect of age, the most important variable to predict support for the radical right is education.

Given the fact that some radical parties in post-communist EU accession countries are very small, the probability that a voter would vote for them is very small as well. Simulations from the rare events logit based on Model 1.3 suggest that the expected value of Y (support for racial right = 1, else = 0) is

Table 7.4 Vote for radical right (= 1) – rare events logit with rare events bias correction

Variable	Estimate (standard error)			
	M.0	*M1.1*	*M1.2*	*M1.3*
Gender (1 = men)	0.26	0.30	0.30	0.33*
	(0.15)	(0.15)	(0.15)	(0.16)
Age		0.06*	0.06*	0.07*
		(0.03)	(0.03)	(0.03)
Age^2/100		−0.07*	−0.08*	−0.08*
		(0.03)	(0.03)	(0.03)
Age at completion of education		−0.27***	−0.26***	−0.25**
		(0.07)	(0.07)	(0.08)
Age at completion of education^2/100		0.56***	0.56***	0.52***
		(0.14)	(0.14)	(0.15)
Income deciles	0.03	0.01	0.03	−0.01
	(0.03)	(0.03)	(0.03)	(0.03)
Occupation			0.13	
All			(0.09)	
Attitudes to immigrants				0.003
				(0.03)
Managers + white collar	0.27			
	(0.41)			
Manual workers + self-employed	0.83*			
	(0.38)			
Unemployed + housekeepers	1.08**			
	(0.40)			
Retired	0.60			
	(0.39)			
Intercept	−4.40***	−1.81	−2.47*	−1.97
	(0.41)	(1.06)	(1.16)	(1.18)
Null deviance	1680.1	1565.3	1564.8	1365.0
Residual deviance	1660.9	1545.1	1542.5	1347.5
AIC	1675	1559	1559	1363

Notes: Baseline for occupation: studying.
Inclusion of income squared does not change the results.
Significance: 0.001 '***', 0.010 '**', 0.050 '*', 0.10 '.'
Results are robust to various controls such as residence, marital status, state employee and church attendance. Other attitudes towards social benefits for asylum seekers and welfare generosity are insignificant in Model 1.3 as well.

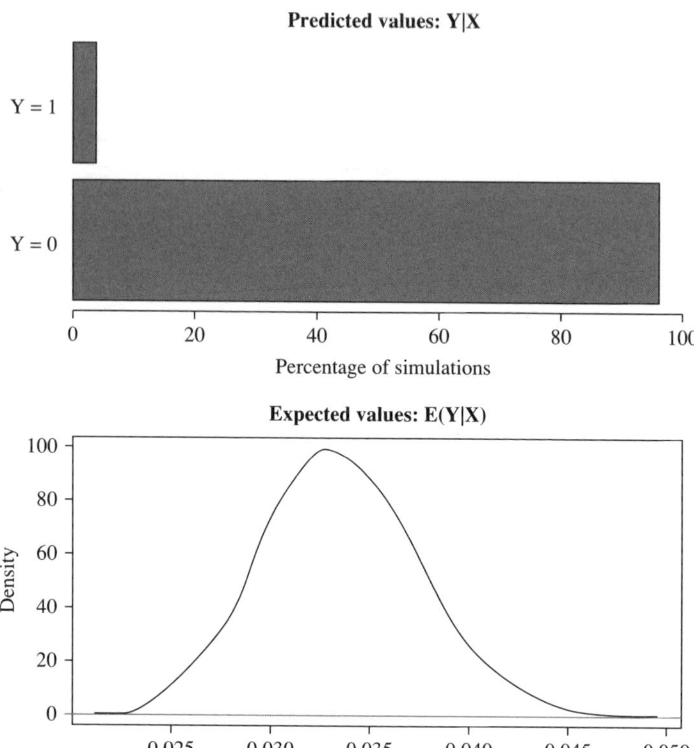

Figure 7.3 Simulation based on Model M1.3 – expected values of
the radical-right vote

Note: Covariates were set at these values: (gender = women, age = 45, age squared/
100 = 23, years of education = 19, years of education squared/100 = 4, income deciles = 5,
anti-immigrant index = 7.5).

about 0.03 (Figure 7.3). In other words, almost nobody is expected to vote for
the radical right. The situation changes when we compare people with low
and high levels of education (Figures 7.4 and 7.5).

Figure 7.4 and Figure 7.5 reveal an absolute difference of 0.11 in the
expected value of Y when we compare a respondent who left school at age
14 to a respondent who left school/college at age 26. Figure 7.5 shows that
a probability of voting for the radical right for someone who left school at
age 26 is practically zero. However, there is an 11 per cent chance that someone who left school at age 14 would vote for the radical right. The risk ratio
of these two scenarios is 27. A person with a low level of education (left
school at age 14) is twenty-seven times more likely to vote for the radical
right party, as compared to someone who left school at age 26. All these
simulations are based on Model 1.3.

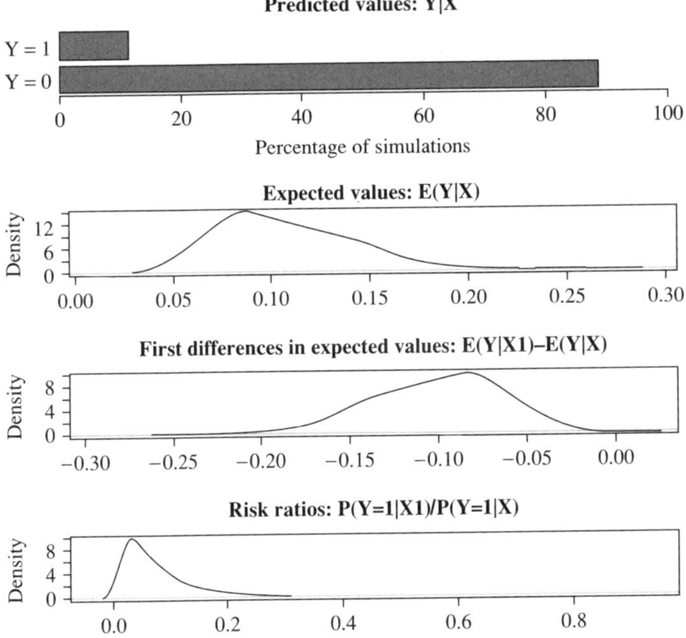

Figure 7.4 Simulation based on Model M1.3 – expected values of the radical right vote: scenario when respondent left school at age 14 (vs at age 26)

These findings illustrate that it is difficult to track socio-demographic profiles of radical-right voters using linear models and standard socio-demographic variables in order to capture a universal profile of a radical-right voter across countries. There is nevertheless a strong and robust relationship between (a lack of) education and vote for the radical right.

Conclusion

Explanatory frameworks in the current literature on the radical right in CEE tend to favour accounts based on political culture. Even if attitudes, such as racism and xenophobia, are entrenched in some segments of CEE societies, these attitudes are ill-equipped to explain change and volatility in support for radical-right parties and cannot explain variation across countries with similar political cultures. We do not mean to imply that cultural heritage is irrelevant. Indeed, we take it seriously and incorporate it into our study of the radical right as part of our understanding of legacies.

By way of contrast, we propose a grid/group framework that captures both the nationalistic and socially illiberal positions of radical-right parties,

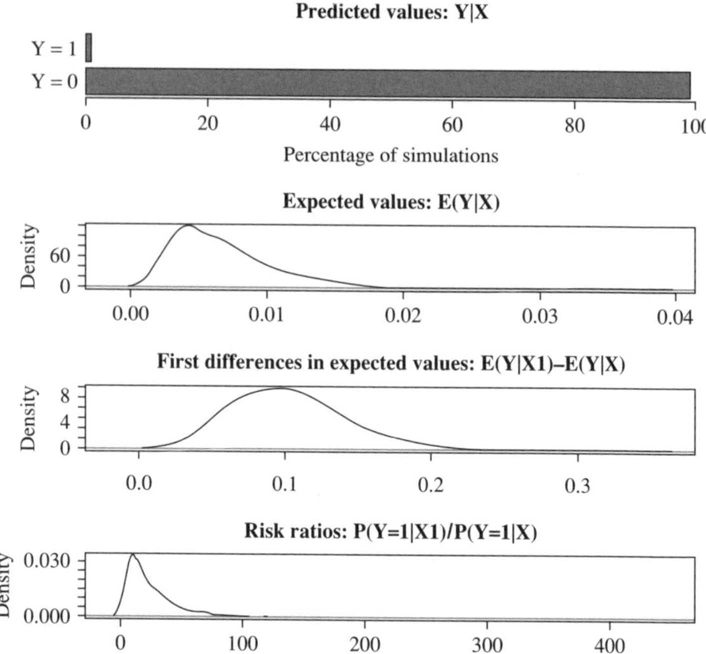

Figure 7.5 Simulation based on Model M1.3 – expected values of the radical right vote: scenario when respondent left school at age 26 (vs at age 14)

and argue that a political-economic perspective is essential to explaining cross-country variation in support for radical-right parties. In particular, we claim that radical right-voters' economic grievances and fears stem from a retrenchment of the welfare state. We link our political-economic framework with the study of communist regime legacies and distinguish the effect of two major legacies in CEE: the legacy of national accommodative communism and the legacy of patrimonial communism. In national accommodative regimes, we argue that the potential for distinctive radical-right parties has always been limited. As a consequence of agreement on economic policies, major political parties incorporated a non-economic dimension into their 'product differentiation', a dimension that builds on distinctive grid/group appeals. In states with patrimonial communist legacies, sharp economic downturns and rising inequality generated much greater potential for the radical right-wing, albeit one that, on the supply side, was partially absorbed by unreconstructed communist successor parties who also invoked exclusionary group and authoritarian grid conceptions of social order. In patrimonial regimes, we argue that the economic axis of party competition is more salient than the axis of party competition capturing socio-cultural issues.

We show that the socio-demographic profiles of radical-right voters are variegated. As a result, it is virtually impossible to create a unified, cross-national profile of a radical-right voter. The only robust predictor associated with support for the radical right is the respondent's education, but the relationship does not follow a linear pattern. Another stable, yet less robust, predictor of the propensity to vote for radical-right parties across countries is the age of the respondent, with older respondents being more likely to vote for radical-right parties. Once we control for education, differences between the occupational profiles of respondents and the possible effects of welfare-chauvinistic attitudes disappear. At the cross-national level of analysis, we argue that the EU accession process contributed to a narrowing of the policy space for new member states and accelerated the convergence of political parties on economic issues. Convergence of established parties on economic issues, we argue, fosters competition on the grid/group dimension of party competition and is associated with radical-right party success.

The full impact of Europeanisation will not become fully apparent until new member states face a more significant economic downturn and drastic welfare retrenchment. The post-Lehman Brothers credit crunch was followed in spring 2009 by the €50 billion bailout of Hungary, Latvia and Romania and the IMF bailout of Belarus, Hungary, Latvia, Romania, Serbia and Ukraine. The financial meltdown exposed both vulnerabilities and dissimilarities among the post-communist economies, since some countries withstood the turmoil relatively well, while others did not. Yet the astonishing success of *Jobbik*, which received 17 per cent of the vote in the first round of the 2010 Hungarian parliamentary elections, is a 'canary in the coalmine' of East European politics. The sovereign-debt time-bomb was not exclusive to Greece; budget imbalances will force some East European governments to further cut social spending. When social policy reforms come to the fore and create new categories of losers, radical-right appeals are likely to gain in prominence in the competitive struggle between the mainstream political parties. If political-economic problems become sufficiently intractable and economic growth falters as centre-left and centre-right parties alternate in government and try to contain fiscal haemorrhage, even socio-cultural polarisation may ultimately be insufficient to counteract defection from the established parties, creating an aperture for new radical-right challengers.

 Europeanising party politics

Appendix

Table 7.A Radical right-wing parties across Central and Eastern Europe

Country	*Party names*
Albania	PBK – BK – Balli Kombëtar [National Front Party]
Bulgaria	BNRP – Bălgarska nacionalna radikalna partija – [Bulgarian National Radical Party] NSA – Nacionalen sayuz Ataka – [National Union Attack, which includes BNRP {Attack Coalition}]
Croatia	HDZ – Hrvatska demokratska zajednica [Croatian Democratic Union] HSP – Hrvatska stranka prava [Croatian Party of Rights]
Czech Republic	SPR-RSČ – Sdružení pro republiku – Republikánská strana Československa (Sládek) RMS – Republikáni Miroslava Sládka – [Republicans of Miroslav Sládek] NS – Národní strana [National Party] NDS – Národně demokratická strana – [National Democratic Party] DS – Dělnická strana; DSSS – Dělnická strana sociální spravedlnosti [Worker's Party]
Estonia	ERSP – Eesti Rahvusliku Sõltumatuse Partei [Estonian National Independence Party] EK – Eesti Kodanik [Estonian Citizens] ERKL – Eesti Rahvuslaste Keskliit [Estonian Nationalists Central League] PE – Parem Eesti [Right Estonia] EIP – Eesti Iseseisvuspartei [Estonian Independence Party]
Hungary	MIÉP – Magyar Igazság és Élet Pártja [Hungarian Justice and Life Party] MIÉP-Jobbik – [MIÉP-Jobbik Magyarországért Mozgalom – Movement for a Better Hungary] Jobbik – Movement for a Better Hungary
Latvia	TB – Tēvzeme un Brīvībai [For Fatherland and Freedom] TB/LNNK – Apvienība Tēvzeme un Brīvībai/LNNK – Alliance For Homeland and Freedom/LNNK – Latvijas Nacionālās Neatkarības Kustība [Latvian National Independence Movement]
Lithuania	LKDS/LTJS – Jaunoji Lietuva susivienijimas uz vieninga Lietuva [Young Lithuania – For United Lithuania] LNP-JL – Lietuvos Nacionaldemokratu Partija – Jaunosios Lietuvos [Lithuanian National Party – Young Lithuania] LlaS – Lithuanian Liberty Union LNDP – Lietuvos nacionaldemokratu partija [Lithuanian National Democratic Party]

Macedonia	VMRO-DPMNE – Vnatreška Makedonska Revolucionerna Organizacija – Demokratska Partija za Makedonsko Nacionalno Edinstvo [Democratic Party for Macedonian National Unity] VMRO-DP – Vnatreška Makedonska Revolucionerna Organizacija – Demokratska Partija DPA – Partia Demokratike Shqiptare; Demokratska Partija na Albancite [Democratic Party of Albanians]
Poland	SN – Stronnictwo Narodowe [National Party] Party X – Party X PWN-PSN – Polska Wspólnota Narodowa – Polskie Stronnictwo Narodowe [Pol. Nat. Commonwealth – Polish Nat. Party] ROP – Ruch Odbudowy Polski [Movement for the Reconstruction of Poland] LPR – Liga Polskich Rodzin [League of Polish Families] LPR – Liga Prawicy Rzeczypospolitej [The League of the Right of the Republic (League of Polish Families (LPR) + Real Politics Union + Right of the Republic)]
Romania	PUNR – Partidul Unității Naționale a Românilor [Party of Romanian Unity] PRM – Partidul (Popular) România Mare [Party for Greater Romania] PNG – Partidul Noua Generație – Creştin Democrat [New Generation Party]
Russia	LDPR – Liberal'no-Demokraticheskaya Partiya Rossii [Liberal-Democratic Party of Russia]
Serbia	SRS – Srpska radikalna stranka [Serbian Radical Party]
Slovakia	PSNS – Pravá Slovenská národná strana [Real Slovak National Party] SNS – Slovenská národná strana [Slovak National Party]
Slovenia	SNS – Slovenska nacionalna stranka [Slovenian National Party]
Ukraine	KUN – Kongres Ukraiins'kikh Natsionalistiv [Congress of Ukrainian Nationalists] Rukh – Narodnyi Rukh Ukrajiny [The People's Movement of Ukraine] Svoboda – [Freedom]

Source: Minkenberg (2002), Mudde (2005), Mudde (2007: 305–8), Pop-Eleches (2010) and other sources.

Notes

1 We would like to thank to Paul G. Lewis, Radek Markowski, Petra Rakusanova-Guasti, David Siroky and an anonymous referee for their helpful comments.

2 For comparative accounts of the radical right in Central and Eastern Europe see especially Held, 1996; Hockenos, 1993; Kopecký and Mudde, 2003; Minkenberg, 2002; Mudde, 2005; Ramet, 1999; Rupnik, 2007. Other recent contributions include: Anastasakis, 2001; Art and Brown, 2007; Alonso and Ruiz-Rufino, 2007; Ekiert, 2006; Enyedi and Eros, 1999; Greskovits, 2007; Ishiyama, 2010; Krastev, 2007; Lewis, 2009b; Mares, 2006; Markowski *et al.*, 2003; Minkenberg and Beichelt, 2001; Minkenberg and Perrineau, 2007; Mudde, 2007; Mungiu-Pippidi, 2007; Norris, 2005; O'Dwyer and Schwartz, 2010; Ost, 2005; Pop-Eleches, 2010; Shafir, 2002; Tismaneau, 2007; Vachudova, 2008; Weaver, 2007.

3 Bulgarian Prime Minister Boyko Borisov. 'Bulgarian Govt relieved by EU Greece bailout, delays ERM II bid.' *Sofia News Agency*, 28 March 2010, www.emg.rs/en/news/region/117523.html.

4 The radical-right parties are often linked to Euroscepticism or Eurorealism (Bielasiak, 2004; Kopecký and Mudde, 2002; Markowski and Tucker, 2010; McManus-Czubinska *et al.*, 2003; Minkenberg and Perrineau, 2007; Taggart and Szczerbiak, 2004).

5 We also assess the strength of the communist party successor with high grid-group appeals. This is what is called a Brown CP (communist party), and examples may be found in the Czech Republic, Russia and Serbia. However, if the successor communist party is either weak or *not* brown (for example if the party transformed itself into a moderate social democratic party) then it falls into a second category: Brown CP < 5\% average or NA. NA means 'not red-brown, only red' (Bustikova, 2009).

6 This is the proposition underlying Meguid (2005).

7 O'Dwyer and Schwartz (2010) see policies related to ethnic and sexual minorities as the source of divergence among the post-communist countries, due to the differences in narratives of national identity and party system institutionalisation.

8 But the Ukrainian – Russian *language-based* cleavage can be as extreme as 50–50 when it comes to the choice of a presidential candidate. In the representative 1997 survey, 56% of respondents declared themselves as Ukrainians, 11% as Russians and 27% as both (Wilson, 2000: 219).

9 The analysis includes these parties: Estonian Pro Patria Union – Isamaaliit, Hungarian MIÉP, Latvian TB/LNNK, Lithuanian JL-NA-PS Young Lithuania, Polish League of Polish Families and Samoobrona, Greater Romania Party, Slovak National Party and the Real Slovak National Party and, finally, the Slovenian National Party. Bulgaria and the Czech Republic were dropped from the analysis, due to the lack of data for the radical right in the Eurobarometer survey.

10 Attitudes towards immigrants is an additive index of three attitudes toward immigration. Each of the questions is asked on a four-point scale from 'completely agree' to 'completely disagree': 1 = Immigration contributes positively to the cultural diversity of our country; 2 = Legal immigrants should have exactly the same rights as [nationality]; 3 = Legal immigrants should have the right to vote in local elections.

11 Model 1.3 has the smallest AIC (Akaike Information Criterion), which suggests the best fit. A smaller AIC indicates a better model.

References

Alonso, S. and R. Ruiz-Rufino (2007), 'Political representation and ethnic conflict in new democracies', *European Journal of Political Research* 46, pp. 237–67.

Anastasakis, O. (2001), 'Post-communist extremism in Eastern Europe: the nature of the phenomenon', *Studies in Ethnicity and Nationalism* 1, pp. 15–26.

Art, D. and D. Brown (2007), 'Making and breaking the radical right in Central Eastern Europe', unpublished manuscript.

Bielasiak, J. (2004), 'Party systems and EU accession: Euroscepticism in Eastern Europe', paper presented at the conference on public opinion about the EU in post-communist Eastern Europe, Bloomington, April 2–3.

Benoit, K. and M. Laver (2006), *Party Policy in Modern Democracies* (London: Routledge).

Bustikova, L. (2009), 'The extreme right in Eastern Europe: EU accession and the quality of governance', *Journal of Contemporary European Studies* 17, pp. 223–39.

Bustikova, L. and H. Kitschelt (2009), 'The radical right in post-communist Europe. Comparative perspectives on legacies and party competition', *Communist and Post-Communist Studies* 42, pp. 459–83.

Dahl, R. (1989), *Democracy and Its Critics* (New Haven: Yale University Press).

Ekiert, G. (2006), 'L'instabilité du système partisan. Le maillon faible de la consolidation démocratique en Pologne', *Pouvoirs: Revue Française D'Etudes Constit. et Polit.* 118, pp. 37–58.

Enyedi, Z. with F. Eros (1999), *Authoritarianism and Prejudice* (Budapest: Central European Press).

Eurobarometer Survey (2003), *Candidate Countries Eurobarometer* 2003.3 (European Union).

Fisher, S., J. Gould, and T. Haughton (2007), 'Slovakia's neoliberal turn', *Europe-Asia Studies* 59, pp. 977–98.

Greskovits, B. (1998), *The Political Economy of Protest and Patience. East European and Latin American Transformations Compared* (Budapest: Central European University Press).

Greskovits, B. (2007), 'Economic woes and political disaffection', *Journal of Democracy* 18, pp. 40–6.

Grzymala-Busse, A. (2007) *Rebuilding Leviathan: Party Competition and State Exploitation in Post-Communist* (Cambridge: Cambridge University Press).

Grzymala-Busse, A. and A. Innes (2003), 'Great expectations: the EU and domestic political competition in East Central Europe', *East European Politics and Societies* 17, pp. 64–73.

Habyarimana, J., M. Humphreys, D. Posner and J. Weinstein (2007), 'Why does ethnic diversity undermine public goods provision?', *American Political Science Review* 101, pp. 709–25.

Hainmueller, J., and M. Hiscox (2007), 'Educated preferences: explaining attitudes toward immigration in Europe', *International Organization* 61, pp. 399–442.

Held, J. (ed.) (1996), *Populism in Eastern Europe. Racism, Nationalism, and Society* (Boulder, CO: East European Monographs).

Hockenos, P. (1993), *Free to Hate: The Rise of the Right in Post-Communist Eastern Europe* (New York: Routledge).

Horowitz, D. (1985), *Ethnic Groups in Conflict* (Berkeley, CA: University of California Press).

Imai, K., G. King, and O. Lau (2007), 'Relogit: rare events logistic regression for dichotomous dependent variables', in K. Imai, G. King and O. Lau, *Zelig: Everyone's Statistical Software*, http://gking.harvard.edu/zelig.

Ishiyama, J. (2010), 'Historical legacies and the size of the red-brown vote in post-communist politics', *Communist and Post-Communist Studies* 42, pp. 485–504.

Johnson, J. (2008), 'The remains of conditionality: the faltering enlargement of the euro zone', *Journal of European Public Policy* 15, pp. 826–41.

Kelley, J. (2004), *Ethnic Politics in Europe* (Princeton, NJ: Princeton University Press).

Kitschelt, H., Z. Mansfeldová, R. Markowski and G. Tóka (1999), *Post-Communist Party Systems: Competition, Representation, and Inter-Party Cooperation* (New York: Cambridge University Press).

Kitschelt, H. with A. McGann (1995), *The Radical Right in Western Europe: A Comparative Analysis* (Ann Arbor, MI: University of Michigan Press).

Kopecký, P. and C. Mudde (2002), 'The two sides of Euroscepticism: party positions on European integration in East Central Europe', *European Union Politics* 3, pp. 297–326.

Kopecký, P. and C. Mudde (eds) (2003), *Uncivil Society? Contentious Politics in Post-Communist Europe* (London: Routledge).

Krastev, I. (2007), 'The strange death of the liberal consensus', *Journal of Democracy* 18, pp. 56–63.

Ladrech, R. (2002), 'Europeanisation and political parties: towards a framework for analysis', *Party Politics* 8, pp. 389–403.

Lewis, P. (2009), 'Party system stabilisation in Central Europe: record and prospects in a changing socio-economic context', ECPR General Conference, Potsdam, 10–12 September.

Mair, P. (2006), 'Political parties and party systems', in P. Graziano and M. P. Vink (eds), *Europeanization: New Research Agendas* (Basingstoke: Palgrave), pp. 154–66.

Mares, M. (2006), 'Transnational networks of extreme right parties in East Central Europe: stimuli and limits of cross-border cooperation', 20th IPSA World Congress, Fukuoka, 9–13 July.

Markowski, R. and J. Tucker (2010), 'Euroskepticism and the emergence of political parties in Poland', *Party Politics*, 16, forthcoming.

McManus-Czubinska, C., W. Miller, R. Markowski, and J. Wasilewski (2003), 'The new Polish "right"?', *The Journal of Communist Studies and Transition Politics* 19, pp. 1–23.

Meguid, B. (2005), 'Competition between unequals: the role of mainstream party strategy in niche party success', *American Political Science Review* 99, pp. 347–59.

Minkenberg, M. (2002), 'The radical right in postsocialist Central and Eastern Europe: comparative observations and interpretations', *East European Politics and Society* 16, pp. 335–62.

Minkenberg, M. (2007), 'Between tradition and transition: the Central European radical right and the new European order', in C. S. Liang (ed.), *Europe for the Europeans: The Foreign and Security Policy of the Populist Radical Right* (Aldershot and Burlington, VT: Ashgate), pp. 261–81.

Minkenberg, M. and T. Beichelt (2001), 'Explaining the radical right in transition, theories of right-wing radicalism and opportunity structures in postsocialist Europe', paper presented at APSA, San Francisco.

Minkenberg, M. and P. Perrineau (2007), 'The radical right in the European elections 2004', *International Political Science Review/Revue internationale de science politique* 28, pp. 29–55.

Mudde, C. (2005), *Racist Extremism in Central and Eastern Europe* (London: Routledge).

Mudde, C. (2007), *Populist Radical Right Parties in Europe* (Cambridge: Cambridge University Press).

Mungiu-Pippidi, A. (2007), 'EU accession is no end of history', *Journal of Democracy* 18, pp. 8–16.

Norris, P. (2005), *Radical Right: Voters and Parties in the Electoral Market* (Cambridge: Cambridge University Press).

O'Dwyer, C. and B. Kovalčík (2007), 'And the last shall be first: party system institutionalization and second-generation economic reform in postcommunist Europe', *Studies in Comparative International Development* 41, pp. 2–26.

O'Dwyer, C. and K. Schwartz (2010), 'Minority rights after EU enlargement: a comparison of anti-gay politics in Poland and Latvia', *Comparative European Politics* 8, forthcoming.

Olzak, S. (1992), *The Dynamic of Ethnic Competition and Conflict* (Stanford, CA: Stanford University Press).

Ost, D. (2005), *The Defeat of Solidarity. Anger and Politics in Postcommunist Europe* (Ithaca, NY: Cornell University Press).

Pop-Eleches, G. (2010), 'Throwing out the bums: protest voting and unorthodox parties after communism', *World Politics* 62, pp. 221–60.

Ramet, S. (ed.) (1999), *The Radical Right in Central and Eastern Europe Since 1989* (Pittsburgh: Pennsylvania State University Press).

Rupnik, J. (2007), 'From democracy fatigue to populist backlash', *Journal of Democracy* 18, pp. 17–25.

Shafir, M. (2002), 'Between denial and "comparative trivialization". Holocaust negotiations in post-communist East Central Europe', *Analysis of Current Trends in Antisemitism* 19, pp. 1–83, available at: http://sicsa.huji.ac.il/shafir19.htm.

Taggart, P. and A. Szczerbiak (2004), 'Contemporary Euroscepticism in the party systems of the European Union candidate states of Central and Eastern Europe', *European Journal of Political Research* 43, pp. 1–27.

Tismaneau, V. (2007), 'Leninist legacies, pluralist dilemmas', *Journal of Democracy* 18, pp. 34–9.

Vachudova, M. (2008), 'Tempered by the EU? Political parties and party systems before and after accession', *Journal of European Public Policy* 15, pp. 861–79.

Vanhuysse, P. (2006), *Divide and Pacify: Strategic Social Policies and Political Protests in Post-Communist Democracies* (Budapest and New York: Central European University Press).

Weaver, E. (2007), 'The communist legacy? – populist but not popular – the foreign policies of the Hungarian radical right', in C. S. Liang (ed.), *Europe for the Europeans: The Foreign and Security Policy of the Populist Radical Right* (Aldershot and Burlington, VT: Ashgate), pp. 177–85.

Wildavsky, A. *et al.* (1990), *Cultural Theory* (Boulder, CO: Westview Press).

Wilson, A. (2000), *The Ukrainians. Unexpected Nation* (New Haven, CT: Yale University Press).

8

The quality of social, partisan and governmental representation

Radoslaw Markowski and Zsolt Enyedi

Introduction

The concept of representation occupies a central place in political science and in contemporary democratic theory. Representative government – from a historical perspective, a relatively new device – is the principal 'organisational tool' of modern democracies, in spite of the increasing popularity of fuzzy 'governance' structures and the spread of various techniques of direct democracy. Some sort of representation is always necessary, due to the simple fact that the formulation and implementation of policies requires a division of labour among citizens.

The process of political representation in complex, developed societies consists of a multitude of actors, of their characteristics, relationships and actions. Citizens, voters, candidates, parties, cabinets, bureaucrats, independent regulatory agencies, courts, ombudsmen, the media – all are linked in the chain, or rather web, of representation. The criteria used to evaluate the quality of representation are also diverse: similarity, communication, accountability and responsiveness are perhaps the most relevant ones. Depending on the values and interests of the evaluators, but also on the fashions of political science, different elements and different criteria are placed in the limelight.

In this chapter we depict many aspects of the development of political representation in Central and Eastern Europe (CEE) across countries, in time and in comparison with Western Europe. It is composed of a rather 'shallow but broad' overview of certain phenomena that – directly or indirectly – are related to the quality of representation and, consequently, to democratic performance. No specific relationship between Europeanisation and representativeness is assumed, although we lean towards a conception of Europeanisation as 'return to Europe' by CEE countries, rather than 'Europeanisation as a consequence of accession'. This particular contribution thus does not analyse and broaden our knowledge of how specific features of EU governance impact on the quality of representation, although we do assume that this kind influence does take place, even if it is seen as indirect. At the same time we share the view of many scholars (see the introductory chapter by Paul Lewis) that the impact of the EU and Europe on political and party systems of the CEE countries is vague and, if detected, only weak.

The phenomenon of political representation is typically focused on the attitudes of voters and of elected representatives. The bulk of the relevant literature is concerned with the similarity of attitudes and values between voters and MPs and with the part played by perception, legislative behaviour and the constituency work of representatives (Miller and Stokes, 1963; Barnes, 1977; Achen, 1978; Kuklinski, 1978; Monroe, 1979; Luttberg, 1981; Page and Shapiro, 1983; Dalton, 1985; Converse and Pierce, 1986; Holmberg, 1989; Powell, 1989; Hill and Hinton-Andersson, 1995; Esaiasson and Holmberg, 1996; Kitschelt *et al.*, 1999; Miller *et al.*, 1999).[1] This focus is understandable, justified and legitimate. But the picture that emerges can only be partial, as other relevant relationships are neglected. For a more accurate assessment one should also consider whether the electorate truly represents the citizenry and whether the government is in tune with the preferences of the voters.

In line with the classical tradition, we contrast voter preferences for particular parties with the attitudes of the elites of the same parties. But in order to balance out the bias of the literature we also look at the representative character of the voters and of the government, thereby complementing existing knowledge with new perspectives and information.

Additionally, we also consider citizens' opinions about the process and actors of representation. To take these evaluations at face value would be a mistake. But to leave them out of the analysis and judge the quality of representation entirely on the similarity of some sort of 'objective' characteristics also smacks of a paternalism that politicians and political scientists should equally try to avoid. We assume that, in order to talk about high-quality representation, citizens are needed who care about politics and who find elections important ('relevance component'). They also must be satisfied with the most fundamental process of representation, parliamentary elections ('satisfaction component'). Finally, they must also trust the principal vehicles of representation, the parties and the party politicians ('trust component').

Since Hannah Pitkin (1967), it is customary to distinguish 'standing-for' and 'acting-for' types of representation.[2] While the first assures a similarity between those represented and their representatives in terms of descriptive, socio-demographic and social-background characteristics, the second projects a principal–agent relationship relating to links between the two units of representation. By analysing the social characteristics of the active part of the electorate and the profile of governments, as well as proximities between elites and voters in selected policy domains, we are able to evaluate both types.

Concerning 'standing for', *descriptive* representation, we focus on the differences between the politically active and passive parts of society, in other words between voters and non-voters in terms of gender, social status (income, class identification and education), ethnicity, religion, residence (urban vs rural) and age. Many of the hypotheses below refer to descriptive representation, or to put it differently, to the inequality of participation. The 'acting-for' type of representation will be assessed through the proximity of voters and governments according to left–right ideological orientation and the EU issue.

The literature on the 'democratic deficit' and on the 'confidence gap' of Western politics is immense (Nye *et al.*, 1997; Pharr and Putnam, 2000, etc.). For CEE one should expect even more significant problems with representative democracy. The speed of social, economic and technological change, the fragility of political parties and the lack of a robust civic culture present major obstacles so far as a smooth linkage between political and social structures is concerned. One might particularly question the relevance of the 'Responsible Party Model' to the region. The model postulates – among other things – that parties compete for voters' confidence and support on the basis of programmes they promise to implement once in office, and that these programmes are distinguishable and comprehensible to the electorate. If parties offer distinctive policy packages citizens can make meaningful choices. But for these choices to be not only meaningful but also consequential one needs parties that can behave as unitary actors and determine government policies by controlling parliament. The model works where party names have real substance, and party systems offer significant policy diversity (Sartori, 1968; Harmel and Janda, 1982: 29; Dalton, 1985; Thomassen, 1994).

The Responsible Party Model is intimately linked to party system institutionalisation. A solid argument can be made in favour of a positive relationship between the accuracy of political representation and the level of party system institutionalisation. Familiar patterns of party politics may help citizens in identifying actors (agents) whom they can trust, while the agents in such systems are in a better position to honour the trust invested in them. But the link between the institutionalisation of party politics and the quality of representation is not as straightforward as might seem from the argument above. Institutionalisation may also mean the freezing of a structure that systematically favours certain groups to the detriment of others. Moreover, institutionalisation is supposed to be accompanied by strong emotional ties between citizens and parties. Ultimately, societies and polities arrive at cleavage structures, in which 'full closure of social relationships' and 'encapsulation of certain groups within political organisations' take place. Such ties may cloud the way of thinking and may thereby loosen the *rational* preference-based links between parties and voters. The analysis below will examine this dilemma by contrasting East and West and by comparing post-communist countries with each other.

Representation happens neither in a historical nor in an institutional vacuum. Characteristics of the political environment – most importantly presidentialism vs parliamentarism, majoritarianism vs proportionalism, concentration vs fragmentation – all have a potential impact on how representation is played out. So does the changing social and political context as the respective countries move from the transition period into the EU-membership era. Our analysis will therefore examine the relationship between the accuracy of representation and political institutional factors, on the one hand, and temporal changes, on the other. Given the large number of aspects and the large number of hypotheses to be investigated, we refrain from complex multivariate analyses and focus on bivariate relations.

The following section contains our specific hypotheses. The hypotheses 'alienation', 'polarisation', 'the role of state', 'economic success', 'institutionalisation' and 'personalistic institutions' refer to subjective aspects of representation. The hypotheses 'capitalism', 'mobilisation' and 'divided societies' take the inequality of electoral participation as dependent variables and are closely identified with the *standing-for* type of representation. The 'saliency', 'majoritarianism', 'maturity' and 'dominance of political phenomena' hypotheses are applied to policy-proximity scores and relate to the *acting-for* type of representation. Finally, the 'democratisation' hypothesis can be investigated at all three levels.

Hypotheses

The hypotheses that structure our research are primarily focused on temporal trends and on intra-regional differences. Concerning the first, the fundamental question is how the quality of representation has changed during the nearly two decades that have passed since the collapse of the communist regimes. This period has also been a period of gradual integration with the EU (cf. Enyedi and Lewis, 2006), so the data analysed reflect on the processes of democratisation, consolidation and Europeanisation. The fundamental hypothesis is that, as time progresses and as the processes listed above advance, the accuracy of representation increases. On the basis of this expectation the match between representatives and represented improves as citizens gradually learn the democratic game and as political institutions adapt to the preferences of citizens.

- *H1. Democratisation hypothesis: The discrepancy between electorates and society gradually decreases, citizens learn to appreciate the functioning of representative democracy and the policy distance between governments and voters declines.*

In spite of the relative success of the transition in terms of economic development and the expansion of freedom, reality cannot match the high hopes. Disappointment and frustration may alienate citizens from politics and lead to a depreciation of the structures of representative democracy. Falling turnout, the success of populist forces and the well-documented spread of distrust and cynicism all make this counter-scenario probable.

- *H2. Alienation hypothesis: Attitudes towards elections as a mechanism of representation gradually turn negative.*

Another pessimistic scenario can be based on the economic aspects of transition. The transition from communism to capitalism entails growing inequalities. Electoral participation tends to be driven by resources (Rosenstone and Hansen, 1993). Social inequalities therefore spill over to the political arena, creating a gradually less representative electorate.

- *H3. Capitalism hypothesis: The discrepancy between electorates and society gradually increases in favour of the high-status groups.*

The history of mobilisation among the poor and the discriminated in the West and the logic of intensive preferences suggest, however, a more positive development. According to this scenario the losers of the transition are particularly motivated to try to alter their fate by collective action, including voting. Those with fewer channels to express their demands are the ones who need the state most, and will therefore participate disproportionately in the elections. They are the ones who need the state most, who have fewer channels to express their demands, and will therefore participate disproportionately in the elections. Time is needed for mobilisation, of course, but by the end of the 1990s we would expect signs of active political engagement.

- *H4. Mobilisation hypothesis: From the end of the 1990s the discrepancy between electorates and society increases in favour of low-status groups.*

Governments and parties may not be representative simultaneously on all possible issues. Representation of the European issue is expected to be worse than that of the left–right dimension. After all, left–right placement is a fundamental organising tool of political discourse in the region (Markowski, 1997), while attitudes to the EU are less central and play a secondary role in electoral campaigns.

- *H5. Saliency hypothesis: Governments and parties will represent voters better on a left–right dimension than on the European issue.*

Concerning the social level, we expect serious problems with representation in the more inegalitarian societies. Inequality has increased in most countries quite radically since the early 1990s, but the country differences are significant. According to the Gini coefficients (see World Bank and CIA websites) the Baltic countries and Poland are the most unequal societies. Hungary, Slovakia, Czech Republic and Slovenia form a more egalitarian group.

- *H6. Divided societies hypothesis: The more inegalitarian (in economic terms) the society is, the more disproportionate the electorate becomes compared to the citizenry.*

From a rationalist perspective, politics is relevant if the stakes are high and if involvement in politics may have a significant impact on the everyday life of citizens. This situation occurs if existing alternatives differ widely and if politicians decide on a wide range of matters (including economic). Accordingly, we propose two hypotheses:

- *H7. Polarisation hypothesis: In countries where sharply divided antagonistic forces rule party competition, more people will think that it matters who is in power and that it is important for whom citizens vote at elections.*
- *H8. The role of state hypothesis: In countries where government intervention in the economy is limited, people will question the relevance of who is in power and for whom citizens vote at elections.*

On the basis of the polarisation hypothesis we expect Hungarians, Bulgarians and Slovaks to have high scores, and Slovenians to have low scores (Estonians would also be expected to care little about politics, but on these questions we have no data on Estonia). The second hypothesis singles out the Czech Republic and Poland (and again Estonia) as countries where the role of government in the economy is moderate and therefore citizens are expected to attribute a low relevance to politics. We expect the 'satisfaction component' to be mainly a function of economic success. In rich and fast-developing countries citizens tend to express satisfaction about political institutions and processes as well.

- *H9. Economic success hypothesis: Satisfaction with elections as a means of representation will be primarily found in rich, economically successful countries.*

In the light of this hypothesis we expect the voters of Slovenia and the Czech Republic to be most satisfied, and Bulgarians and Romanians to be most negative. The 'trust component' can be measured against two different attitude objects: parties and party leaders. We expect parties to fulfil their representative function well in institutionalised party systems. The Czech Republic and Hungary have the most institutionalised party politics in the region, and therefore we expect Czechs and Hungarians to value parties particularly.

- *H10. Institutionalisation hypothesis: Parties are appreciated as the instruments of representation in countries that have consolidated party systems.*

Party leaders are expected, however, to play an acknowledged role in the representation process in systems where institutional factors facilitate personalistic politics. This is to be expected particularly in Lithuania, Poland and Romania, where presidents are directly elected and have considerable power.

- *H11. Personalistic institutions hypothesis: Party leaders are seen as fulfilling a representative role in systems that contain elements of semi-presidentialism.*

Finally, we apply institutional hypotheses to intra-regional differences in the representative quality of governments. According to the studies of Lijphart and Powell, societies that have fewer parties and have a more majoritarian institutional system are more likely to produce unrepresentative governments. In our sample Hungary, Lithuania and, if one counts strong presidents as majoritarian institutions, Romania constitute the more majoritarian bloc. Party system fragmentation, not representing a constitutionally defined feature, also reflects on the majoritarian nature of a country's political life. If the fragmentation of the party system shapes the quality of representation, then we should expect representative governments in Bulgaria, Hungary and the Czech Republic, and very unrepresentative ones in Latvia and Slovenia.

- *H12. Majoritarianism hypothesis: Countries with majoritarian electoral systems, strong presidents and few parties have less representative governments.*

In terms of party–voter proximity, the quality of representation is expected to be higher in the West than in the East. The deficiencies of political culture, the fluidity of party landscapes and the simple lack of time most likely prevent post-communist societies from developing accurate matches between masses and elites.

- *H13. Maturity hypothesis: Stable democracies have better party–voter proximity scores than the newcomer CEE societies.*

Finally, in both regions party–voter proximity scores are likely to be shaped primarily by political factors. Social background (primarily education) will most probably contribute to high-quality representation, but we expect various political orientations (party identification, political attitudes etc.) to play a more decisive role.

- *H14. The dominance of political phenomena hypothesis: Purely political factors have a larger role in shaping the quality of representation than do social structural factors.*

Analysis

Representation as proportional participation of socio-demographic groups

Tables 8.1A through 8.1I show how the electoral participation of selected socio-demographic groups developed between 1995 and 2007 (the time points, in most cases, were 1995, 1999, 2004 and 2007, but for some of the variables we have only two time points).

As far as gender participation is concerned, the differences between men and women stayed statistically significant throughout the period, but then decreased gradually (the Adjusted Residuals went down from 4.1 in 1995 to 2.9 in 2007). More importantly and more interestingly, the original male over-representation not only diminishes but turns into over-representation of women by 2007.

In terms of age, we note significant differences in the voter–non-voter ratio. The youngest cohort (18–35) is highly under-represented and – if anything – their relative absence at elections increases rather than declines over time. The middle-aged and the oldest cohort (60+) have been systematically over-represented, and the latter group has increased its share significantly during the twelve years between 1995 and 2007.

The results show a weak but significant positive relationship between educational attainment and participation. University graduates exert far more influence on parliamentary representation than people with primary education and, as time passes, the unrepresentativeness of the system increases. For the class factor, unfortunately we have only two time points – 1999 and 2007. Contrasting them indicates the growing under-representation of the working class and over-representation of the upper-middle class. The differences are not extraordinarily strong, but they are significant. A related factor – household income per capita – reconfirms the asymmetry between the rich and the poor, and the moderate tendency for this phenomenon to become more robust over time.

For religiosity/church attendance there has been a discontinuity in the wording of the question. For 1999[3] we used the only available question in the data set, one that asks in a rather 'nominal' way about the respondents' attitude towards religion; the data for 2004 and 2007 use the classical 'ordinal' question about the frequency of church attendance. The overall message is complicated because in 2004 we see no statistically significant differences among the religious groups. But the overall picture is one of slight over-representation of more religious citizens. The much talked-about urban–rural divide hardly appears in our data, although in 1999 there was some over-representation of the rural population.

Table 8.1A Electoral participation by sex

Sex		1995 vote (intention)			1999 vote			2004 vote (intention)			2007 vote		
		NV	VT	Total	NV	VT	Total	NV	VT	Total	NV	VT	Total
Male	%	43.6	48.3	46.9	45.3	49.1	48.0	44.9	48.1	46.8	50.3	46.2	47.3
	N =	1156	3100	4256	1295	3765	5060	1622	2481	4103	812	2075	2887
Female	%	56.4	51.7	53.1	54.7	50.9	52.0	55.1	51.9	53.2	49.7	53.8	52.7
	N =	1494	3317	4811	1562	3910	5472	1992	2681	4673	801	2418	3219
Total	%	100.0	100.0	100.0	100.0	100.0	100.0	100.0	100.0	100.0	100.0	100.0	100.0
	N =	2650	6417	9067	2857	7675	10532	3614	5162	8776	1613	4493	6106

Note: All statistically significant.

Table 8.1B Electoral participation by age (3 groups)

Age		1995 vote (intention)			1999 vote			2004 vote (intention)			2007 vote		
		NV	VT	Total	NV	VT	Total	NV	VT	Total	NV	VT	Total
18 → 35	%	41.8	32.4	35.1	48.3	28.7	34.0	34.9	33.2	33.9	44.7	28.0	32.4
	N =	1106	2076	3182	1375	2188	3563	1259	1712	2971	721	1259	1980
36 → 60	%	39.0	44.9	43.2	34.3	47.3	43.8	42.2	43.0	42.6	38.2	45.7	43.7
	N =	1033	2879	3912	976	3614	4590	1521	2217	3738	616	2052	2668
61 → …	%	19.3	22.8	19.3	17.4	24.0	22.2	22.9	23.9	23.5	17.1	26.3	23.9
	N =	510	1461	510	976	3614	4590	827	1232	2059	276	1181	1457
Total	%	100.0	100.0	100.0	100.0	100.0	100.0	100.0	100.0	100.0	100.0	100.0	100.0
	N =	2649	6416	9065	2845	7633	10478	3607	5161	8768	1613	4492	6105

Note: Statistically insignificant marked in grey.

Table 8.1C Electoral participation by education (3 groups)

Education		1995 vote (intention)			1999 vote			2004 vote (intention)			2007 vote		
		NV	*VT*	*Total*	*NV*	*VT*	*Total*	*NV*	*VT*	*Total*	*NV*	*VT*	*Total*
Primary	%	32.1	30.7	31.1	32.5	29.0	29.9	29.0	23.1	25.5	10.6	7.5	8.3
	N =	*847*	*1961*	*2808*	*922*	*2219*	*3141*	*1044*	*1188*	*2232*	*171*	*336*	*507*
Secondary	%	59.6	58.4	58.8	56.0	55.2	55.4	62.4	60.8	61.5	75.8	70.9	72.2
(+ uncompleted)	*N =*	*1573*	*3730*	*5303*	*1590*	*4225*	*5815*	*2242*	*3128*	*5370*	*1223*	*3187*	*4410*
Higher	%	8.3	10.9	10.1	11.5	15.8	14.6	8.6	16.1	13.0	13.6	21.6	19.5
	N =	*220*	*694*	*914*	*327*	*1205*	*1532*	*308*	*826*	*1134*	*220*	*970*	*1190*
Total	%	100.0	100.0	100.0	100.0	100.0	100.0	100.0	100.0	100.0	100.0	100.0	100.0
	N =	*2640*	*6385*	*9025*	*2839*	*7649*	*10488*	*3594*	*5142*	*8736*	*1614*	*4493*	*6107*

Note: Statistically insignificant marked in grey.

Table 8.1D Electoral participation by subjective class (4 groups)

Class		1999 vote			2007 vote		
		NV	VT	Total	NV	VT	Total
Working	%	54.5	50.9	51.9	45.6	37.3	39.5
	N =	1346	3647	4993	736	1675	2411
Lower middle	%	35.2	38.3	37.5	37.8	40.6	39.8
	N =	868	2739	3607	610	1823	2433
Upper middle	%	9.6	10.1	10.0	15.4	20.6	19.2
	N =	238	720	958	248	927	1175
Upper	%	.6	.8	.7	1.2	1.5	1.4
	N =	16	54	70	19	68	87
Total	%	100.0	100.0	100.0	100.0	100.0	100.0
	N =	2468	7160	9628	1613	4493	6106

Note: Statistically insignificant marked in grey.

On ethnicity the contrast between 1995 and 2004 reveals that the balance has shifted in favour of ethnic majorities. Given the cross-country differences and the fundamental differences in the character of various minorities, we must take a closer look at the trajectories of individual countries. One group – composed of the Czech Republic, Romania and Slovakia – shows a decrease in disproportionality. In all three cases it is the minorities' over-representation that disappears. Another group – Estonia, Lithuania and Latvia – shows significant differences between majorities and minorities (mainly Russian-speakers), with the majority being considerably over-represented. In the first two cases there is virtually no change over time, while in Latvia the majority's over-representation increased between 1995 and 2004. Finally, Bulgaria is a separate case, because in this country minorities are consistently over-represented at elections and the difference has even increased in favour of minorities.

To conclude this part of our analysis, the Democratisation and Mobilisation hypotheses receive little support, while the Capitalism hypothesis has been largely confirmed. Gender and ethnicity turn out to be exceptions; in their case representative accuracy increased and one could even see the over-representation of the weaker social groups. In two other instances (religion and urban–rural divide) there was no indication of poor representation. The slight over-representation of religious groups also fits the Mobilisation frame. But in most cases the trend was towards a decline in the quality of representation, although the level of misrepresentation has never become dramatic.

Table 8.1E Electoral participation by household income (4 groups, each year different income)

Household income		1995 vote (intention)			1999 vote			2004 vote (intention)		
		NV	VT	Total	NV	VT	Total	NV	VT	Total
Lower 22% (1995)	%	23.4	21.6	22.1	32.9	23.9	26.3	31.6	25.4	28.0
Lower 26% (1999)	N =	525	1254	1779	845	1749	2594	939	1084	2023
Lower 25% (2004)										
22–55% (1995)	%	33.5	34.7	34.4	38.6	40.1	39.7	28.0	27.2	27.5
26–66% (1999)	N =	752	2012	2764	990	2926	3916	833	1159	1992
25–53% (2004)										
55–80% (1995)	%	23.2	24.9	24.5	17.1	21.4	20.3	21.9	23.4	22.8
66–86% (1999)	N =	521	1446	1967	440	1561	2001	651	998	1649
53–76% (2004)										
Upper 20% (1995)	%	19.8	18.7	19.0	11.3	14.6	13.8	18.5	24.0	21.7
Upper 14% (1999)	N =	444	1084	1528	291	1069	1360	549	1022	1571
Upper 24% (2004)										
Total	%	100.0	100.0	100.0	100.0	100.0	100.0	100.0	100.0	100.0
	N =	2242	5796	8038	2566	7305	9871	2972	4263	7235
Lower 26% (1999)	N =	100.0	100.0	100.0	100.0	100.0	100.0	100.0	100.0	100.0

Note: Statistically insignificant marked in grey.

Table 8.1F Electoral participation by place of residence (rural/urban)

Place of residence		1995 vote (intention)			1999 vote			2004 vote (intention)			2007 vote		
		NV	VT	Total	NV	VT	Total	NV	VT	Total	NV	VT	Total
Rural	%	39.8	42.4	41.7	25.6	27.2	26.8	34.9	37.0	36.1	20.4	20.6	20.5
	N =	1056	2721	3777	731	2078	2809	1259	1902	3161	271	777	1048
Urban	%	60.2	57.6	58.3	74.4	72.8	73.2	65.1	63.0	63.9	79.6	79.4	79.5
	N =	1594	3695	5289	2120	5562	7682	2345	3242	5587	1056	3002	4058
Total	%	100.0	100.0	100.0	100.0	100.0	100.0	100.0	100.0	100.0	100.0	100.0	100.0
	N =	2650	6416	9066	2851	7640	10491	3604	5144	8748	1327	3779	5106

Note: Statistically insignificant marked in grey.

Table 8.1G Electoral participation by religiosity (1999)/church attendance (2004, 2007)

Religiosity/church attendance		1999 vote			2004 vote (intention)			2007 vote		
		NV	*VT*	*Total*	*NV*	*VT*	*Total*	*NV*	*VT*	*Total*
Churches are wrong (relig.–1999)	%	5.2	4.1	4.4	26.1	27.6	27.0	23.2	21.6	22.0
Never (2004, 2007)	*N =*	*143*	*304*	*447*	*917*	*1399*	*2316*	*359*	*942*	*1301*
Not interested (religiosity–1999)	%	15.4	10.4	11.7	21.5	21.1	21.3	23.8	21.0	21.7
Once a year (2004, 2007)	*N =*	*426*	*778*	*1204*	*753*	*1071*	*1824*	*369*	*917*	*1286*
Cannot say (relig.–1999)	%	15.0	12.2	12.9	32.4	32.3	32.3	36.7	35.1	35.6
Few times a year (2004, 2007)	*N =*	*415*	*911*	*1326*	*1137*	*1636*	*2773*	*569*	*1535*	*2104*
In own way (relig.–1999)	%	39.7	46.0	44.3	17.0	15.7	16.2	13.9	18.1	17.0
Once a week (2004, 2007)	*N =*	*1099*	*3444*	*4543*	*596*	*797*	*1393*	*216*	*791*	*1007*
Follow the teachings (relig.–1999)	%	24.7	27.4	26.7	3.0	3.3	3.1	2.4	4.2	3.7
Several times a week (2004, 2007)	*N =*	*684*	*2052*	*2736*	*104*	*166*	*270*	*37*	*183*	*220*
Total	%	100.0	100.0	100.0	100.0	100.0	100.0	100.0	100.0	100.0
	N =	*2767*	*7489*	*10256*	*3507*	*5069*	*8576*	*1550*	*4368*	*5918*

Note: Statistically insignificant marked in grey.

Table 8.1H Electoral participation by left–right self-identification (3 groups)

L–R scale		1999 vote			2004 vote (intention)			2007 vote		
		NV	VT	Total	NV	VT	Total	NV	VT	Total
Left	%	28.0	29.5	29.1	26.4	27.7	27.2	16.5	22.3	20.7
	N =	506	1738	2244	641	1182	1823	266	1000	1266
Center	%	51.2	43.2	45.1	53.2	39.1	44.2	66.4	50.4	54.6
	N =	925	2544	3469	1291	1670	2961	1071	2266	3337
Right	%	20.8	27.3	25.8	20.4	33.2	28.6	17.2	27.3	24.6
	N =	375	1612	1987	495	1417	1912	277	1227	1504
Total	%	100.0	100.0	100.0	100.0	100.0	100.0	100.0	100.0	100.0
	N =	1806	5894	7700	2427	4269	6696	1614	4493	6107

Note: Statistically insignificant marked in grey.

Table 8.1I Electoral participation by ethnic group membership

Ethnic group		1995 vote (intention)			2004 vote (intention)		
		NV	*VT*	*Total*	*NV*	*VT*	*Total*
Main	%	90.0	89.6	89.7	84.7	89.3	87.4
	N =	*2386*	*5740*	*8126*	*3057*	*4603*	*7660*
Other	%	10.0	10.4	10.3	15.3	10.7	12.6
	N =	*264*	*669*	*933*	*554*	*550*	*1104*
Total	%	100.0	100.0	100.0	100.0	100.0	100.0
	N =	*2650*	*6409*	*9059*	*3611*	*5153*	*8764*

Note: Statistically insignificant marked in grey.

Subjective evaluations of system-representativeness

The subjective aspect of representation is typically discussed under the heading of political efficacy, political cynicism and/or political alienation. One of the questions in the Comparative Study of Electoral Systems (CSES) data set that pertains to these characteristics is 'whether who is in power makes a difference or not'. Tables 8.2A through 8.2C show both the percentage distributions of the five-point scale and the means at two points in time in particular Central and East European countries.

Fewer citizens think that 'who is in power matters' in the early new millennium years than did so in the late 1990s. The differences are clear and significant. This result strengthens the Alienation hypothesis and casts doubt on the Democratisation hypothesis. The change towards cynicism is particularly spectacular in the Czech Republic and Poland. These two countries were joined in the Module 2 CSES data set by Bulgaria. The opposite trend is exemplified only by Hungary. On average, there is a contrast between the high scorers, Romania and Hungary, and the low scorers, the Czech Republic, Poland and Bulgaria.

A related question is whether 'who people vote for makes a difference'. Tables 8.3A through 8.3C show both the between-country and the temporal patterns. The temporal trend shows a slight decline in the belief of the meaningfulness of the vote. That is, the tests point again in the direction of the Alienation hypothesis. The decline in the belief in voting as an effective procedural democratic tool is most visible among Czechs, followed by Poles; at the same time the trust of Hungarians and Slovenes in the electoral game has increased. The highest support for the relevance of voting was found in Romania, Hungary and Slovenia, the lowest in Poland and Lithuania.

Table 8.2A Responses to statement: 'Who is in power can make a difference' (CSES, Module 1, 1996–2002)

	Czech Republic		Hungary		Lithuania		Poland		Romania		Slovenia	
	N	%	N	%	N	%	N	%	N	%	N	%
1. It makes a difference who is in power.	939	59.1	673	42.8	832	53.2	812	53.9	1114	70.8	1045	66.7
2. -----------	439	27.6	414	26.4	363	23.2	356	23.6	158	10.0	284	18.2
3. -----------	142	8.9	265	16.9	189	12.1	172	11.4	101	6.4	138	8.8
4. -----------	48	3.0	82	5.3	80	5.1	71	4.7	57	3.6	46	3.0
5. It doesn't make a difference who is in power.	21	1.3	136	8.7	101	6.5	96	6.4	143	9.1	53	3.4
Total	1589	100.0	1570	100.0	1565	100.0	1508	100.0	1573	100.0	1566	100.0
5. who is in power.	1589	100.0	1570	100.0	1565	100.0	1508	100.0	1573	100.0	1566	100.0

Table 8.2B Responses 2001–6 (CSES, Module 2)

	Czech Republic		Hungary		Lithuania		Poland		Romania		Slovenia		Bulgaria	
1. It makes a difference who is in power.	385	24.7	817	53.1	–	–	533	35.8	865	56.7	804	52.6	617	43.2
2. ------------	501	32.1	357	23.2	–	–	381	25.6	300	19.7	338	22.1	309	21.7
3. ------------	384	24.6	232	15.1	–	–	299	20.1	174	11.4	170	11.2	211	14.7
4. ------------	159	10.2	61	4.0	–	–	121	8.1	75	4.9	69	4.5	122	8.6
5. It doesn't make a difference who is in power.	134	8.6	71	4.6	–	–	156	10.5	111	7.3	147	9.6	168	11.8
Total	1562	100.0	1537	100.0	–	–	1491	100.0	1525	100.0	1528	100.0	1428	100.0

Table 8.2C Mean responses to statement: 'Who is in power can make difference' (CSES, Modules 1 and 2), Central and East European countries

'Who is in power can make difference'

(1. It makes a difference who is in power . . . 5. It doesn't make a difference who is in power)

Countries	Module 1	Module 2	Statistical significance of differences between two points of time in each country (t-test)
	Mean	*Mean*	
Czech Republic	1.6	2.5	***
Hungary	2.1	1.8	***
Lithuania	1.9	–	***
Poland	1.9	2.3	***
Romania	1.7	1.9	***
Slovenia	1.6	2.0	***
Bulgaria (2001)	–	2.2	***
Total	1.8	2.1	
Eta^2	.03	.04	
Statistical significance of differences between countries in each module (one-way anova)	***	***	

Note: *** sig. < .01; ** .01 < sig. ≤ .05; * .05 < sig. < .1.

The tendency in Hungary towards the growing recognition of the relevance of politics fits the Polarisation hypothesis, but we expected Bulgaria and Slovakia to score high as well, and Slovenia should have been particularly low. The low status of Poland is in line with the Role of State hypothesis. The shift of the Czech Republic and Poland in the direction of depoliticisation also strengthens the latter approach. The third CSES question, 'How well voters' views are represented in elections' taps the 'satisfaction component' of subjective representation. Tables 8.4A and 8.4B show robust cross-country differences.

According to the results, the citizens of Bulgaria, Hungary, Poland and Romania are more enthusiastic about elections than the citizens of Slovenia and, especially, the Czech Republic (the difference is statistically significant as the between-country differences explain 4 per cent of the variance.) This ranking directly contradicts our Economic Success hypothesis. Perhaps in rich and successful countries citizens are more critical towards political

Table 8.3A Responses to statement: 'Who people vote for makes a difference' (CSES, Module 1)

	Czech Republic		Hungary		Lithuania		Poland		Romania		Slovenia	
	N	%	N	%	N	%	N	%	N	%	N	%
1. Who people vote for won't make a difference	66	4.2	81	5.2	142	9.1	176	11.8	163	10.3	139	9.0
2. -----------	128	8.1	70	4.5	158	10.2	128	8.6	39	2.5	110	7.2
3. -----------	230	14.6	257	16.4	248	15.9	253	17.0	123	7.8	205	13.3
4. -----------	462	29.2	461	29.4	382	24.6	450	30.2	192	12.2	323	21.0
5. Who people vote for can make a difference	697	44.0	700	44.6	623	40.1	483	32.4	1062	67.2	764	49.6
Total	1583	100.0	1569	100.0	1553	100.0	1489	100.0	1580	100.0	1541	100.0

Table 8.3B Responses 2001–6 (CSES, Module 2)

	Czech Republic		Hungary		Lithuania		Poland		Romania		Slovenia		Bulgaria	
1. Who people vote for won't make a difference	142	9.1	45	3.0	–	–	241	16.2	104	6.8	106	7.0	124	9.3
2. -----------	220	14.1	44	2.8	–	–	190	12.8	80	5.2	83	5.4	141	10.5
3. -----------	458	29.3	221	14.4	–	–	334	22.5	206	13.5	185	12.1	265	19.7
4. -----------	516	33.0	364	23.7	–	–	375	25.3	324	21.1	353	23.2	338	25.1
5. Who people vote for can make a difference	226	14.5	859	56.0	–	–	346	23.3	818	53.4	799	52.4	476	35.4
Total	1562	100.0	1533	100.0	–	–	1486	100.0	1533	100.0	1527	100.0	1344	100.0

Table 8.3C Mean responses to statement: 'Who people vote for makes a difference' (Modules 1 and 2), Central and East European countries

'Who people vote for makes a difference'

(1. Who people vote for won't make a difference . . . 5. Who people vote for can make a difference)

Countries	Module 1	Module 2	Statistical significance of differences between two points of time in each country (t-test)
	Mean	*Mean*	
Czech Republic	4.0	3.3	***
Hungary	4.0	4.3	***
Lithuania	3.8		***
Poland	3.6	3.3	***
Romania	4.2	4.1	**
Slovenia	4.0	4.1	**
Bulgaria (2001)		3.7	***
Total	3.9	3.9	
Eta^2	.0	.1	
Statistical significance of differences between countries in each module (one-way anova)	***	***	

Note: *** sig. < .01; ** .01< sig. ≤ .05; * .05 < sig. < .1.

processes precisely because they are used to higher standards in their economic activities.

Finally, CSES respondents could express their evaluation of the process of representation by grading parties and party leaders. The answers to the question 'whether there are parties that represent citizens' views reasonably well' are to be found in Tables 8.5A and 8.5B. Hungarians and Czechs stand out, followed by Bulgarians and Romanians, as relatively satisfied with the representative capacity of their parties. The other end of the continuum is occupied by Slovenes. The distance between Slovenia and the other CEE countries is surprisingly large. The cross-country differences are statistically significant and explain 12 per cent of the dependent variable variance (Table 8.5B). The high scores of Hungary and the Czech Republic are in line with the Institutionalisation hypothesis, but the scores of Bulgaria and, especially, Romania were expected to be lower.

Table 8.4A Answers to question: 'How well are voters' views are represented in elections?' (CSES, Module 2)

	Bulgaria (2001)		Czech Republic (2002)		Hungary (2002)		Poland (2001)		Romania (2004)		Slovenia (2004)	
	N	%	N	%	N	%	N	%	N	%	N	%
1. Very well	128	14.0	15	1.1	48	3.3	78	5.6	89	9.7	39	2.9
2. Quite well	356	38.8	360	27.3	709	48.4	605	42.9	256	27.6	335	24.8
3. Not very well	290	31.6	681	51.6	611	41.7	580	41.2	552	59.7	865	64.0
4. Not well at all	144	15.7	265	20.0	96	6.5	146	10.4	28	3.0	113	8.3
Total	918	100.0	1321	100.0	1465	100.0	1409	100.0	925	100.0	1351	100.0

Table 8.4B Mean differences between CEE countries and their statistical significance in answers to question (see below)

How well voters' views are represented in elections?

(1. Very well . . . 4. Not well at all)

Countries	Module 2
	Mean
Bulgaria (2001)	2.5
Czech Republic (2002)	2.9
Hungary (2002)	2.5
Poland (2001)	2.6
Romania (2004)	2.6
Slovenia (2004)	2.8
Total	2.6
	$Eta^2 = .0$
Statistical significance of differences between countries (one-way anova)	***

Note: *** sig. < .01; ** .01 < sig. ≤ .05; * .05 < sig. < .1.

Table 8.5A Answers to question: 'Does any of the parties represent your views reasonably well?' (CSES, Module 2)

	Bulgaria (2001)		Czech Republic (2002)		Hungary (2002)	
	N	*%*	*N*	*%*	*N*	*%*
0. No	*842*	53.7	*250*	22.1	*420*	27.4
1. Yes	*725*	46.3	*881*	77.9	*1113*	72.6
Total	*1567*	100.0	*1131*	100.0	*1534*	100.0
	Poland (2001)		Romania (2004)		Slovenia (2004)	
	N	*%*	*N*	*%*	*N*	*%*
0. No	*803*	59.6	*755*	55.0	*827*	71.1
1. Yes	*544*	40.4	*618*	45.0	*336*	28.9
Total	*1347*	100.0	*1373*	100.0	*1164*	100.0

Table 8.5B Mean differences between CEE countries and their statistical
significance in answers to question (see below)

Does any of the parties represent your views reasonably well?

(0 = no; 1 = yes)

Countries	Module 2
	Mean
Bulgaria (2001)	.5
Czech Republic (2002)	.7
Hungary (2002)	.7
Poland (2001)	.4
Romania (2004)	.5
Slovenia (2004)	.3
Total	.5
	$Eta^2 = .1$
Statistical significance of differences between countries (one-way anova)	***

Note: *** sig. < .01; ** .01 < sig. ≤ .05; * .05 < sig. < .1.

The distribution of the answers to the question whether there are 'party
leaders that represent voters' views reasonably well' is displayed in Tables 8.6A
and 8.6B. Hungarians and Czechs are absolute leaders in believing that their
politicians represent their views fairly well and, again, the Slovenes (and the
Poles) question the representative capacities of their leading politicians.
These results are at odds with the Personalistic Institutions hypothesis and fit
more the Institutionalisation hypothesis. It seems that in consolidated party
systems both parties and party leaders are highly regarded by the public.

Government representation

In the following section we look at the relationship between the median
voter and the government. With information on the programmatic position
of the parties, and knowing the partisan composition of the government, the
Comparative Manifesto Project allows for the reconstruction of the position
of governments on important policy issues. The government's policy position
is calculated as the weighted mean score of the government parties' positions.
The latest volume of the Group's data (Klingemann *et al.*, 2006) presents
the median voter's position as well, derived from the party manifestos as:
L + [(50 − C)/F] * W, where L is the lower end (ideological score) of the

Table 8.6A Answers to question: 'Does any of the party leaders represent your views reasonably well?' (CSES, Module 2)

	Bulgaria (2001)		Czech Republic (2002)		Hungary (2002)	
	N	%	N	%	N	%
0. No	881	56.3	466	44.3	299	19.7
1. Yes	685	43.7	585	55.7	1217	80.3
Total	1566	100.0	1051	100.0	1516	100.0
	Poland (2001)		Romania (2004)		Slovenia (2004)	
	N	%	N	%	N	%
0. No	815	60.4	702	51.9	727	64.7
1. Yes	534	39.6	651	48.1	397	35.3
Total	1349	100.0	1353	100.0	1125	100.0

Table 8.6B Mean differences between CEE countries and their statistical significance in answers to question (see below)

Does any of party leaders represent your views reasonably well?

(0 = no; 1 = yes)

Countries	Module 2
	Mean
Bulgaria (2001)	.4
Czech Republic (2002)	.6
Hungary (2002)	.8
Poland (2001)	.4
Romania (2004)	.5
Slovenia (2004)	.4
Total	.5
	Eta^2 = .1
Statistical significance of differences between countries (one-way anova)	***

Note: *** sig. < .01; ** .01 < sig. ≤ .05; * .05 < sig. < .1.

interval containing the median, C is the cumulative frequency (vote share) up to the interval containing the median, F is the frequency (vote share) in the interval containing the median, and W is the width of the interval containing the median (for details see also Kim and Fording, 2001). The left–right scale has been constructed by Klingemann *et al.*, by deducting left-wing quasi-sentences from right-wing ones, while the EU position was calculated by deducting hostile references to EU from favourable references in party programmes. We now (Tables 8.7A and 8.7B) take the difference between the two numbers (the absolute value) as the indicator of the representative nature of the government.

As Tables 8.7A and 8.7B indicate, there is little covariation between time and the accuracy of representation. This is true both in general[4] and within individual countries. The Democratisation hypothesis thus suffers a last and final blow. Actually, in a number of countries there is a tendency towards deterioration. In Estonia, as far as the EU issue is concerned, every new election brought a government that was less representative than its predecessor. The development on the left–right dimension was less linear, but also on this dimension the last-recorded government (2003) was the least representative. The same negative, though less steep, tendency can be witnessed in Poland on both left–right and EU. In Bulgaria, Latvia, Lithuania and Slovenia there has been an improvement on the EU issue, while on left–right the latest figures are promising for the Czech Republic and Slovenia.

Table 8.8 averages the scores for the countries (this is a meaningful exercise, because the countries differ significantly in terms of the quality of representation[5]). According to these results the most accurate representation on the EU dimension is in Bulgaria, Slovenia and Lithuania, while the largest distance between the voters and the government is in the Czech Republic and Estonia. On the left–right dimension, again Bulgaria is the country with the smallest distance, while Romania and Slovenia are located at the opposite extreme.

Most surprisingly, the EU issue is better represented than the left–right position in the majority of the countries (Romania, Slovenia, Lithuania, Poland, Slovakia, and Bulgaria) while the left–right dimension strongly outperforms the EU only in the Czech Republic and Estonia (weakly also in Hungary and Latvia). This means that the Saliency hypothesis, as formulated at the beginning of this chapter, must be rejected. It seems that the logic of party competition presses parties to develop more homogeneous and more extreme profiles on salient issues than on other issues, and on these issues they must also construct government coalitions that can be unambiguously identified with one of the sides of the debate. The loser in this process is the median voter.

Since left–right positioning is a super-issue, a dimension that is supposed to absorb most of the specific political conflicts, one can regard the distance

Table 8.7A Government–voter policy distance in the CEE countries on the EU issue (data ordered by the size of the 'distance' for each country separately)

Countries	*Year*	*Distance – EU issue*
Bulgaria	1997	.0
	2001	.1
	1990	.1
	1994	.2
Czech Republic	1996	.1
	1992	.2
	1990	1.0
	2002	1.1
	1998	2.1
Estonia	1992	.6
	1995	.7
	1999	1.0
	2003	1.5
Hungary	1994	.0
	1990	.3
	2002	.6
Latvia	2002	.0
	1995	.1
	1998	.1
	1993	1.2
Lithuania	2000	.0
	1992	.3
Poland	1991	.1
	1997	.1
	2001	.5
Romania	1992	.2
	1990	.3
	2000	.3
	1996	.5
Slovakia	1994	.0
	1998	.1
	1990	.3
	2002	.3
Slovenia	1996	.0
	2000	.1
	1990	.2
	1992	.2

Notes: Bulgaria 1991, Hungary 1998, Lithuania 1996, Poland 1993, Romania 2000, Slovakia 1992 are missing. The left–right position was calculated by subtracting the percentages of party programmes devoted to leftist categories from the percentages attributed to right-wing categories: (per104 + per201 + per203 + per305 + per401 + per402 + per407 + per414 + per505 + per601 + per603 + per605 + per606) – (per103 + per105 + per106 + per107 + per403 + per404 + per406 + per412 + per413 + per504 + per506 + per701 + per202). (See Michael Laver and Ian Budge (eds) *Party Policy and Government Coalitions*, Houndmills, Basingstoke: Macmillan 1992.) The calculus of the EU position was: per108 – per110. Because of the differences between the structure of the left–right and the EU scales the results have been standardised.

Table 8.7B Government–voter policy distance in the CEE countries on the left–right dimension (data ordered by size of the 'distance' for each country separately)

Countries	Year	Distance – LR
Bulgaria	1994	.0
	2001	.2
	1990	.2
	1997	.3
Czech Republic	2002	.1
	1992	.2
	1990	.2
	1998	.2
	1996	.8
Estonia	1995	.3
	1999	.4
	1992	.5
	2003	.6
Hungary	1994	.0
	1990	.1
	2002	.7
Latvia	1995	.2
	1998	.2
	2002	.3
	1993	.4
Lithuania	1992	.6
	2000	.8
Poland	1997	.1
	1991	.3
	2001	.9
Romania	1990	.8
	2000	.8
	1992	1.4
	1996	2.3
Slovakia	1998	.0
	2002	.2
	1990	.2
	1994	1.0
Slovenia	2000	.4
	1990	.7
	1996	.8
	1992	1.9

Table 8.8 Government–voter policy distances and party system fragmentation

Countries	Government–voter distance on EU	Government–voter distance on left–right	Governmental representation (measured as average government–voter policy distance on left–right)	Average effective number of parliamentary parties
Bulgaria	.1	.2	Very high	3.1
Hungary	.3	.2	High	3
Latvia	.3	.3	High	5.8
Czech Republic	.9	.3	High	3.9
Slovakia	.1	.4	High	4.7
Estonia	.9	.4	Median	4.9
Poland	.2	.4	Median	4.7
Lithuania	.2	.7	Low	4
Slovenia	.1	.9	Low	5.5
Romania	.4	1.5	very low	4

between voters and governments on this dimension as a good proxy for the quality of governmental representation. The ranking of the countries on left–right moderately supports the Majoritarianism hypothesis. The unrepresentative nature of Romanian governments may have something to do with the strong role of presidents, and the good performance of Bulgaria may be a result of the proportionality of its institutional regime, but the overall ranking of countries differs from what we had expected. Party system fragmentation is a better predictor of the quality of representation than the legally defined political institutions. If Latvia had had larger, and Romania and Lithuania somewhat smaller, policy distances between governments and voters, the match would have been perfect.

As Table 8.9 shows, the negative correlation between fragmentation and the quality of governmental representation has developed gradually. It seems that party system characteristics, like fragmentation, need time to have an impact on the process of government formation, but in the end the relationship detected accords with the prevailing wisdom in the theoretical and comparative literature.

Party–voter proximity

This last part of the analysis employs the classical (cf. Miller and Stokes, 1963; Converse and Pierce, 1986; Kitschelt *et al.*, 1999) approach to the study of the quality of representation – it depicts and evaluates the fit between elites and followers of particular parties on ideology, salient issues and policy areas. We test the proximity between party elites and their voters on the left–right dimension and on their preferences concerning EU unification,[6] i.e. whether the EU project should be 'strengthened', on the one hand, or has already 'gone too far', on the other.

Table 8.9 Correlation between fragmentation and governmental representation (measured as average government–voter policy distance on left–right at three stages of democratic consolidation)

	*Distance on left–right issue * fragmentation*
1990–94	.2
	11
1995–99	−.1
	11
2000–3	−.3
	10

First, we start by depicting simple distributions concerning the average left–right position and 'strengthening EU' distances between elites and masses in CEE and Western European democracies. The underlying query concerns the extent to which new fragile democracies differ from the more established ones, those which are presumably more 'Europeanised'. Surprisingly, in left–right terms there is no difference between the two groups, while on EU-issues CEE citizens are far better represented by their respective parties than are their Western European fellow citizens (the detailed distributions for particular countries are not shown here but are available upon request from the authors). The latter difference is significant at the .000 level, although eta-squared equals only .014. The average distance between parties and their voters in Western Europe is 2.44 (standard deviation = 1.88) and in CEE polities it is 1.97 (sd = 1.48), which indicates that the latter region is both better represented and more cohesive.

As a next step we examine the causes of proximity. Our models explained Western European proximity scores much better than the CEE scores and the left–right dimension better than the EU dimension. When we entered only socio-demographic independent variables into the regressions, education and political sophistication appeared as significant factors in both regions. But when tested in a more multivariate design their direct impact disappeared in the CEE countries. In both regions sociological factors were considerably weaker than the political ones, confirming the dominance of the Political Phenomena hypothesis.

Representation on the left–right axis is shaped in the West by national and party identity. Citizens showing strong affective inclination towards either the nation or parties are less proximate to their parties. In other words, both types of identity impede the positional calculation and lead the voters further away from their parties. Satisfaction with the performance of democracy is positively related to accurate representation. For CEE polities we found only a few significant predictors. Weak, non-significant relationships were detected between education and proximity. Left–right proximities were influenced by the preference of the respondents towards an EU that 'provides better social security for all' (rather than one that is 'economically competitive').

Table 8.10 presents our final regression model with interaction terms, where the 'interaction variable' is citizenship in a country with a *communist past* (COMPAST).

The most straightforward message from Table 8.10 is that the two parts of the European continent differ in terms of representational fit on the left–right dimension because of the different impact of (a) party identification and (b) the preference for an competitive-liberal or social EU (whether its main aim should be to foster competitiveness or provide better social security for all). Party identification in stable democracies impedes the left–right representational

Table 8.10 Determinants of left–right proximity (data: INTUNE)

Dep var: proximity left–right	*Coefficient*	*Robust standard error (clustered by country)*	*t*
COMPAST	−.30	.21	−1.39
Age	.00	.07	−.02
COMPAST*Age	.16	.10	1.70
Education	−.20***	.02	−8.20
COMPAST*Education	.07	.06	1.22
Class	−.01	.05	−.18
COMPAST*Class	.11	.07	1.53
PID	.28**	.09	3.31
COMPAST*PID	−.40*	.16	−2.57
Demsat	−.12*	.05	−2.57
COMPAST*Demsat	.06	.06	.96
Social_eu	.04	.04	.88
COMPAST*Social_eu	.15**	.05	2.83
Nat_id	.03***	.01	3.44
COMPAST*Nat_id	−.03	.02	−1.50
Sophist	−.03*	.01	−2.50
COMPAST*Sophist	−.01	.02	−.39
Const.	2.42***	.20	12.30
N =	5803		
R^2 =	4%		

Note: * p < .05; ** p < .01; *** p < .001.

fit, that is, party identifiers are further away from the positions of their parties on the left–right dimension. In new, post-communist democracies this factor works in the opposite way, but the relationship is not significant. The phenomenon of cue-taking by voters from party positions seems to be more robust in new democracies. Alternatively, one might say that in long-established democracies political socialisation and durable identifications, either national or party, are encapsulating citizens into relationships that restrict their calculative potential concerning the assessment of party positions.

The other significant difference between 'the West and the East' concerns the relationship between the social or economic approach to EU and left–right proximity. In CEE post-communist countries citizens who are in favour of a social-redistributive Europe are poorly represented (on the left–right dimension) by their chosen parties, while in Western democracies there is no relationship between the two (the difference between the regions is significant, see interaction term of 'COMP*Soc_eu' in Table 8.10).

Replacing representation on the left–right axis with representation on the EU issue as the dependent variable, we found that among the socio-demographic variables only education matters, i.e. has a positive impact on the accuracy of representation (and this only in Western Europe). Regressing our dependent variable on political factors shows that the more satisfied the citizens are with the national performance of democracy, the more likely they are close to their party on this issue – in both parts of Europe. The remaining factors were either insignificantly or variously associated with our proximity measure in the West and the East.

The coefficients and interaction terms (full model) in Table 8.11 confirm that education is an extremely important factor, but only in the West. The difference between the two regions is significant. Second, satisfaction with democracy is significant in both parts of EU and its directional impact is the same – satisfaction is associated with a high level of representation. The regions differ, however, in the strength of this relationship. Finally, there is

Table 8.11 Determinants of proximity on the EU issue (data: INTUNE)

Dep var: proximity strengthening EU	*Coefficient*	*Robust standard error (clustered by country)*	*t*
COMPAST	−1.83***	.34	−5.34
Age	.10	.10	1.07
COMPAST*Age	−.15	.15	−.99
Education	−.21***	.03	−7.77
COMPAST*Education	.25***	.06	4.27
Class	−.05	.06	−.87
COMPAST*Class	.01	.08	.09
PID	−.01	.08	−.13
COMPAST*PID	.23*	.10	2.27
Demsat	−.28***	.04	−6.47
COMPAST*Demsat	.12*	.06	2.2
Social_eu	−.13**	.04	−3.23
COMPAST*Social_eu	.13	.12	1.14
Nat_id	−.01	.02	−.62
COMPAST*Nat_id	.04	.03	1.15
Sophist	−.01	.01	−.99
COMPAST*Sophist	.00	.02	−.17
Const.	3.93***	.30	13.22
N =	5803		
R^2 =	4%		

Note: * p < .05; ** p < .01; *** p < .001.

one more significant difference between the two regions – party identification is unrelated to the quality of representation in the West, but it is influential in the East.

Conclusions

Perhaps the most important conclusion is that the optimistic Democratisation hypothesis must be rejected. CEE post-communist party systems are moving in the direction of deteriorating representation. Particularly worrying is that, with the passing of time, poorer segments of the population withdraw from influencing the composition of the parliaments. Alienation and inegalitarian capitalist structures counterbalance the opening up of political opportunities.

Income, class and education, or to use sociological jargon, aspects of *achieved status*, contribute to growing misrepresentation. But *ascribed status* (sex, place of residence, religiosity) of citizens receives a fairly proportional representation. In case of religious and ethnic groups one can even notice a readiness for (counter-)mobilisation. Ethnicity is the factor that can be least described in terms of universal patterns. In countries where the party of the ethnic minority is a crucial and much sought-after player (like Bulgaria), minority voters are particularly active, while political processes that are biased in favour of majorities (cf. Estonia) alienate minority voters. The over- and under-represented segments do not coincide perfectly with the winners and losers of the transition. This is perhaps most obvious concerning age. The elderly are typically discussed as victims of the neo-liberal reforms, but in CEE they seem to take more advantage of democratic procedures than other groups. The two observations are not in contradiction: the state, under pressure from the pensioner voters, mitigates the negative impact of the free market but in most cases it cannot eliminate it.

The results of the present investigation attest to the fact that representation is a multi-dimensional concept. Different nations score high on different dimensions of representation. Bulgarians find elections representative and have governments that deviate little from the median voter. Hungarians, together with Romanians, attribute high relevance to politics, are pretty satisfied with how elections work, and the former can also find at least one party and party leader that they can be enthusiastic about. In this regard they are joined by the Czechs. But the Czechs tend to have little interest in or respect for the political process.

It is noteworthy that on several issues it is the Slovenes and the Czechs, the wealthiest two nations in the region, who display the most cynical, politically alienated attitudes towards their polities. It seems the alienation can coexist with, or is even fuelled by, economic success. There is no deterministic link between how the representative linkage functions and the kind of political institutions that operate in a country. But more 'semi-presidential' regimes (Poland, Lithuania, Romania) have often had bad scores on representation, while the most typically high scorers, Bulgaria and Hungary, belong to the least presidential and most purely unicameral regimes of the region. The institutionalisation of party politics has most likely helped the Czech Republic and Hungary to accept parties and party politicians. In these two cases strong political personalities like Orban and Klaus put their energy into consolidating a polarised party-political landscape (Enyedi, 2006).

Government representation on the EU issue proved to be better than expected and better than on the salient left–right dimension. Governments seem to be further away from the median voter on the most relevant political dimension precisely because parties may be particularly keen to match the taste of their clientele on the salient issues. This is, of course, only a speculation, but it is in accordance with the mandate theories of representation and directional theories of voting.

The superiority of the West in terms of accurate matches between party elites and electorates did not materialise. Post-communist citizens are in fact able, on average, to find parties that are close to their views. But we are better able to explain for the West than for the East why some citizens are able to choose the 'right' party. Citizens who are educated, sophisticated, satisfied with democracy and have relatively few national and partisan attachments are represented better by parties. The peculiarity of the East is that those who are for a 'social' Europe tend to end up with parties that are in fact ideologically very distant from them.

Notes

1 Note that the American (Anglo-Saxon) tradition is more concerned with policy outputs, for example budget expenditures on certain policies (Brooks 1985; 1990; Bartels 1991; Petry 1999).

2 She also introduced the differentiation between *formalistic* (conceived of in terms of 'authorisation' and 'accountability'), *symbolic, descriptive and substantive* – as she calls them – 'views' of representation. The agenda of empirically oriented scholars have been dominated by the last two categories.

3 Unfortunately no data were available for 1995.

4 There was no significant correlation between year and policy distance.

5 According to the ANOVA test the 'country' variable's impact on Euroscepticism is around the border of the traditional .05 significance level (it is .057), while on left–right it is at the .01 level. The eta squared figures were .431 and .525. Due to the low number of cases the LSD post-hoc comparisons show significant differences only for the minority of the relations: on left–right between Romania and the rest of the countries (with the exception of Slovenia) and between Slovenia and Bulgaria and Slovenia and Latvia. On the EU issue between Estonia and the Czech

Republic, on the one hand, and Lithuania, Poland, Slovakia, Bulgaria and Slovenia, on the other.

6 The question reads: 'Some say European unification has already gone too far. Others say it should be strengthened. What is your opinion? Please indicate your views using a 10-point scale. On this scale, "0" means unification "has already gone too far" and "10" means "should be strengthened". What number on this scale describes your position?' Both issues/questions – the left–right self-positioning and the attitudes concerning EU, utilise the elite and mass surveys of the INTUNE project.

References

Achen, Ch. (1978), 'Measuring representation', *American Journal of Political Science* 22, pp. 475–510.

Barnes, S. (1977), *Representation in Italy: Institutional Tradition and Electoral Choice* (Chicago: University of Chicago Press).

Bartels, L. (1991), 'Constituency opinion and congressional policy making: the Reagan defense buildup', *American Political Science Review* 85, pp. 457–74.

Brooks, J. E. (1985), 'Democratic frustration in the Anglo-American polities: a quantification of inconsistency between mass public opinion and public policy', *Western Political Quarterly* 38, pp. 250–61.

Brooks, J. E. (1990), 'The opinion–policy nexus in Germany', *Public Opinion Quarterly* 54, pp. 508–29.

Converse, Ph. and R. Pierce (1986), *Political Representation in France* (Cambridge: The Belknap Press of Harvard University Press).

Dalton, R. (1985), 'Political parties and political representation: party supporters and party elites in nine nations', *Comparative Political Studies* 18, pp. 267–99.

Enyedi, Z. (2006), 'Party politics in post-communist transition', in W. Crotty and R. Katz (eds), *Handbook of Political Parties* (London: Sage), pp. 228–38.

Enyedi, Z. and P. G. Lewis (2006), 'The Impact of the European Union on party politics in Central and Eastern Europe', in P. G. Lewis and Z. Mansfeldová (eds), *The European Union and Party Politics in East Central Europe* (Houndmills: Palgrave Macmillan), pp. 247–68.

Esaiasson, P. and S. Holmberg (1996), *Representation from Above. Members of Parliament and Representative Democracy in Sweden* (Aldershot: Dartmouth).

Harmel, R. and K. Janda (1982), *Parties and Their Environments: Limits to Reform?* (New York and London: Longman).

Hill, K. Q. and A. Hinton-Andersson (1995), 'Pathways of representation: a causal analysis of public opinion–policy linkages', *American Journal of Political Science* 39, pp. 924–35.

Holmberg, S. (1989), 'Political Representation in Sweden', *Scandinavian Political Studies* 12, pp. 1–36.

Kim, H. and R. C. Fording (2001), 'Extending party estimates to governments and electors', in I. Budge, *et al.* (eds), *Mapping Policy Preferences: Estimates for Parties, Electors, and Governments, 1945–1998* (London: Oxford University Press), pp. 157–78.

Kitschelt, H., Z. Mansfeldová, R. Markowski and G. Tóka (1999), *Post-communist Party Systems: Competition, Representation and Inter-party Cooperation* (Cambridge: Cambridge University Press).

Klingemann, H.-D., R. Hofferbert and I. Budge (1994), *Parties, Policies and Democracy* (Boulder, CO: Westview Press).

Klingemann, H.-D., A. Volkens, I. Budge, J. Bara and M. McDonald (2006), *Mapping Policy Preferences II: Parties, Electorates and Governments in Eastern Europe and the OECD 1990–2003* (Oxford: Oxford University Press).

Kuklinski, J. H. (1978), 'Representativeness and elections: a policy analysis', *American Political Science Review* 72, pp. 165–77.

Luttberg, N. R. (1981), *Public Opinion and Public Policy: Models of Political Linkage* (Itasca: Peacock).

Markowski, R. (1997), 'Political parties and ideological spaces in East Central Europe', *Communist and Post-communist Studies* 3, pp. 221–54.

Miller, W. and D. Stokes (1963), 'Constituency influence in Congress', *American Political Science Review* 57, pp. 45–56.

Miller, W., R. Pierce, J. Thomassen, R. Herrera, S. Holmberg, P. Esaiasson and B. Wessels (1999), *Policy Representation in Western Democracies* (Oxford: Oxford University Press).

Monroe, A. (1979), 'Consistency between constituency preferences and national policy decisions', *American Politics Quarterly* 12, pp. 3–19.

Nye, J. S., Ph. Zelikow and D. C. King (eds) (1997), *Why People Don't Trust Government?* (Cambridge, MA: Harvard University Press).

Page, B. I. and R. Y. Shapiro (1983), 'Effects of public opinion on policy', *American Political Science Review* 77, pp. 175–90.

Petry, F. (1999), 'The opinion–policy relationship in Canada', *The Journal of Politics* 61, pp. 540–50.

Pharr, S. and R. Putnam (eds) (2000), *Disaffected Democracies: What's Troubling the Trilateral Democracies?* (Princeton, NJ: Princeton University Press).

Pitkin, H. (1967), *The Concept of Representation* (Berkeley, CA: University of California Press).

Powell, G. B. (1989), 'Constitutional design and citizen electoral control', *Journal of Theoretical Politics* 1, pp. 107–30.

Rosenstone, S. J. and J. M. Hansen (1993), *Mobilization, Participation, and Democracy in America* (New York: Macmillan Publishing Company).

Sartori, G. (1968), 'Political development and political engineering', in J. D. Montgomery and A. O. Hirschman (eds), *Public Policy, Vol. 17* (Cambridge, MA: Cambridge University Press), pp. 261–98.

Strom, K. (1984), 'Minority governments in parliamentary democracies', *Comparative Political Studies* 17, 199–227.

Thomassen, J. (1994), 'Empirical research into political representation: failing democracy or failing models?', in M. Kent Jennings and T. E. Mann (eds), *Elections at Home and Abroad: Essays in Honor of Warren E. Miller* (Ann Arbor, MI: University of Michigan Press).

9

(Shallow) Europeanisation and party system instability in post-communist states: how changing constraints undermine the development of stable partisan linkages

Robert Ladrech

The European Union (EU) has had a profound effect upon the democratising countries of post-communist Central and Eastern Europe (CEE). Indeed, the specific direction of their political-economic development as well as social welfare provision – both emphasising market mechanisms – has been inextricably tied to the decision to join the EU, and subsequent efforts to 'download' the EU's *acquis communautaire* have imparted a liberal conception of state–society relations. In the realm of politics in particular, the EU has also had a significant effect, primarily through the terms of its political conditionality. In the end, the overwhelming desire by most political elites in post-communist countries to gain membership in the EU, as soon as possible, acted as a form of self-discipline for these governments to meet the conditions the EU set for membership. In the process, minority rights were protected and strengthened, elections were monitored for their fairness, and in some cases, such as that of Slovakia at the end of the 1990s, the EU may have been a critical factor in preventing a return to authoritarian government.

More specifically, in the case of political parties, the *indirect* influence of the EU can be ascertained in various domains, for example in national party finance legislation designed to counter potential corruption; in campaign technique and party organisational development through relations with respective transnational party federations; and in the pattern of party system competition that emerged, due to the marked support for Eurosceptic parties, a phenomenon especially notable from the late 1990s onward. In general, mostly positive attributes have been associated with the influence of the EU on the political development of post-communist countries, especially those that chose to apply for eventual EU membership. On the other hand, closer scrutiny of political dynamics in these countries reveals a slightly more complex and perhaps mixed picture; that is, after nearly twenty years since the process of democratisation began, there are certain indicators that point to continuing instability, especially in regard to the degree of party system institutionalisation (PSI), suggesting that these party systems have not (yet) acquired the full characteristics of Western European party systems. The main question this chapter confronts is whether the EU can be implicated in this partial failure of the party systems to reach levels of stability that approximate those in Western Europe.

This chapter argues that the EU has been a contributing factor in the inability of CEE party systems in general to acquire the attributes of an institutionalised party system. However, it will be proposed that the EU effect upon CEE party systems has not been static, that it has changed over time, and that it is based on the perception by CEE party elites of the effectiveness of EU-induced constraints on their behaviour. This analysis therefore fits into the emerging-party Europeanisation literature (see Ladrech 2009 for an overview) as well as the literature on party system development in post-communist political systems (e.g. Lewis 2006; Haughton, 2009). On the one hand, the party Europeanisation approach is concerned with determining whether the EU can be isolated as a causal factor in domestic change. On the other hand, party system analysis tries to explain why, after nearly twenty years since the end of the previous regime, CEE party systems continue to exhibit relatively high levels of electoral volatility and party fragmentation. This chapter attempts to bridge these two different approaches by presenting an external or international factor into post-communist party system analysis as well as to add to the present body of Europeanisation studies in the area of party change.

The thesis advanced in this chapter is as follows: the party elites of most of the main parties of government that emerged by the mid-1990s signalled their strong desire to join the EU as soon as possible. This goal was shared by the party leaderships of both the (putative) centre-left and centre-right, and produced an almost immediate consequence: the displacement of socio-economic partisan conflict or cleavage between them by political-cultural issues. In other words, by collaborating on the main outlines of their emerging socio-economic systems in the process of adapting to the EU's *acquis communautaire*, which had the effect of significantly influencing relations between state and economy – in particular the emphasis on competitiveness and a de-emphasis on state aid – the main parties of government removed this dimension of policy as an area of competition, thereby allowing parties to their far left or far right as well as political entrepreneurs, i.e. new parties, to exploit this lacuna in left–right political competition.

However, this seemingly self-imposed conformity lessened, the more confident party leaderships became that the goal of membership was a certainty – after the announcement in 2000 of those countries with which the European Commission would begin official accession negotiations, and after membership itself, i.e. post-2004. The effect of weakening conformity on the socio-economic policy dimension was to allow party leaderships to repackage their parties' electoral appeal, including the introduction of a more nationalist discourse. This process of changing party policy profiles over the period of the mid-1990s to the present has had the result, it is argued, of preventing the development of stable linkages between voters and these parties, and thereby explaining a portion of the continuing low levels of party system institutionalisation in CEE countries. In terms of party Europeanisation findings, this chapter contributes further evidence of the differential outcomes of the Europeanisation process, in this case between the older party systems in Western Europe and those of the post-communist member states.

Theoretical and contextual background

The literature that has developed concerning party system institutionalisation in Third Wave democracies, with much of the initial assumptions developed by Mainwaring and others (*inter alia*, Mainwaring and Torcal, 2006), does not incorporate external, that is, international, variables into their research questions. Although international actors do of course play a role in issues related to political stability in areas such as Latin America – one can easily bring to mind the IMF, the USA, and programmes such as the North American Free Trade Association – none of these external actors approaches the fundamental influence of the EU in the political developments that have unfolded since the transition phase in post-communist East and Central Europe. To be specific, I am not recalling the efforts of external actors in the transition to democracy per se; rather, the extent to which they contribute to the stabilisation of the party system according to the criteria put forward by Mainwaring *et al*. There is a clear case to be made, and it has been articulated by a number of commentators, that the EU's political conditionality played a critical role – the degree to which is debatable – in the stabilisation of democratic practice.

The question this chapter focuses upon is, then, more precise: has the EU been a factor in the persistence of low levels of party system institutionalisation in post-communist states, both pre- and post-accession? This chapter argues in the affirmative, and explains the contribution made by the EU to this 'condition' by focusing on a hypothesised incongruence between policy preferences pursued by party elites and those of voters. The components of the argument are: *first*, the decision to obtain EU membership as soon as possible, by most parties, and especially by nominally centre-left and centre-right parties, locked in a policy direction in terms of socio-economic choices that had direct consequences for party competition; *second*, the nature of party competition by government and main challenger parties therefore emphasised political-cultural over economic choices – as the space for policy innovation was circumscribed by EU *acquis communautaire* – but economic choices in Eurosceptical tones by 'extreme parties' were also on offer; *third*, EU political conditionality further exerted policy conformity on governmental parties; *fourth*, opportunities for new party formation were generated by the policy space left 'vacant' by the main parties; *fifth*, the constraints on major parties on socio-economic issues begin to decrease, the closer to accession; and finally, *sixth*, the preceding points are predicated on party-elite manipulation of party policy positions.

The result of this evolving state of affairs was to prevent rapid voter loyalty/partisan identification because major parties continued to 'sample' policies as conditions altered; that is, as EU constraints lessened, these parties produced new policy profiles in order to capture a larger portion of the electoral market. As Tavits (2008a: 67) suggests, '[g]iven this continuous adaptation by elites and voters, it is not surprising that instability in this region has been sustained for more than 15 years'. The contention of this paper is that strategic elite behaviour was at least partly influenced by the desire to join the EU, and as political conditionality (i.e. constraints) decreased the closer accession neared, and especially in the post-accession period, party-elite behaviour reverted to more unhindered office-seeking strategies. The paper elaborates these points in more detail.

The transition from communist one-party, command economies to systems characterised fundamentally by a market economy and political pluralism has no immediate antecedent. The literature specifically dealing with the establishment and consolidation of democratic political systems outside of Europe acknowledges the sometime critical support of international actors, especially in the consolidation phase of a fragile political system. Within a European context, as for instance in the cases of Spain and Portugal, the desire by certain elites to ensure stability of their post-authoritarian regimes involved European Community (EC) and NATO membership (EC membership, in particular, for reasons of economic and structural modernisation). But a fundamental difference between the Spanish and Portuguese cases and those of post-communist countries is the former's possession of a market economy (no matter the degree of isolation from the wider international capitalist system) and ideological positioning of new and reformed parties that allowed relatively rapid voter alignment with these parties. In the case of parties emerging in post-communist systems, transition and consolidation involved both a shift toward market mechanisms (with all of the implications deriving from the methods pursued, e.g. so-called 'shock therapy') and initial voter alignments based on the position of parties relative to the previous regime, i.e. anti-communist opponents etc., not left–right ideological polarisation or social cleavage representation.

It is this context that made the decision to attempt EU membership as soon as possible so fateful. At the time of official pronouncements by these governments that joining the EU was a fundamental, national-interest goal, the parties and party systems were characterised by weak cleavage structures with which to support party systems (Mair, 1997); weak programmatic identities (Kitschelt, 1995); parliamentary elite-dominated party organisation; and electoral volatility between elections, together with parties appearing and disappearing after only one or two elections. This set of characteristics describes the condition of parties and party systems during the first decade of postcommunist competitive party systems, but what explains the persistence of electoral volatility (see Webb and White (2007) for additional indicators)?

The expectation of party system institutionalisation is that there ought to have appeared a trend towards stability in terms of more predictable behaviour of voters toward parties, and this has not occurred widely enough to be taken as a rule. Electoral rather than partisan mobilisation characterised early mobilisation, with the price paid being weak linkages between party and voters (van Biezen, 2003). Although Kitschelt *et al.* (1999) found evidence of programmatic crystallisation, i.e. social protectionist vs market liberalisation, the parameters within which these two mainstream components of the party system actually differed, once commitment to EU membership became the norm for both, was minimised (though not neutralised).[1] Attachment to EU membership by all major parties further lessened macroeconomic distinctions, thereby putting a premium on other factors, including leadership qualities of party elites and factors pertinent to individual country cases. Another effect, also slowing PSI, may be the less-efficient representation of social cleavages, a prime function of parties as they developed in Western European party systems. McAllister and White (2007) suggest that although much progress has been made, there remains a notable difference between voters' positions on the left–right scale within parties in emerging democracies, as compared to those in established ones.

It has been asserted that one result of the Europeanisation of West European party systems is a reduction in competition – a narrowing of competitive space – in the realm of economic policies, as the room for manoeuvre by member state governments is circumscribed by membership in the eurozone – with the consequent inability to manipulate interest rates, limits on budget deficits and less-overt interventionist policies, due to constraints on state aid, etc. Ladrech (2002) and Mair (2006) have argued that the narrow policy space has a consequent indirect effect on parties' positions in competitive elections, with Mair (2007) also suggesting that the effect leads to a 'de-politicisation' over time. The contrast with post-communist experiences is stark. The intensity or impact of accommodating the *acquis communautaire* for already-existing liberal-democratic market economies was slight compared to that of the post-communist member states, for whom downloading of the *acquis* was a condition of membership. Additionally, in the West, prospective members could negotiate and upload preferences to the EU. This was the case, for example, from the 1986 enlargement incorporating Spain and Portugal to the 1995 enlargement that included Finland, Sweden and Austria.

In the East, Commission monitoring and accession conditionality – which were *not* part of the older states' experience – ensured an adaptation 'from above'. Deeply embedded domestic structures in the West could resist or shape EU directives, whilst Eastern counterparts, still weakly structured, were less resistant. If domestic change related to the influence of the EU (i.e. Europeanisation) in the West was deemed to be 'accommodation' or 'adaptation', in the East 'transformation' better qualified the set of outcomes (Börzel, 2005). Thus, if the EU has had an effect at all on Western parties through an indirect process of internalising EU single-market norms and regulations at the level of government, the much more 'directed (some would call it coercive) process of rule transfer' (Börzel, 2006: 164) in post-communist countries would suggest a definite impact on parties. But in exactly what manner could the EU impact on new parties in post-communist states?

From the mid-1990s, post-communist governments in most Eastern and Central European countries made clear their intention of gaining membership in the EU. In 2000 the EU indicated which states would begin formal accession negotiations, but the handful of years prior to this date saw governments striving to position themselves to be 'acceptable' to the Commission – the political and electoral changes in Slovakia are seen by some as but one example of the influence exerted by the domestic desire to make the 'cut'. The clearly pro-EU parties, which included the major centre-right and centre-left parties in most cases, were obliged to signal their acceptance of the main thrusts of EU development to date, this being encapsulated by the *acquis communautaire*. By signalling acceptance of this blueprint for their evolving political economies, and further, forming cross-parliamentary party pacts to speed the necessary legislation through their respective national parliaments, these parties took potential socio-economic policy differences between themselves off the competitive political spectrum. The desire to join, which was largely enjoyed by these party elites and a majority of the public, temporarily deflected scrutiny of this economic policy-convergence expedience. For some, this 'de-politicisation' could have negative consequences, for example 'arresting party developments by excluding from political competition those substantive, grass-roots, ideological policy conflicts around which western European party systems have evolved' (Innes, 2002: 101–2).

One could also add that, in addition to conditionality 'locking in' the macro-economic policy direction and thus reducing the policy space between main parties, most of these parties took advantage of the assistance offered by Western-based transnational party federations to shape party policy and ideology. Affiliation with these so-called Euro-parties, such as the Party of European Socialists and the European People's Party, was seen as an extra resource to develop networks and gain advice on compatible European political behaviour (Lewis, 2005; Pridham, 2005). Spirova (2008: 805) argues that legitimacy 'derived from the EU level was so important that parties chose strategies that might not have been entirely to their benefit in terms of office-seeking ambitions, but that satisfied the will of the Europarties'. The point here is that party elites had to combine two fundamental goals, portraying their parties and, by extension, governments as appropriate potential members of the EU, *and* getting elected, that is, attracting voters. Put into principal–agent terminology, these party elites served two principals.[2] Their primary attraction to voters in the late 1990s, but wearing off in the early 2000s, was their fundamental support for the 'return to Europe' sentiment. The EU, in particular the Commission, was the other actor, requiring a demonstration of their conformity to EU norms and political behaviour in addition to policy and institutional development, through the publication of continual progress reports. Two consequences for party systems emerged from this situation, an accent on political-cultural factors in party competition and a space, small at first, for Eurosceptic parties at the extreme ends of the party system.

With major left vs right conflict over economic direction minimised once EU membership became the overarching aim, political-cultural issues came to play a perhaps larger role in party competition than might have been the case. Personality issues, attesting to the weakness of party organisational roots in society, also emerged as factors in electioneering. Historical grievances, ethnic division, relations with the previous regime etc. all combined to become issues upon which major parties were obliged to invest time and effort. With macro-economic issues displaced during the mid-to-late 1990s, the policy space was filled with alternative issues.

Secondly, parties that contested the drive for EU membership, including some old regime parties such as the Czech KSCM or right-wing nationalist parties such as the Hungarian MIÉP, were able to tap into Eurosceptic sentiment and challenge the economic policy compact between the main parties. Marks *et al.* (2006) refer to these parties according to their placement on two axes, left and right representing the economic dimension, and a political dimension portrayed as *gal* (green, alternative, libertarian) and *tan* (traditional, authoritarian, nationalist). Interestingly, the major opposition to the EU in the 1990s was from left-*tan* parties such as KSCM. These parties were able to exploit the decision not to challenge some of the basic economic-policy fundamentals of the EU, especially those aspects of liberalising economies. In this respect they represented a 'left' position but also incorporated features of the *tan* categorisation, namely 'nationalist'. Yet, at least in the early-to-mid 1990s, widespread Eurosceptic opinion was relatively low. As the decade progressed, and especially after formal accession negotiations began in 2000, Eurosceptic sentiment expanded, at least the so-called 'soft' Euroscepticism. The electoral fortune of some left-*tan* parties improved, but equally significant was the emergence of rhetoric in some mainstream parties mildly critical of the EU, such as the Czech ODS and the Polish PiS (Taggart and Szczerbiak, 2004).

Both of these factors, mainstream-party aversion to clear differences over economic policy allowing greater salience to political-cultural issues, and the ability of left-*tan* parties to challenge EU economic policy in the name of the 'losers' of the transition to market economies, created a competitive policy spectrum that ill-served those voters politically pro-EU but wary of some aspects of EU-mandated economic change and the resulting effects on social welfare (in the West, this is represented by a portion of the social democratic electorate and party activists). Recognising that there exist a variety of Eurosceptic positions (as witnessed not least by different classifications on offer; see Kopecký and Mudde, 2002 and special issue of *Acta Politica*, 2007) that a party system conceptualised as either a basic pro- and anti-EU may not adequately reflect, it is not difficult to recognise the policy vacuum from the mid-1990s onwards. The difference between Western and Eastern party systems in regard to Europeanisation is the much more clearly defined line of accountability between the EU's policy orientation and domestic government economic policy in post-communist countries. In the West, political parties that are generally pro-EU – which is essentially most mainstream parties – (a) have policy stances developed well before the onset of a more policy-intrusive EU (post-Single European Act, 1986), and (b) have been able to maintain policy autonomy in their public profile through the marginalising of the EU in daily political life. The opposite is true for most post-communist parties, and therefore the impact of the EU can be more directly linked to policy change among parties.

This brings the argument to its next stage, that is, new party formation. In an environment in which the 'pull' of EU membership created policy vacuums for voter preferences, this impacts on strategic entry calculations by new parties. Many parties that entered, and then disappeared one or two elections later, may have been able to enter in the first place because of where they positioned themselves vis-à-vis existing parties and the manner in which they were able to manipulate or politicise an issue (Tavits, 2008a). More specifically for the present argument, it is assumed that, beginning in the late 1990s and continuing up to at least accession in 2004, a defining aspect of the policy profile of some challenger parties may be to position themselves where the hypothesised policy vacuum exists, that is, between general support for EU membership and critical stances vis-à-vis economic-policy issues – what Marks *et al.* might label left-*gal*. Vachudova (2008: 862) underlines this indirectly by stating that, based on the 'content of the requirements for EU membership, we know that the EU expects parties in the East to take positions that tend toward the *right* and toward *gal*'. However, parties to the right of the right-*gal*, that is, parties for whom EU membership stimulates a nationalist backlash and that are not linked with the former regime, what Marks *et al.* could label right-*tan*, also position themselves for stealing voters from the main centre-right parties. Both of these dimensions of party competition are small areas, but nevertheless, if voter volatility and the number of parties are indicators of PSI, then they should not be dismissed. Their brief life span, again underlining the PSI nature of the argument, is explained in the final stage of this chapter's argument.

To recap the argument so far: from the mid-1990s onwards, most 'mainstream' parties in post-communist states signalled their intention to become members of the EU as soon as possible. Most of these parties had political credentials based on their role in the transition from the old regime. In addition, most had also supported a transition to a market economy, although in the early 1990s the routes to this goal varied among the new governments. Once these party/coalition governments made their EU decision, the outline of their macro-economic policy direction became EU-directed, thereby removing from party competition the space for differences over the type or mix of economic and related policies. This indirect effect of the EU, self-induced, is the factor that this chapter argues contributed to the shape of party systems from the mid-1990s up to accession in 2004, for it allowed anti-EU parties, small at first, to exploit the reticence of major parties to take more nationalist or 'soft' left stances in pre-accession negotiations. It also made the party system environment more conducive for new parties to position themselves in such policy proximity to these major parties so as to 'steal voters'.

The next stage of the argument is as follows: the constraint on pro-EU parties on economic policy differentiation and on 'soft' nationalist positions begins to ebb or decrease after formal negotiations open in 2000 and accelerate after accession in 2004. The decrease in perceived constraints is by no means an indication that *all* parties begin to adapt their ideological profiles to the altered environment, simply that the *conditions* are such that party leaderships may take advantage to pursue more unhindered vote-maximising strategies.

A basic premise of this argument is that pro-EU party elites had as a major goal for their country the successful and speedy entry into EU membership. Once this became a possibility – mid-1990s to 2000 – party/government leaderships strenuously portrayed themselves to the EU, politically and in economic policy terms, as compatible with EU norms and policy orientations. In domestic party competition, sometimes major parties promoted themselves as better able to steer their country toward EU membership. This is a rationalist, if not rational institutionalist perspective, and fits in with the thrust of Europeanisation studies of post-communist states (Sedelmeier, 2006). Ágh (2003) refers to this as 'anticipatory Europeanization'. Once certain countries made the initial 'cut' (all but Bulgaria and Romania), the critical EU-related question was now *when* membership would be achieved rather than *if*, and this state of affairs represents the initial decrease in externally generated constraints, although this is a domestic-leadership perception rather than an easing of conditionality or surveillance on the transposition of the *acquis communautaire* by the European Commission. This explanation, of a reaction or interpretation by party leaderships of an altered environment, also fits into the Europeanisation research paradigm, though here a constructivist approach is invoked to explain how party leaders may weigh the costs and benefits to themselves in a competitive situation.

After accession in 2004, a further reduction in perceived constraints could be expected to lead to (a) new coalition possibilities and (b) nuanced shifts in pro-EU positions. Empirical evidence seems to support, in the realm of party politics, the hypothesis of a 'shallow Europeanisation'. As Goetz (2005: 262) suggests, rationalist arguments suggesting a 'pattern of wide-ranging, but relatively shallow, effects are underscored by more constructivist understandings of Europeanization, which stress the importance of learning and socialization and note that institutions are not just constructed around interests, but norms and values'. The top-down nature of EU political conditionality and the underdevelopment of societal agents pushing for integration 'did not leave much room for socialization through processes of social learning and policy emulation. Moreover, it undermined the overall legitimacy of Europeanization since the candidate countries had no say in the creation of the rules that they were expected to adopt and the EU required them to comply with rules that did not apply to the old member states. . . . With sociological mechanisms being largely absent, we should not be too surprised to find "shallow Europeanization" . . .' (Börzel, 2006: 166). The result of less time and 'outsider' status in relation to EU actors and institutions meant that with 'shallow institutionalization, fluidity and uncertainty . . . strategic interest-based "rational" behaviour by domestic actors is more likely . . .' (262).

Applied to the strategic calculations of party leaders in government or aspiring to government, placating and convincing the EU of their suitability or readiness in the latter half of the 1990s demanded conformity; achievement of formal accession in 2004 removes or greatly decreases the constraint over behaviour, and it could be expected that options which could not be pursued before, for example in terms of acceptable coalition partners or more soft Eurosceptic rhetoric to target more voters, would increase as each individual party system demanded. The Europeanisation argument thus retains the understanding of a differential response to the end of the self-perceived constraint on political strategic considerations, and helps therefore to explain the lack of a convergence among parties. This argument corresponds in general with that of Vachudova (2008), who argues that a weakening of conditionality witnesses ideological repositioning of certain types of parties. The argument presented here consequently adds to an actor-centred analysis of these changes, with some pre-suppositions regarding party leadership behaviour.

The argument above is based on an understanding of the internal organisation of most post-communist parties, especially those created after the end of the previous regime, where party leaderships are mostly unhindered by the membership (the party on the ground), extra-parliamentary party officials (the party in central office) or by affiliated organisations. Of course the reason for this dominance is the underdevelopment of all three areas of party life. In other words, the dominant segment of parties, the party in public office (van Biezen, 2003; Mair, 1997), is relatively autonomous in setting out changes, whether in government or opposition, that reflect perceived opportunities for electoral mobilisation. This relative autonomy facilitates changes in rhetoric, tactical moves regarding coalition partners, or expressed policy positions. The opportunity to exercise this degree of manoeuvrability expands as the external EU-generated constraints weaken. The unintended consequence is an arrest or slower development of stable partisan identification, a key factor in party system institutionalisation.

Another consequence of more unhindered major party ideological (re)positioning would be the increased capacity to politicise issues whose salience had been beneficial to minor parties; the logic of this should be a further step toward the future stabilisation of the party system. Hanley *et al.* (2008, 429), in an analysis of comparative centre-right party success in post-communist CEE, also point to the significance of parties being able to repackage their appeal, noting in particular that with new party elites in place, 'the subsequent ability of such elites to (re)fashion broad integrative ideological narratives relating post-communist transformation to earlier conservative, nationalist and anti-communist traditions' appears to have explanatory power over macro-institutional and historical-structural explanations. We argue here, observing the timing of the successful 're-fashioning' of

Fidesz in Hungary and ODS in the Czech Republic in the Hanley *et al.* sample, that the EU factor plays a role in the ability to formulate and express certain positions that during the period *before* 2000 may have raised concern in Brussels, threatening the formal opening of accession negotiations (witness the coalition government led by the Slovak Smer in 2006, which registered less overt concern than the actions of the earlier Mečiar government in the late 1990s or even the Austrian ÖVP-FPÖ coalition in 2000). Indeed, incorporating the EU as an intervening factor in the analysis of PSI contributes to the research agenda, suggesting that 'if elites dominate party system stabilisation, we need to understand their incentive structures' (Tavits, 2008b: 549).

Finally, it is possible to illustrate the same phenomenon with post-communist parties other than the set of countries in CEE that have been the focus of this study, i.e. those that eventually joined in 2004 and 2007. The case of Croatia demonstrates, albeit with modified conditions specifically relevant to its democratisation process – war and nationalist government until 2000 – the principle of instrumental party elite behaviour in relation to perceived constraints transmitted by EU conditionality. Croatia officially applied to join the EU in 2003, and practically speaking, is already accepted as the first country to be added to the EU after the Lisbon Treaty situation is finally resolved (remaining issues surround a border dispute with Slovenia and the broader Balkan affliction of corruption). The main difference between Croatia and the CEE countries as candidates is the lower degree of the power asymmetry between it and the EU (on the issue of power asymmetry between the EU and former Yugoslav states, apart from Slovenia, see Ladrech, 2008). That is, to be blunt, the EU has signalled the critical importance of Croatia (and for that matter Serbia) eventually becoming members because of urgent security reasons, i.e. the possibility of new Balkan war(s) and potential EU involvement.

This fact represents a fundamental difference between the EU and the CEE countries in the 1990s, where although security concerns were also expressed at the time, it was a more abstract possibility (the conflict in the former Yugoslavia in the 1990s and subsequent EU involvement definitely alter the relationship). Political elites in Croatia are aware of the EU security perspective, and although there is the same set of political conditionality and chapters of the *acquis communautaire* to successfully engage, and added pressure due to the requirement to capture and turn over alleged war criminals to the International Criminal Tribunal, party discourse has followed a pattern where diluted constraints allow more pronounced EU-wariness on the part of the two major parties, depending on government–opposition positions. That is, the party in government promotes itself as the best-placed party to guide Croatia into successful and rapid membership, yet when in opposition accuses the incumbent party of giving away too much of Croatian sovereignty to the EU in negotiations. This dynamic characterises both major parties, the Social Democrats and HDZ.

How does this reflect on the phenomenon described above with CEE countries? In the first place, the perception that EU membership is not in doubt, only the timing of entry, allows party elites to more closely correspond to voters' positions, including sovereignty issues bound up with EU membership (that is, a soft Eurosceptic position). Employing once more the principal–agent construct, Croatian party leaders, having signalled their intent to join the EU as soon as possible, find themselves steering their government toward completion of the various chapters of the *acquis communautaire*, that is, meeting European Commission requirements.

At the same time, though, they must 'temper' their enthusiasm for EU membership by the recognition that the Croatian public, *from the beginning of Croatia's application to join the EU*, whilst supportive of EU membership and aware of EU conditionality, are nevertheless suspicious of certain EU demands, obliging party leaders to placate them in their pro-EU discourse. Fink-Hafner (2008: 180) summarises this phenomenon as follows:

> The party system has been institutionalized enough to be able to respond to dual pro-Europeanization pressures (voters' preferences as well as EU actors' pressures) at a satisfactory level. As voters' preferences have not been homogenous (in particular, some reservations regarding Croatia's collaboration with the ICTY have been strongly opposed in public on behalf of the anti-Hague lobby, including war veteran interest groups and for some time even part of the military leadership in some interest groups) and since some remains of ethno-politics still persist, the process of EU integration has involved a push-pull relationship parallel to the Croatian government's two-level game.

Again, under modified conditions, the Croatian example serves to illustrate how party leaderships consciously balance the need to meet EU conditions while responding to the dynamics of party competition. Unlike in CEE countries in the 1990s, the leaderships of the two main Croatian parties positioned their parties' discourse in such a way to keep the EU on board (but in a context in which they realised the EU was willing to be relatively more 'lenient' in some matters in order to keep Croatia in line to join – reflecting an EU self-interest), but also signalling from the start a critical embrace of EU membership. Party-elite incentives and power within their organisation are the similarities between the two cases of CEE and Croatia.

East–West comparison revisited

Let us return to the West–East comparison. The present argument underlines an important external environmental factor in the structuring of the policy space of post-communist party systems, i.e. the mutual embrace of the EU by certain party leaderships in the latter half of the 1990s. The analysis traces a dynamic interaction in which the weakening influence of the EU allows more strategic options to become available to parties and, dominated as they are by their party-in-public office, changes can be attempted without significant resistance by party members or affiliated organisations (both of which are comparatively weak). The argument of a hollowing out of the Western European state, and a corresponding reduction in policy differences among major centre-left and centre-right parties, due to the migration of certain policy competence to the EU level, would seem to follow a slightly opposite dynamic.

As stated above, the development of stable patterns in Western party systems preceded the EU, and certainly well before the EU expanded its policy competence from the mid-1980s onwards. As Webb (2002) makes clear, the rise in indicators of greater electoral volatility and number of effective parties has been low but persistent, and has appeared since the 1970s. One reason for the persistence, however, of the main contours of Western European party systems is the still-effective influence of socio-structural factors such as cleavages. Here we have a difference with Eastern, post-communist parties, for whom party elites may have more sway in attempting to re-orient party strategies and ideological profiles than their Western counterparts. Secondly, the general parameters of Western parties' policy positions also preceded the expansion of EU influence in the domestic policy realm, although there is evidence of an ideological policy-driven shift, beginning in the 1980s, that cannot be traced solely to the EU, but which EU developments in the late 1980s and 1990s may have consolidated.

This is the globalisation argument, in which the liberalisation of global financial markets, a widespread emphasis on budgetary discipline, corresponding policies of deregulation and privatisation, explain a rightward shift in social democratic and Christian democratic parties. The EU, seen as a regional response to global changes, exerts a rule-bound adaptation to this perceived state of affairs. Therefore the EU is not necessarily seen as the instigator or inculcator of neo-liberal approaches to political economy, but served as a vehicle to their practice by both centre-left and centre-right parties. The challenge of Europeanisation research is precisely to isolate the EU factor in change. In the context of this chapter's discussion, the question is whether these large but gradual changes in the political-economic environment 'trickle down' to the arena of party competition. One could say that if both centre-left and centre-right parties shift somewhat to the right, space is opened up for opportunistic parties on the margins (in particular to the left of social democratic parties). It is precisely parties of the far left and far right that since the mid-1990s have become established components of many

Western European party systems – entering parliaments in the 1980s and 1990s – which both contest the apparent condominium between the main parties of the centre-left and centre-right in major economic policy matters (what the French label '*la pensée unique*').

Although analysts do not go so far as to say these parties' success is attributable to a reaction against the EU, that is, a Eurosceptic voter backlash against mainstream parties (most of which are pro-EU), it is the case that a common Eurosceptic thread does link these parties, whether on the right, e.g. the Austrian FPÖ, or the left, e.g. the Dutch Socialist Party. The common critique of these parties is an accusation of policy conformity to the EU's general neo-liberal economic orientation. As a member of the newly formed French New Anti-Capitalist Party phrased it, 'there is no question of the Socialist Party ushering in a neo-liberal policy framework, simply that its institutionalisation will be slower than that of the UMP' (*Le Monde*, 1 September 2008). Another difference is the place of party leaderships in most mainstream Western parties. Although membership has been decreasing in most parties, and though some speak of a presidentialisation (Poguntke and Webb, 2005) of party leaders/prime ministers, it remains the case that attempts to alter party programmes are a slow and complicated process, involving not only internal rules integrating activists and the party-in-central office, but also trade-offs in terms of multi-party coalitions (Heidar and Koole, 2000 on the strength of parliamentary parties vis-à-vis other party components; for social democratic parties in particular, see Kitschelt, 1999). That change in the profile of major Western parties is difficult to execute versus those in post-communist states may also contribute to the lower levels of party system instability, and conversely, as this paper argues, the relative ease for leaderships in this endeavour has contributed toward or prevented the development of stable bonds between voters and parties in the East.

Conclusion

Most work in the area of party system institutionalisation and post-communist party systems that seeks to answer the question why institutionalisation has not proceeded as much as expected, focuses on institutional issues – electoral system design, party organisation and issues related to voters – partisanship, cleavage patterns, ideology. The argument of this chapter has paid particular attention to the actions of party leaderships, in particular how and why they have altered their individual party profiles since the mid-1990s. The argument here is that movement by parties – that is, the fact that many have been essentially 'ideological moving targets' – acts as a factor in preventing stable partisan identification. Furthermore, although it may be expected that party positioning would be initially fluid in party systems without clear prior patterns of voter–party alignments, this chapter has argued that the EU played an important role in party leaderships' calculations as to the relative positioning of party identity through the 'pull' of possible membership. The result of this was reduced competition between mainstream parties over socio-economic issues and the consequent stress on political-cultural ones.

The waning of EU conditionality, marked in two stages, official pre-accession candidacy in 2000 and accession in 2004, released party leaderships from the constraint of overt conformity to EU norms, especially in political matters. For example, in the case of Slovakian politics, the 2006 parliamentary election saw the return of conflict over socio-economic themes (Haughton and Rybář, 2008). This 'condition' may be described then as 'shallow' Europeanisation. This paper therefore adds the gradual shift of party identity, as engineered by party leaderships influenced by the goal of EU membership, as a contributing factor to party system instability. It would suggest that post-communist member states – that is, after accession – would be relatively freer in allowing domestic factors to shape their party systems and eventual institutionalisation, and at the same time raise the prospect of certain types of conflict with the European Commission over prior agreed conditions.

Notes

1 It should be noted that the research for *Post-Communist Party Systems: Competition, Representation, and Inter-Party Cooperation* took place in 1993 and 1994, and this paper focuses on party changes beginning at the end of this period.
2 This argument therefore complicates the picture presented by Lane and Ersson (2007).

References

Acta Politica (2007), special issue: Understanding Euroscepticism, 42 (July).

Ágh, A. (2003), *Anticipatory and Adaptive Europeanization in Hungary* (Budapest: Hungarian Centre for Democracy Studies).

Börzel, T. (2005), 'Europeanization: how the European Union interacts with its member states', in Bulmer and Lequesne (eds), *The Member States of the European Union*, pp. 45–69.

Börzel, T. (2006), 'Deep impact? Europeanisation meets Eastern enlargement', in A. Ágh and A. Ferencz (eds), *Deepening and Widening in an Enlarged Europe: The Impact of the Eastern Enlargement* (Budapest: 'Together for Europe' Research Centre of the Hungarian Academy of Sciences), pp. 161–72.

Bulmer, S. and C. Lequesne (eds) (2005), *The Member States of the European Union* (Oxford: Oxford University Press).

Fink-Hafner, D. (2008), 'Europeanization and party system mechanics: comparing Croatia, Serbia and Montenegro', *Journal of Southern Europe and the Balkans*, 10, pp. 167–82.

Goetz, K. H. (2005), 'The new member states and the EU: responding to Europe', in Bulmer and Lequesne (eds), *The Member States of the European Union*, pp. 254–84.

Hanley, S., A. Szczerbiak, T. Haughton and B. Fowler (2008), 'Sticking together: explaining comparative centre-right party success in post-communist Central and Eastern Europe', *Party Politics* 14, pp. 407–34.

Haughton, T. (2009), 'Driver, conductor or fellow passenger? EU membership and party politics in Central and Eastern Europe', *Journal of Communist Studies and Transition Politics* 25, pp. 413–26.

Haughton, T. and M. Rybář (2008), 'A change of direction: the 2006 parliamentary elections and party politics in Slovakia', *Journal of Communist Studies and Transition Politics* 24, pp. 232–55.

Heidar, K. and R. Koole (eds) (2000), *Parliamentary Party Groups in European Democracies: Political Parties Behind Closed Doors* (London: Routledge).

Innes, A. (2002), 'Party competition in post-communist Europe', *Comparative Politics* 35, pp. 85–104.

Kitschelt, H. (1995), 'Formation of party cleavages in post-communist democracies', *Party Politics* 1, pp. 447–72.

Kitschelt, H. (1999), 'European social democracy between political economy and electoral competition', in H. Kitschelt *et al.* (eds), *Continuity and Change in Contemporary Capitalism* (Cambridge: Cambridge University Press), pp. 317–45.

Kitschelt, H., Z. Mansfeldová, R. Markowski and G. Tóka (1999), *Post-Communist Party Systems: Competition, Representation, and Inter-Party Cooperation* (Cambridge: Cambridge University Press).

Kopecký, P. and Mudde, C. (2002), 'The two sides of Euroscepticism: party positions on European integration in East Central Europe', *European Union Politics* 3, pp. 297–326.

Ladrech, R. (2002), 'Europeanization and political parties: towards a framework for analysis', *Party Politics* 8, pp. 389–403.

Ladrech, R. (2008), 'Europeanization and the variable influence of the EU: national parties and party systems in Western and Eastern Europe', *Journal of Southern Europe and the Balkans* 10, pp. 139–50.

Ladrech, R. (2009), 'Europeanization and political parties', *Living Reviews in European Governance* 4, available at www.livingreview.org/lreg-2009-1.

Lane, J.-E. and S. Ersson (2007), 'Party system instability in Europe: persistent differences in volatility between the west and east', *Democratization* 14, pp. 92–110.

Lewis, P. G. (2005), 'EU enlargement and party systems in Central Europe', *Journal of Communist Studies and Transition Politics* 21, pp. 171–99.

Lewis, P. G. (2006), 'Party systems in post-communist Central Europe: patterns of stability and consolidation', *Democratization* 13, pp. 562–83.

Mainwaring, S. and M. Torcal (2006), 'Party system institutionalization and party system theory after the third wave of democratization', in R. Katz and W. Crotty (eds), *Handbook of Party Politics* (London: Sage), pp. 204–27.

Mair, P. (1997), *Party System Change: Approaches and Interpretations* (Oxford: Oxford University Press).

Mair, P. (2006), 'Political parties and party systems', in P. Graziano and M. P. Vink (eds), *Europeanization: New Research Agendas* (Basingstoke: Palgrave Macmillan), pp. 154–66.

Mair, P. (2007), 'Political opposition and the European Union', *Government and Opposition* 42, pp. 1–17.

Marks, G., L. Hooghe, M. Nelson, and E. Edwards (2006), 'Party competition and European integration in the East and West: different structure, same causality', *Comparative Political Studies* 39, pp. 155–75.

McAllister, I. and S. White (2007), 'Political parties and democratic consolidation in post-communist societies', *Party Politics* 13, pp. 197–216.

Poguntke, T. and P. Webb (2005), *The Presidentialization of Politics: A Comparative Study of Modern Democracies* (Oxford: Oxford University Press).

Pridham, G. (2005), *Designing Democracy: EU Enlargement and Regime Change in Post-Communist Europe* (Basingstoke: Palgrave).

Sedelmeier, U. (2006), 'Europeanisation in new member and candidate states', *Living Reviews in European Governance* 1, available at www.livingreviews.ord/lreg-2006-3.

Spirova, M. (2008), 'Europarties and party development in EU-candidate states: the case of Bulgaria', *Europe-Asia Studies* 60, pp. 791–808.

Taggart, P. and A. Szczerbiak (2004), 'Contemporary Euroscepticism in the systems of the European Union candidate states of Central and Eastern Europe', *European Journal of Political Research* 43, pp. 1–27.

Tavits, M. (2008a), 'Policy positions, issue importance, and party competition in new democracies', *Comparative Political Studies* 41, pp. 48–72.

Tavits, M. (2008b), 'On the linkage between electoral volatility and party system instability in central and eastern Europe', *European Journal of Political Research* 47, pp. 537–55.

Vachudova, M. (2008), 'Tempered by the EU? Political parties and party systems before and after accession', *Journal of European Public Policy* 15, pp. 861–79.

van Beizen, I. (2003), *Political Parties in New Democracies: Party Organization in Southern and East-Central Europe* (Basingstoke: Palgrave Macmillan).

Webb, P. (2002), 'Conclusion: political parties and democratic control in advanced industrial societies', in P. Webb, D. M. Farrell and I. Holliday (eds), *Political Parties in Advanced Industrial Democracies* (Oxford: Oxford University Press), pp. 438–60.

Webb, P. and S. White (2007), 'Political parties in new democracies: trajectories of development and implications for democracy', in P. Webb and S. White (eds), *Party Politics in New Democracies* (Oxford: Oxford University Press), pp. 345–70.

10

Conclusion

Radoslaw Markowski

Work on this book began with the intention of contributing to the understanding of the complicated relations between, on the one hand, the significant process of macro-change that was the accession to the European Union (EU) by a number of Central and East European (CEE) states and, on the other, certain domestic political phenomena within these countries, i.e. the transformation of their political system, specifically in relation to the party system. We were aware of the challenge that lay before us: the large amount of existing work on the subject made clear to us the fact that not only does the process of Europeanisation remain particularly vague but also various manifestations of the ongoing changes are extremely difficult to attribute unambiguously to the influence of the EU or the accession conditions set by it.

For this reason, as spelled out in the Introduction, we set out in this book to explore a range of comparative perspectives on CEE party politics to see exactly what has been achieved after twenty or so years of post-communist development and to establish the similarities and differences that do seem to have emerged between the new and old democracies of Western Europe. Most of these older democracies are, of course, also established members of the EU. The task was understood to be that much more feasible at this juncture by virtue of the wide range of empirical material currently available, the extent of the comparative research that has been conducted in the area of European politics in recent years, and the selection of new data sets that can now be used. All the chapters in the book are therefore comparative in nature, and most base their analysis on new empirical data and a wide variety of new sources. Having established the parameters of CEE party politics in a number of key comparative areas we are now in a better situation to consider whether the differences between East and Western Europe, the new and old democracies of the region, can indeed be attributed to EU influences in one way or another.

This concluding chapter is divided into two parts. In the first, a general overview of the broad approach is discussed, and some of the more debatable findings are commented upon. An effort is made to locate the topic of this volume in the broader Europeanisation landscape, its sequential stages and characteristic features. Comments on some of the more problematic results as well as an attempt to frame them in a slightly different light and from a different angle than the usual one are offered. The second part concentrates on the detailed conclusions presented by particular authors.

General conclusions

The introductory chapter presented a very broad overview of the literature on the topic. 'Europeanisation' is nevertheless such a complex and dynamic phenomenon that new empirical data, new findings and the outcomes of new analyses sometimes – *post factum* – suggest that they should be looked at from yet another perspective. This is, in my view, the case with this volume, and I think it is worth looking at the results obtained from yet another perspective delineating the 'Europeanisation' process. Two authors (Olsen, 2002, 2007; Radaelli, 2003) clearly depict the various facets of Europeanisation.

Olsen (2002: 923–6) enumerates five general phenomena encompassed by the term of Europeanisation: (a) changes in the external boundaries of Europe, especially of the EU, mainly through the process of enlargement ('Europe' as a geographical entity); (b) institution building and the development of common norms at the European level, especially, but not only, in the EU ('Europe' as a distinct system of governance); (c) domestic impacts of European-level institutions and norms, and thus the penetration of national systems of governance, feeding into the literature on multi-level governance (adaptation of national systems of governance to EU institutions and norms); (d) the export of certain forms of political organisation to political systems outside Europe; (e) a project of political unification, whereby Europe should be a strong and unified political entity (a normative approach). The process is expressed somewhat differently by Radaelli (2003: 30), who postulates that: 'Europeanization consists of processes of (a) construction (b) diffusion and (c) institutionalization of formal and informal rules, procedures, policy paradigms, styles, "ways of doing things" and shared beliefs and norms which are first defined and consolidated in the EU policy process and then incorporated in the logic of domestic discourse, political structures and public choices.'

Most reliable analyses of the phenomenon summarise their endeavour in a similar way to Olsen in his recent work: 'In spite of a considerable number of empirical studies, there is limited agreement on the degree to which Europeanization as the development of institutions at the European level creates Europeanization in the sense of domestic institutions [. . .] a main finding is that there has been no radical change in any of the national systems and no significant convergence towards a common institutional model which homogenizes the domestic structures of the European states' (2007: 81–2). And this conclusion applies to countries most of which had been exposed to the direct impact of EU institutions for several decades. This volume largely focuses on aspects (b) and (c) as characterised by Olsen and the processes of diffusion and institutionalisation as put forward by Radaelli.

The problem of accurate description and explanation of the impact of 'Europeanisation' becomes particularly complicated in relation to the countries of CEE, largely due to the fact that the process is *de facto* a dual one. On the one hand it is about a return to European roots and traditions which overlaps as a process, on the other hand, with the political-institutional enterprise of EU-isation, that is, the formal accession and adaptation of new members to an already-existing pan-European order. This, in turn, coincides temporarily with the liberalising, cosmopolitan and democratic opening up of these countries and with the omnipresent, but often nebulous, impact of globalisation. This complication clearly relates to our independent variable.

The chapters in this collection undoubtedly demonstrate one fact: that it is exceptionally difficult to assess this impact. To a greater or lesser extent, I concur with Peter Mair (2006), who, when differentiating between the 'direct' and 'indirect' impact on European party systems, believes that the former manifests itself by the establishment of new parties which are often unfavourably disposed to the EU, openly Eurosceptic or even anti-European. Similar processes can be seen in CEE, although their durability (excluding some countries) is doubtful (Markowski and Tucker, 2010; Deegan-Krause and Haughton, 2009). 'Indirect' impact appears to be more significant and is principally visible in the restrictions placed on the freedom of EU member states, their governments and individual parties in shaping particular sectoral policies.

No less complicated are the relations at work within what it is we are attempting to define, that is, the changes taking place in the policies, political systems and party systems of the new CEE democracies. These processes are both confused and complex, due to the fact that West European countries themselves are experiencing a period of great change in their party systems, societal-political relations and the attitude of voters to their parties. These changes are by no means trivial. Strong ties between social classes and their organisations are now a thing of the past; socio-political cleavages begin to 'melt', their encapsulating forces decline. In almost all of the countries of Western Europe voter volatility has been rising to unprecedented levels for several decades, with voters regularly changing party allegiances. Simultaneously, party membership is on the decline. We have witnessed a gradual yet systematic drop in electoral participation in elections both to national parliaments and also to the European Parliament (EP), despite the increasing political role of the latter.

The chapters in this volume – as outlined in the introductory chapter – apart from comparing between CEE countries, ask to what extent the contemporary party systems of the region are moving closer (and in a sense become more similar) to those in the western part of the continent. In doing this, we have assumed that the greater resemblance between the party systems of the two parts of Europe, the more likely it is that Europeanisation has had an impact, especially if temporal events substantiate the resemblance, i.e. if one can prove that such changes are logically linked to the major events of the last two decades. However, because of the turbulent developments within the West European party systems over the last dozen years or so, this line of reasoning is becoming doubtful. Such an assumption might well have been pertinent in the mid-1990s, when the party systems of West European democracies were characterised by stability and the hypothesis put forward by Lipset and Rokkan in the 1960s of the 'freezing of party systems and the socio-political cleavages in Europe' was still applicable. This, however, is not true in 2010. One of the factors exemplifying this is the significant rise in voter volatility, exceeding 20 per cent in some West European countries (for example, France, Italy and the Netherlands). The latter country is particularly symptomatic, where voter volatility was about 5 per cent in the 1960s, increasing to over 10 per cent in the 1970s and 1980s, rising to 20 per cent in the 1990s and reaching a level of 34 per cent in 2004.

Additionally, in Western Europe class–party relationships have become considerably weaker, and so-called 'class voting' is a marginal phenomenon nowadays. Ideological polarisation has also begun to atrophy and has thus weakened the identification of a party's electorate in this area. The number of parties and the fragmentation of the party system have begun to increase in Western Europe, thus increasing the costs of forming multi-party coalitions and, in turn, hampering the accountability of successive governments. Entrenched coalition governments (for example, the social democrats in Scandinavia or the Christian democrats in many of the corporate capitalist countries of continental Europe) no longer exist. At present, relatively frequent changes in ruling coalitions are common. Together with the process of party proliferation in coalition governments, increasingly fewer parties have never been in government (Tóka, 2006). Typologies of party systems and the mechanisms that lead to their formation also seem to be a thing of the past. So-called two-party systems have disappeared, and it is difficult even to demonstrate the existence of a classic polarised pluralism à la Sartori which blocks the alternation of power, as was the case in France and Italy, as well as Finland and Denmark.

If the above description, although necessarily simplified, is consistent with reality, then it is valid to ask ourselves the question whether we are able or not to free ourselves of the stereotypical belief in the stability of West European party systems and their constitutive features. Is it not the case that whatever the party systems of CEE are implored to emulate simply no longer exists? Perhaps a different question is now apposite. Is it not the case that in recent years the systems of Western Europe have in fact begun to resemble those in CEE, and not vice versa? To be sure, I am not claiming that there is an opposite causal relationship at work here, nor that the above description is a deliberate mark of imitation on the part of the systems of Western Europe. But that if we take the established factors describing party systems (voter volatility, fractionalisation, power alternation, the effective number of parties and level of polarisation of the system) and their variability in time, it is difficult not to pose this question. At least we can detect some convergence.

Indeed, the party systems of CEE were formed as a result of the 'transition' of the early 1990s, in a period marked by the strong decomposition of social structure, the decay of social classes, secularisation and the mediatisation of politics. This explains the difficulty in attempting to find a fixed point of reference for social interests in party politics. In all probability, the formation of political parties on the basis of strong rootedness in social groups was simply not possible in CEE. Whether this really was the case, of course, we will never be able to discover. However, there is no question that if the political parties of CEE had had the intention of building their support and future stability on the basis of social rootedness they would have had, objectively speaking, an immensely difficult task, largely due to the fact that the social structure, the position of the individual on the labour market and its consequences, as well as their chances in life and the nature of their career ambitions were constantly in a state of flux during the first post-transition decade. This made citizens very confused so far as policies related to the economy and income redistribution were concerned. In consequence, from the very onset of the transition period, in most CEE countries (with the exception of the Czech Republic) voters' political decisions and the main dimension of competition were dominated by a socio-cultural rather than an economic-redistribution domain. This phenomenon precedes the 'narrowing of economic political choices' mentioned in some of the chapters of this publication, which is supposed to be a mark of EU conditionality.

Another hypothesis concerning the impact of EU conditionality claims that in the period following the decision to join the EU, which took place in most of the countries under examination here in the mid-1990s, the accession process was characterised, on the one hand, by the standards unilaterally set by the EU which had to be met by the applicant countries and, on the other, by the readiness of these countries to meet these requirements (a position more precisely involving their respective governments and in turn the main parties, including both the centre-right and centre-left). This readiness – goes the story – on the part of the applicant countries supposedly caused the narrowing of economic political choices and the direction of attention and orientation of competition to the socio-cultural dimension. Due to the fact that these governments were engrossed in following centrist economic policies, the formation of more radical parties (which were to a greater or lesser degree Eurosceptic) became possible on both the left and the right.

I believe that many of the misunderstandings related to the role of the EU in the process of CEE party system formation stem from the above (or similar) assumptions. What is so problematic about them? Firstly and most notably, let us specify the sequence of events and their significance. In the countries of the region the most important macro-economic decisions, concerning their scope, depth and substance, decisions favouring full economic liberalisation, free market economics and the democratisation of the public sphere, were undertaken before anyone had even begun to think about EU accession. In 1989 and 1990, most of the countries of the region made the choice, under the influence and with the partnership of experts mainly from the World Bank and IMF, although also the EU, as to which path of reform their economies should take. It was then that these countries decided not to experiment with visions of a 'third way' (although some did try) but to make the most important political choices concerning economic reform from among mainstream liberal economic traditions.

This included the choices made by Balcerowicz in Poland, Klaus in the Czech Republic and their respective economist colleagues in other countries. These blueprints, ranging from Balcerowicz's monetaristic market vision to Klaus's 'kuponovka', were both systemic and path-dependent enterprises limiting the political alternatives of their competitors to a minimum. In Poland, prior to any serious preparation for EU accession, at least two governments won power whilst being openly critical of the 'Balcerowicz Plan'. What is more, these same two governments were unable to change anything of substance in the mechanisms of the 'Plan' (although they did manage to slow the reforms down a bit). Even Hungary's most significant economic reform, known as the 'Bokros Package' of early 1995 (thus relatively late on), was not created due to pressure from the EU or due to EU conditionality but was an entirely domestic Hungarian matter played out between the trio Gyula Horn, László Békesi and Lajos Bokros or, if one prefers a more institutional narrative, between the liberals of the SZDSZ, the dominant socialists of the MSZP and the Hungarian Central Bank.

If I were to risk an assessment, I would say that the lion's share of all decisions taken in the first two to three years after the collapse of the *ancien régime* were related to those issues which, several years later, were also foregrounded by the EU in its formal accession requirements for the CEE applicant countries. These decisions moulded the main political opposition groups which are still active and exist in almost the same form today. In 2005, the success of Law and Justice (PiS) and the Kaczyński brothers in Poland had little to do with the country's accession to the EU and the conditions set by the EU, but rather the Kaczyńskis' idea of a 'Fourth Republic', which was deeply rooted in – what they believed to be – the alleged malpractices of the transition, in particular the Balcerowicz reforms and their consequences (Markowski, 2006; 2008). The great change in inter-party competition in Hungary caused by the strategic decision of Viktor Orbán to move Fidesz from the liberal to the conservative camp and unite the Hungarian right-wing under one leadership also had little to do with EU conditionality but rather more with the supply and demand of the Hungarian political scene in the latter half of the 1990s, as well as Orbán's strategic intuition and skilful leadership (Enyedi, 2005). In the Czech Republic, Klaus's 'Euroscepticism' was not in any way a response to external influence either in its earlier period or during the accession period or after. The only member of the Visegrád Four in which the mechanism of conditionality had an effect was Slovakia.

Secondly, the centrism of Hungarian and Polish parties in the field of economic competition was clear to see as early as the first half of the 1990s (Markowski, 1997; Kitschelt *et al.*, 1999) and, again, had little in common with EU conditionality. In Hungary, prior to the Bokros Package, it was an indicator of the desire to implement gradual reforms and the conviction of the most important parties of the system that a reformed and quasi-free market version of Hungarian socialism could gradually transform into a fully fledged market economy without the need, as in Poland, for 'shock therapy' economics. In Poland, it was triggered by both the initial positive effects of the Balcerowicz Plan and strong competition of a symbolic socio-cultural nature in relation to issues like abortion, the public role of the Catholic church and recent Polish history. Virtually no EU effects have been recorded.

Thirdly, the hypothesis concerning the restriction of economic and political choices through the implementation of the *acquis communautaire* needs to be examined further. Although we can agree that these requirements caused a narrowing of economic choice, this only applies when considered as an absolute concept, in strategic areas and macro-economics, and – most of all – the very issue of accession itself. However, if we consider this from a relative point of view and take a look at the real debates and political conflicts related to the acceptance and implementation of the EU requirements, we can see that economic policy related to EU accession had in fact broadened and become enriched with multiple new issues and problems which were not hitherto considered. It is problematic therefore to speak of 'a narrowing' of choices; rather, we have witnessed a rich development of new, perhaps overly detailed, economic issues which CEE political parties debated with the same eloquence as they did macro-economic issues.

Fourthly, it is true that the period of accession can be described in terms of the desire of CEE states to join the EU after fulfilling certain conditions. However, this process was also a pan-European project and the then members of the EU (particularly Germany) put all their prestige behind the project so that it might be successful. In the largest countries of the region, those which had definitely contributed to the collapse of communism and – in consequence – to German unification, there was an overwhelming belief (not entirely unjustified) that, independent of the fulfilment of the EU accession requirements, EU enlargement was simply not possible politically without the inclusion of countries like Poland or Hungary. The negotiations in Copenhagen at the beginning of the second millennium demonstrated the level of determination with which Germany wanted to help the process right up to the very last moment, when one of the CEE countries did not wish to withdraw its demands. The point of the above example is not to highlight a situation particular to one or other applicant country, but to remind us of the fact that the enlargement process was not a unilateral enterprise, seen by some as a simple relationship between supplicant and benefactor.

Finally, a little imagination is needed in relation to the next point. Let us imagine that some of the applicant CEE countries had decided to stay outside the EU. What economic policies, norms and procedures would they have had to implement as countries outside of the EU but still wanting to remain fully fledged members of the international, liberal and democratic community? It is hard to believe that such a country would differ a great deal in socio-economic solutions and policies implemented from those required by the EU, or in a wider context, the conditions set by the North American Free Trade Association, Mercosur, the World Trade Organisation or any other organisation functioning in the global economy. In this context, what are the specific EU stipulations and conditions, and how large a proportion of the 'general' requirements do they constitute? In my opinion, not a large one at all. This conclusion is substantiated by the regulations implemented by Norway and Switzerland, as well as by the attempts made (mostly unsuccessfully) by Ukraine or Turkey.

Detailed conclusions

The comparison between the two parts of Europe and within CEE countries is, of course, not exhaustive and the book has focused on a few key areas. Two initial chapters focus on the developing institutional context of post-communist party politics. In the first, Kopecký and Spirova direct attention to party–state relations, the management of parties by the state and the degree to which the post-communist state is subject to colonisation by political parties. They find that state support for, and regulation of, parties, has been quite extensive and that this close relation has, further, been widely used by parties to provide their members and supporters with selective benefits. Moreover, the colonisation of the state by parties may facilitate the institutionalisation of party systems, certainly in the short term, although long-term implications remain uncertain. The chapter shows that between-country differences in the region might indeed be significant.

The impact of the EU on party systems, although chiefly on parties themselves, can be seen to some extent in Chapter 3, concerning *transnational cooperation*. Indeed, the author indicates many mechanisms which show CEE parties moving in the direction of their sister parties in the West. This phenomenon is, however, extremely difficult to study, and focusing purely on a qualitative approach and treating high-ranking party politicians as 'experts' in the description and explanation of the process is as much necessary as it is insufficient. But cooperation does exist and in certain situations, and to some extent, it does have an impact on the parties of CEE countries. Nevertheless, the phenomenon is pretty complex and the exact effects are difficult to estimate. Firstly, there is a relatively high proportion of newly elected MEPs from CEE countries who find themselves in the rather smaller (if not marginal) party groups of the EP that have very little to say or create new party groups within the EP. Secondly, the fact that turnout in the EP elections is incredibly low in these countries. Both facts seem to point to a pretty weak effect of the EU mainstream parties. If the impact of this cooperation were significant we might expect the elections to the EP to leave an indelible mark on party systems and particular parties in this region. In fact, no such impact can be seen, and if it does exist it is both weak and short lived.

Let us now move on to the detailed topics discussed in Chapters 4 and 5. They concern electoral (and more generally political) participation and demonstrate, firstly, that political participation takes on a rather traditionally institutional guise and, secondly, that it has very little in common with EU-isation and that if it does, then it manifests itself in a rather perverse correlation – indicated by Czesnik – whereby the lower the voter turnout, the higher the support for the EU and pro-European policies. Political exclusion is thus conducive to the success of the pan-European project. From a practical point of view, one critical question that needs to be answered is whether the reluctance to engage with European issues occurs because citizens of the new member states do not like specific EU policies or because they are not favourably disposed to the very idea of Europeanisation. It is most likely a transitory phenomenon, although if it persists it does not bode well for the future of the pan-European entity. One cannot fail to notice that a hidden factor determining this correlation is the level of education and general social status of the individual. The comparative analysis of Hafner-Fink *et al.* suggests that patterns of political participation mainly differ between old and new democracies and change only over the long term, regardless of whether they are EU members or not. The process of accession itself seems to make little difference.

The institutionalisation of party systems and the patterns of competition is one of the main subjects of this book. Chapter 6 is concerned with this problem and finds that it in no way relates to the impacts of the EU, and its authors (Enyedi and Bertoa) do not feel it appropriate to discuss EU influences. This is not an oversight but a conscious decision on their part. Their results show that no single pattern of competition can be identified in the CEE region. Their findings on coalition-building strategies and the stability of alliances are inconclusive, although there is a general tendency towards less fragmentation and the volatility indicators show pretty high scores. But they fluctuate over time, while in some larger countries of the region a decline in voter volatility is registered. The region as a whole is deeply divided – Hungary and the Czech Republic differ significantly from Latvia, Bulgaria and Estonia. But even these differences seem to be determined chiefly by domestic influences rather than by any EU impact.

Political radicalism, Euroscepticism, populism and – especially – the fate of radical right-wing parties have all been hot topics on the Continent for at least the last two decades. Chapter 7 of this volume advances an interesting theoretical proposition and scrupulously tests it, inclining us, like the majority of the other chapters here, to take a sceptical view of the impact that the EU and the process of accession have had on the formation of radical right-wing parties. The nuanced and multi-faceted analysis emphasises the role of old-regime legacies, pointing out that EU integrations should be treated as an intervening mechanism in more sense than one. The impact of the economic downturn and welfare retrenchment has taken particular force and form in the context of EU membership, and further developments in these areas are likely to unveil the full impact of Europeanisation. The actual reason for the appearance, and also the speedy disappearance (Markowski and Tucker, 2010; Deegan-Krause, 2009), of Eurosceptic and usually radical-right parties of this type is largely due to particular currents of domestic politics. If any more fundamental determinants exist, then they can be found rather in historical events and the various types of socialist legacies that existed.

Two further chapters are concerned more with the output dimension of politics. In Chapter 8 the phenomenon of political representativeness and how it changes over time is presented. Firstly, it registers the fact that the general representativeness of social groups is declining over time. Not everyone is adequately represented, disproportionality increases to the detriment of

those at the 'bottom' of the social ladder and the poorest and most marginalised people on the labour market withdraw from making any impact
on parliamentary bodies. Secondly (a point that is particularly revealing and
worth further study), according to the factors that constitute *ascribed status*
no significant disproportionality is found, while if the factors constituting
achieved status are combined, then disproportionality does become significant.
Finally, comparison of the countries of CEE with the countries of Western
Europe with regard to representativeness measured in terms of policy con-
gruence shows that, yet again (as mentioned above), in this regard the
countries of CEE do not have to 'catch up with' the developed West at all,
although significant regional diversity exists. One major finding, however, is
that the democratisation hypothesis has to be rejected; the passage of time
and the alleged effects of consolidating mechanisms do not work as expected
for the quality of representation.

Chapter 9 points to a mechanism widely discussed in the first part of these
conclusions – the sequence and timing of the EU aspirations of the CEE
countries. Ladrech vigorously argues in favour of a profound effect of the EU
on the development of CEE party politics. Weakly defined party identities
and low levels of ideologisation have been – in the narrative of this chapter –
a direct result of strong commitment of CEE mainstream parties to EU conditionality. This results in limited competition over socio-economic issues
and the overemphasis of political-cultural ones prior to EU accession, as well
as the subsequent opening of the economic dimension of competition after
membership has been achieved. There is, consequently, high party system
fluidity.

In conclusion, let us state that in researching socio-political phenomena
time is needed. We are not always aware of how the ontology of studied phenomena will present itself over time. The attentive reader will undoubtedly
not be satisfied with the answers offered in this volume on the relationship
between the impact of the EU and Europe in general on the party politics of
CEE. However, I believe that it could not have been otherwise. In the future,
this volume will serve as evidence of the doubtful structural and cultural
impact of the EU on the new member states in the period immediately prior
to, during and shortly after accession. This does not mean that this impact
will not reveal itself by 2015–2020. However, for this to happen, theoretical
reflection, sound research, deep practical knowledge and a large amount of
empirical testing of our new European situation is needed. Literary parables
may help, but they will not give us convincing answers.

Let me conclude by borrowing a sentence from another publication
reporting on a project I happen to participate in and which is similar in its
general design, concentrating on the effects of political institutions on the
political behaviour of individuals. The editor of the volume (Klingemann,

2009) citing one of the authors, concluded that 'Institutions matter, but not that much.' I am inclined to suggest an almost identical conclusion: 'The EU matters, but not that much.' At least, not in the way in which some of us may have suspected.

References

Deegan-Krause, K. and T. Haughton (2009), 'Toward a more useful conceptualization of populism: types and degrees of populist appeal in the case of Slovakia', *Politics and Policy* 37, pp. 821–42.

Enyedi, Zsolt (2005), 'The role of agency in cleavage formation', *European Journal of Political Research*, 44, pp. 697–720.

Kitschelt, H., Z. Mansfeldová, R. Markowski and G. Tóka (1999), *Post-communist Party Systems* (Cambridge: Cambridge University Press).

Klingemann, H.-D. (2009), *The Comparative Study of Electoral Systems* (Oxford: Oxford University Press).

Mair, P. (2006), 'Political parties and party systems', in P. Graziano and M. P. Vink (eds), *Europeanization: New Research Agendas* (Basingstoke: Palgrave Macmillan).

Markowski, R. (1997), 'Political parties and ideological spaces in East Central Europe', *Communist and Post-Communist Studies* 30, pp. 221–54.

Markowski, R. (2006), 'The Polish elections of 2005: pure chaos or a restructuring of the party system', *West European Politics* 29, pp. 814–32.

Markowski, R. (2008), 'The 2007 Polish parliamentary election: some structuring, still a lot of chaos', *West European Politics* 31, pp. 1055–68.

Markowski, R. and J. Tucker (2010), 'Euroskepticism and the emergence of political parties in Poland', *Party Politics* (forthcoming).

Olsen, J. P. (2002), 'The many faces of Europeanisation', *Journal of Common Market Studies* 40, pp. 921–52.

Olsen, J. P. (2007), *Europe in Search of Political Order* (Oxford: Oxford University Press).

Radaelli, C. M. (2003), 'The Europeanization of public policy', in K. Featherstone and C. M. Radaelli (eds), *The Politics of Europeanization* (Oxford: Oxford University Press).

Toka, G. (2006), 'Elections and representation', in P. M. Heywood, E. Jones, M. Rhodes and U. Sedelmeier (eds), *Developments in European Politics* (London: Palgrave).

Index